MU
WITH

Brian Marriner

TRUE CRIME Library

True Crime Library – No. 4
A Forum Press Book
by the Paperback Division of
Forum Design,
P.O. Box 158, London SE20 7QA.

An Imprint of True Crime Library/Forum Press
© 1993 by Brian Marriner
All rights reserved

Typeset by T.S. Typesetting,
1 Park Avenue, West Wickham, Kent BR4 9JU.
Printed and bound in Great Britain by
HarperCollins Manufacturing, Glasgow.

ISBN No. 1 874358 04 4

To my wife Barbara

In the True Crime Library series:

An expert in criminology and forensic science, Brian Marriner has established himself as one of Britain's leading true crime authors. He is a regular contributor to the top non-fiction crime magazines: *True Detective, True Crime Monthly, Master Detective* and the quarterly journal *Murder Most Foul.* His best-selling book *A Century of Sex Killers* is recognised by many students of criminology as a modern classic.

CONTENTS

Page

Foreword by
COLIN WILSON

The late John Dunning described one of the most unusual cases of poisoning that I have ever come across.

In New Zealand in January 1979, a woman named Freda Wilson began to complain of stomach pains; a few months later she died in agony. The post mortem showed, as her doctor suspected, that she had died of arsenic poisoning – arsenic administered in fairly small doses over a long period.

There was only one suspect: her husband James Wilson. What is more, he was also suspected of killing his first wife Norah, with strychnine. Norah Wilson had been found dead in front of the television set, with a bottle of lemonade in front of her. Her husband had a perfect alibi. He had been away on business that day. But he admitted that her death was probably his fault. He kept some strychnine for killing pests on his farm, and moreover, he kept it in a lemonade bottle in the kitchen. Somehow, his wife had mistaken the strychnine for lemonade as she sat watching television.

It had been impossible to disprove Wilson's assertion that it had been an accident, and the police were unable to charge him with her murder.

Soon after the death of his first wife – from whom he inherited the farm – James Wilson married Freda. He had been having an affair with her for some time before

Norah's death – another reason for the police to believe that he murdered Norah.

And now his second wife had died of arsenic poisoning. The Auckland police soon uncovered a motive – Wilson had been having an affair with a beautiful young girl who lived nearby. History, it seemed, was repeating itself.

Wilson denied that he had poisoned Freda. He insisted that he did not even possess any arsenic. But under pressing police interrogation, he finally admitted that he *had* murdered his first wife Norah. They were childless, and she refused to have sex with him. He met Freda at a trade fair, and within hours the couple were in bed. They seemed made for one another. And one day, James Wilson told her he had decided to kill his wife. She owned the farm – he was penniless when he met her – and if he simply ran away with Freda, he would be penniless again. So he had evolved a simple and foolproof plan. Every afternoon, Norah watched television and drank a bottle of lemonade – she kept a row of them on the larder shelf. All he had to do was to introduce strychnine into one of the bottles, and make an appointment for the day she would drink it – she always drank the bottles in sequence. This is how he had come to be in Wellington while Norah died in agony.

Yet even though he had now confessed to killing Norah, James Wilson continued to deny poisoning Freda with arsenic. It made no difference. The jury still found him guilty of murdering Freda, and in April 1980, he was sentenced to life imprisonment. He immediately had a heart attack. In the following month, he had another in his prison cell and this time died.

And now, Freda Wilson's best – and only – friend came forward with the true solution. Jessica Lacey, the owner of a small grocery shop, told how Freda had learned of her husband's affair with a younger woman. She had been driving along the road when she saw her husband's car parked near some bushes. She stopped to see what was happening. On the other side of the bushes, her husband was sitting beside a stream, and the naked younger woman was bathing in it. James Wilson was begging her not to keep him waiting. Minutes later, the younger woman came out of the stream, and they made love on the grass. . .

Freda Wilson had chosen an interesting method of getting her revenge. She had poisoned herself with small doses of arsenic, knowing that her husband would be charged with her murder. For the pleasure of destroying her husband's love affair, she had endured agonising pain over many months, until she died in torment. The only person to whom she confided her secret was her friend Jessica, the only woman in the area who did not ostracise her. And Jessica kept silent until her friend's revenge was complete.

What is interesting about this story – apart from the tangled emotions of the protagonists – is the fact that there was never any doubt that this was death by poison. For in the late 20th century, nobody but an idiot or a highly skilled toxicologist would use poison if he wanted to get away with murder. James Wilson knew that his only chance of escaping conviction for killing Norah was to make it look like an accident.

In fact, in spite of appearances, the police who investigated the death of his second wife strongly suspected that he must be innocent, since there was no reason why anyone should do anything so obvious. Ever since 1836, when an English chemist named James Marsh invented an incredibly sensitive test for arsenic, the poison has been as dangerous to the murderer as to the victim. And for the past century and a half, the same has applied to hundreds of other poisons.

It was not always so, as Brian Marriner – one of the most intelligent of modern students of criminology – tells in this absorbing book. Almost since the beginning of civilisation, poison was the favourite of all methods of assassination, since there was virtually no method of proving that it had been used.

The great revolutionary in the detection of poisons was a Spaniard named Mathieu Orfila. A brilliant and intensely ambitious young medical student, Orfila came to Paris determined to make a name for himself. But he had no idea of how to go about it. One day in 1813, lecturing to a small class of students about poisons, Orfila told them that there was an infallible method of detecting arsenic, because when it was mixed with liquids like wine, broth or coffee there would always be a telltale white deposit. At which he poured arsenious acid into some coffee. Instead of a white deposit, there was a dirty grey one. He tried another demonstration, and it also turned the wrong colour. Orfila was not the kind of man who liked to look ridiculous; he cleared his throat and told his students that there must be some impurities in the arsenic. And as soon as he was alone, he tried pouring arsenious acid into various liquids, such as wine, soup and urine. And as the expected reactions failed to appear, Orfila realised that most of the so-called "infallible" tests were hopelessly flawed. The science of toxicology was virtually non-existent.

In that moment, Orfila knew he had discovered his route to fame. He went to a publisher, and asked if he would be willing to publish a two-volume work on poisons. Then, with the contract in his pocket, he rushed back to his laboratory, and started from scratch. He worked so feverishly that less than a year later, in1814, the first volume of his *Treatise on Poison, or General Toxicology*, was published. It made him famous. Death by poison was still commonplace, and most ordinary doctors had no idea of how to go about investigating it. Orfila's volume – at a mere six francs a copy – provided the answer. Every doctor in France – and soon in Europe – felt he had to have a copy on his shelf.

The young celebrity married a wealthy girl, became head of the Faculty of Medicine in Paris, and was soon France's leading forensic toxicologist. But it was twenty years later that he reached the apex of his fame with a case which became a *cause célèbre* all over Europe. In 1840, an attractive – if somewhat neurotic – young woman called Marie Lafarge was accused of poisoning her husband by giving him large quantities of arsenic concealed in a cake and a glass of eggnog. A local chemist declared that he had detected arsenic, but his methods were so incompetent that the defence had no difficulty in ridiculing him.

Marie aroused much sympathy because her husband was a bankrupt who had married her for her money, representing himself as wealthy, and had then taken her to live in a rat-hole of a farm in the provinces, where his mother ruled the roost. The general feeling was that he deserved to be poisoned. Even when it emerged that Marie was a thief who had stolen a diamond tiara from a wealthier acquaintance, the public took her side when the husband took Marie to court, feeling that she had troubles enough. The defence lawyer was an old friend of Orfila, and when he showed Orfila the medical evidence, the great toxicologist was contemptuous, and declared that it should not be possible to condemn a dog on tests performed with such monstrous incompetence. More tests were carried out by provincial "experts", and when these failed to reveal arsenic it began to look as though Marie would be acquitted.

Unfortunately, the defence refused to leave well alone, and asked Orfila to come and perform his tests in front of the local experts, just to show them how it should be done. Orfila obliged and immediately discovered large quantities of arsenic in the contents of the dead man's stomach. The defence was shattered, and Marie was condemned to hard labour for life. Yet although Orfila had brought about her downfall, no one could blame him. He was a man of science, and had no alternative. . . For the rest of the 19th century the name of Orfila became a synonym for brilliant and logical detective work, like that of his fictional counterpart Sherlock Holmes.

Arsenic deserves an important place in the history of

forensic medicine because it was the first poison that chemists learned to detect. In 1775, a chemist named Karl Scheele learned how to make arsenious acid by dissolving arsenic in nitric acid. He then found that when zinc was dropped into arsenious acid, a gas that stank of garlic was given off. The tests were refined until chemists learned how to make an 'arsenic mirror' by heating arsenic compounds and holding a cold plate above them. In 1806, Dr Valentine Rose cut up the stomach of a suspected poison victim, boiled it in water, and then demonstrated the presence of arsenic by obtaining an 'arsenic mirror'.

It was Rose's gruesome method that led to the conviction of one of Germany's most notorious poisoners, while Orfila was still a schoolboy. Anna Zwanziger started life as a romantic young woman who had come down in the world as a result of marrying an alcoholic lawyer, and was forced to take jobs as a housekeeper. She decided that the best way to become a 'lady' again was to marry her employer, a judge named Glaser – who, unfortunately, already had a wife. Frau Glaser died in agony, but her husband showed no sign of wanting to marry his sallow, ugly housekeeper, and after he too suffered intense stomach pains, he got rid of her. Another judge who employed Anna also died suddenly. So did the wife of her next employer, who also took warning and dismissed her. Soon after Anna left the house, most people in it became violently ill; the cause was traced to the salt box, which proved to contain a quantity of arsenic.

Arrested in 1809, Anna denied everything. But at this point the corpse of Frau Glaser was exhumed and the stomach sliced up and boiled in the manner prescribed by Valentine Rose. A huge dose of arsenic was found. When this evidence was produced in court, Anna fell to the floor in convulsions and had to be carried out. But she knew denial was now pointless, and confessed to a whole string of poisonings and attempted poisonings. What shocked everyone was that many of these had been carried out without motive – apparently she had so enjoyed the sense of power induced by watching her victims swallow the poison that she began to do it for fun. She told the judge that 'poison was her truest friend', and it is recorded that her eyes lit up when they fell upon arsenic. Anna Zwanziger was beheaded – by sword – in 1811.

Three more women were apparently bitten by the 'poisoning for fun' bug in the next few decades. Gesina Gottfried poisoned a brutal husband, then went on to poison various members of the households in which she became a servant. Finally, one of her employers wondered about the white powder she had sprinkled on a leg of pork and took it to the police to be analysed; when it proved to be arsenic, Gesina Gottfried confessed to a number of murders, and was executed in 1828. Hélène Jegado, a Breton peasant woman, poisoned up to twenty-three victims over a twenty-year period, including seven people in one household. When a servant of whom she was jealous died in agony, the police went to interview her, and before they could speak, Hélène cried: "I am innocent!" "Of what?" asked the detective, "no one has accused you", and placed her under arrest. She was executed in 1852. A Dutch nurse named van den Linden killed more than a hundred – although, regrettably, little is known of her beyond her name and her sentence. These were all 'serial killers' in the modern sense – 'repeat killers' who murder for pleasure.

Now that arsenic was so easily detectable, 19th century murderers tried other poisons. One homicidal doctor – William Palmer – decided that strychnine was safer, because its symptoms could be confused with tetanus. Palmer, who lived in Rugeley, poisoned a friend called Cook, to whom he was heavily in debt because of their mutual devotion to horse racing. Because of the crudity of forensic analysis in that period (1855), although an autopsy found traces of antimony, the strychnine proved undetectable. But since Palmer had a string of other mysterious deaths to his credit – eleven in all – the jury decided he was guilty on circumstantial evidence and sentenced him to death. Ten years later, the vain and mendacious Dr Edward Pritchard chose a mixture of antimony and aconite – presumably to confuse the investigators – to murder his wife and mother-in-law, but was promptly detected and hanged.

Three Victorian poisoners who, against all the odds, escaped with their lives, were Madeleine Smith, Florence Bravo and Adelaide Bartlett. Madeleine poisoned her lover, who was trying to prevent an arranged marriage to an older man by blackmailing her, but no one could work out how she had separated out the arsenic in the rat poison from the soot with which it was coloured by law, so she was given the benefit of the doubt. Florence Bravo's husband Charles died in agony after drinking a bottle of Burgundy, which seems to have been laced with tartar emetic (antimony.) A jury decided that Bravo had been murdered, but again there was not quite enough evidence to fix it on the accused. The case of Adelaide Bartlett, which is described in this book, is one of the great poison mysteries, since chloroform – which killed her husband – is very corrosive and has such a powerful odour that it would be virtually undrinkable. My own belief is that Adelaide persuaded him to drink it to kill off the worms which he believed were eating away his intestines; at all events, Adelaide, like the others, escaped the hangman by the skin of her teeth.

Perhaps the most amazing story in the history of poisoning is the Bocarmé case, also related here by Brian Marriner, in which a brilliant young chemist had to devise his own method of detecting the highly unusual poison – nicotine – that had killed Gustave Fougnies. I will not spoil it by telling the reader how it was done.

Other poisoners who deserve a mention are Dr Edmé Castaing, the first to use morphine (which he administered to an acquaintance in mulled wine), Dr Eustachy, who injected atropine into some thrushes which he sent a rival as a present, Quaker John Tawell, who poisoned his mistress with prussic acid (and was the first murderer to be arrested through the use of the new electric telegraph), and Frau Martha Marek, a beautiful Viennese who poisoned a number of people – including her husband – for their insurance money and who anticipated Graham Young in using the rare poison thallium.

In spite of its detectability, modern serial killers have by no means abandoned poison. In Cincinatti in 1987, a nursing attendant named Donald Harvey was sentenced to life imprisonment for poisoning twenty-four of his patients with arsenic and cyanide, simply for the pleasure of seeing them suffer. In 1989, Michaela Rosa, a nurse nicknamed "the Angel of Death", was charged with killing seventeen of her patients by injecting them with Catra-presan, a blood pressure drug. Also in 1989, five nurses in Vienna were charged with killing elderly patients – the figure mentioned was forty-nine – with various types of injection. As a profession, nursing still seems to offer the serial killer a certain temporary immunity.

The real comprehensive history of poisoning has still to be written. But Brian Marriner has taken an important step in that direction with this book which includes sixteen celebrated murder cases and a study of each of the poisons used. It reinforces Marriner's claim to be one of the most distinguished living crime writers.

1
GEORGE CHAPMAN
The Cruel Casanova

*"I have never seen such a villain. He looked like some
evil wild beast" – Sir Edward Carson KC*

To describe George Chapman as a womaniser is a little
like saying that Al Capone was a bad man or that Rocke-
feller was reasonably well off. It rather understates the
case.

Chapman could apparently lure women into his bed at
will. And as soon as one affair was under way, he would
be eagerly seeking another. The long line of lovers was
seemingly endless.

Yet this was no matinee idol. To judge from surviving
photographs, Chapman was an ugly man of meagre
physique with a skin rough in texture and dull in colour,
hair coarse and a moustache so long that it drooped some
four or five inches below his mouth.

He has even been described as being 'baboon-like'.
And Sir Edward Carson, who prosecuted him during his
murder trial, recounted, "I have never seen such a villain.
He looked like some evil wild beast. I almost expected
him to leap over the dock and attack me."

The 'wild beast' description may have been more apt
than Sir Edward imagined at the time. It was later
discovered that before Chapman came to England, he had

married a woman in Poland and beheaded her; and he has always been a prime candidate for the bloodstained role of Jack the Ripper, the suggestion being that he simply changed his *modus operandi* from that of murder by the knife to that of murder by poison. Women were still the victims and the crimes still seemingly motiveless.

This is the real mystery that Chapman left unanswered. Just why did he kill? Sir Edward Carson tackled this point in his closing speech to the jury by saying, "Learned counsel for the defence has commented on the absence of motive, but what is the use of seeking for motive when we have the actual fact of murder? In this instance there was the most ample motive, for the prisoner's was a history of unbridled, heartless and cruel lust."

This is unconvincing. No motive was proved, and to contend that a skilled seducer like Chapman would murder for sex is ludicrous. A publican by trade, he bedded many of his barmaids, and then sent them packing. He was not legally married to any of his three known victims, and they had no claim on him. He could have kicked them out at any time he wished. There was no need to kill. And he certainly didn't murder for money, since he had insured none of his victims. Yet kill he did.

H.L.Adams writes of Chapman's obsession as the pursuit, capture and destruction of women. That explanation is an over-simplification. We must seek another. We must also seek to explain Chapman's sheer *carelessness*.

His real name was Severin Klosowski, and he was born in Poland on December 14th, 1865. He had adopted an English name from one of his mistresses, Annie Chapman, and given the nature of his murderous enterprises, one would suppose that such a cunning killer would seek to cover up his real identity and all proof of his crimes. Yet following his arrest and when police searched his room, they found documents giving his true name and a receipt for the purchase of the poison used. Police also discovered the existence of two previous victims only because Chapman had kept the undertaker's bills. Was he contemptuous of the law and the possibility of capture, or just plain foolhardy?

Many killers have made such stupid blunders that it seems possible that they wanted to be caught, but Chapman's carelessness perhaps stemmed from naive arrogance. He had fooled so many doctors, having had extensive medical training himself, that he thought he was invincible.

Suspicion that he was Jack the Ripper stems from the fact that Chapman/Klosowski was a *feldscher*, or "barber-surgeon", having been apprenticed to a surgeon in Poland for six years. He had the necessary anatomical skill to have removed the organs which were missing from the bodies of some of the Ripper's victims. He arrived in London from Poland in 1888 and lived and worked in Whitechapel just when the series of murders began. The Ripper had surgical knowledge. . .

Chapman's physical description fits that of the man seen with the last of the Ripper's victims, Mary Jane Kelly, found dissected in her lodgings. The American-style phrases used in the Ripper's letters to the press and police would also have fitted Chapman, who often passed himself off as an American and used American slang.

Chapman *did* go to America in May 1890, and is said to have opened a barber's shop in Jersey City. It has been further alleged that a series of Ripper-type killings then occurred in the locality of Jersey City, ceasing only when Chapman returned to London in May 1892. However, there is no historical confirmation of the Jersey City murders.

Chief Inspector Abberline, who headed inquiries into the Whitechapel murders, was convinced that Chapman was the real Jack the Ripper. When Chapman was arrested by Inspector Godley, who had also been involved in the Ripper investigation, Abberline told Godley: "You've got Jack the Ripper at last!"

The objection to the Chapman/Ripper theory is the difference in *style*. Why would a homicidal killer who liked to rip his female victims open, turn instead to poisoning them? Some killers, notably Peter Kürten, the Düsseldorf Vampire, have changed their *modus operandi* in a deliberate attempt to fool the police, but it seems unlikely that the unknown Ripper, whose frenzy could only be appeased with hot blood, would become a mere poisoner.

We know little about Chapman, almost nothing about his character or state of mind. As he never confessed, he left no clues to his motives. But we do not necessarily need a man's own words to compose his biography; often it is possible to construct a man's inner life from his habits and deeds, and of these we have details in plenty.

Of his early life in Europe, we know that he eventually worked as an assistant-surgeon in a hospital in Prague, and got married, spending eighteen months in the Russian army before travelling to England in 1888. Aged twenty-three, he got a job in a barber's shop in the High Street, Whitechapel. Eventually he obtained a shop of his own, but when that failed he went back to working for other barbers.

Of his emotional life, we know that Chapman already had a wife in Poland when he went through a form of marriage with another Polish woman, Lucy Baderski, in London in 1889. For a time they lived together in Cable Street, and when his real wife arrived in England, both women shared Chapman's home, until the first wife moved out.

Chapman and his second wife, Lucy, went to America, but she returned alone in February 1891. In early 1892 Chapman returned to London and again worked in the East End as a barber. His wife and two children had left him, no doubt because of his numerous affairs. He met Annie Chapman in 1893, began living with her, and even changed his name to hers, but she left him after only a year, tired of his philandering.

While working in Leytonstone in 1895, Chapman met his first known English victim, Mary Spink. She was married to a railway porter, who left her because of her excessive drinking. Pressured by the persistent badgering of her relatives, Chapman went through a form of marriage with Mary Spink in October 1895, and afterwards the couple lived together as man and wife.

Mary Spink had private means. Her grandfather had left her £600 in trust, and Chapman soon got his hands on this money, buying his own hairdressing salon in Hastings in 1897. At first the wife attempted shaving his male customers, quite a novelty for the time, but later she played the piano for customers. These "musical shaves" proved to be very popular, but not enough to keep the business afloat. While at Hastings Chapman had his own little sailing dinghy, and liked to boast of his nautical prowess.

Lying is one of the principal traits of the criminal, and Chapman never told the truth when a lie would suffice. He boasted of having been a big-game hunter, a noted surgeon in Warsaw, and gave the impression he could have sailed the Atlantic single-handed. He had grandiose fantasies, a rich inner life in which he was the hero of his own biography.

One of Chapman's customers was a local chemist, a Mr Davidson, who was so impressed by the extent of Chapman's medical knowledge that he had no qualms in selling him an ounce of tartar emetic, a form of antimony. However, he ensured that Chapman signed the Poisons Register. An ounce, costing twopence, contained enough grains to kill a dozen people or more. The purchase was made in Spring, 1897.

Chapman's business failed, despite the musical shaves, and after six months the couple sold up and moved back to London, where Chapman became landlord of the Prince of Wales tavern in Bartholomew Square, off City Road. Until this time Mrs Spink, aged forty-one, had always seemed a healthy woman, despite her heavy drinking. Now, however, she became ill, suffering from severe vomiting attacks. Chapman hired a neighbouring woman to nurse his wife, and called in a Dr Rogers, who prescribed medicine. Chapman also nursed her himself, giving her glasses of brandy, but she died later in 1897. Dr Rogers signed a certificate listing phthisis as the cause of death.

Chapman then advertised for a barmaid, selecting Bessie Taylor from the list of applicants. She had been a domestic servant and was a farmer's daughter: a fine, healthy girl. Within a few months Chapman went through a form of marriage with her, but there was no honeymoon. The same night the newly-weds were serving behind the bar. Soon afterwards the new Mrs Chapman's health began to fail. She began to waste away.

Chapman gave up the Prince of Wales and took over another pub, the Grapes, at Bishops Stortford. Bessie had to go into hospital for an operation, and when she returned home Chapman's manner towards her had changed. He became cruel and abusive. Once he threatened her with a loaded revolver.

The couple moved again, this time to the Monument Tavern in Union Street. Bessie became thinner. Several doctors were called in, but all were baffled by her constant vomiting. A Dr Stoker had some minor success with her. Bessie had a nurse in constant attendance, and one day Dr Stoker arrived at the pub to find Bessie sitting up and playing the piano. "Capital!" he said, and went away pleased with his patient's recovery. The nurse was sent home. Two days later Bessie was near to death, finally succumbing on February 13th, 1901. Dr Stoker signed the certificate, attributing death to "exhaustion from vomiting and diarrhoea." Bessie was duly buried at Lym, in Cheshire, aged thirty-six.

In August 1901 Chapman spotted an advertisement in a newspaper placed by a young woman named Maud Marsh, nineteen, who was seeking a position as a barmaid. Chapman contacted her and engaged her to work at the Monument Tavern. Maud had been living with her parents in Croydon. Her father was a labourer, and her mother went with Maud to the interview, to satisfy herself that the job was decent and above board.

Chapman said he was bachelor and did not live alone in the pub, as a family occupied the top floor. Both statements were untrue. Within weeks Maud was secretly writing home: "Dear Mother, just a line to say on the QT. Mr has gone out, so I now write this to you to say that George says if I do not let him have what he wants he will give me £35 and send me home. What shall I do?" She also intimated in her letter that she and Chapman were engaged.

Maud's parents, anxious about their daughter, visited her at the pub, where Maud told them that Chapman had been "paying her attentions" and had proposed marriage. Chapman, anxious to impress the parents, visited them in Croydon to assure them that his intentions were honourable, and made out a will in their presence, witnessed by Mrs Marsh, leaving Maud £400.

Later, when Mr Marsh lay ill in hospital, Maud visited him and he noticed a ring on her finger. He asked her if she was married and she said yes. Chapman had married her in a Roman Catholic "room" in Bishopsgate Street, Chapman being of that faith. But all Chapman's weddings in England were bogus, and the women themselves must have known it and been willing participants in the charade.

Mrs Marsh never did trust Chapman, and that mistrust was to be his undoing. She asked to see the marriage certificate, but Maud said Chapman "had it in his safekeeping." Early in 1902 Maud began to sicken, experiencing the same symptoms as Bessie Taylor. A short stay in Guy's Hospital led to a brief recovery, but she became ill again when she returned home.

Chapman moved yet again, and became landlord of the Crown public house, also in Union Street, in the Borough. Maud's mother came to nurse her ailing daughter, keeping day and night bedside vigil, but Maud grew steadily worse. The same Dr Stoker who had treated Bessie Taylor was now called in to attend her replacement. He did not think it odd that two of Chapman's wives should display the same symptoms. He prescribed medicine and liquid nourishment to be injected, yet Maud continued to vomit and fail rapidly. Chapman insisted on preparing all the food and drink for the patient, often giving her a glass of brandy and soda. Once, when Maud was unable to drink this, Mrs Marsh and the nurse finished it off between them. Both women suffered painful attacks of vomiting and diarrhoea afterwards.

Chapman himself acted the part of doctor, often taking Maud's pulse and listening to her chest with a stethoscope. Once, asked by a customer how his wife was, Chapman replied bluntly: "She's dying."

Maud herself had suggested that a rabbit she had eaten the previous Sunday might have been "off", but as her mother pointed out, no one else who had eaten that rabbit had been taken ill. Mrs Marsh had become convinced that her daughter was being slowly poisoned. She contacted her own physician, Dr Grapnel of Croydon, telling him of her suspicions. He went to visit the patient at the Crown, much to Chapman's resentment, and quickly concluded that Maud was indeed being poisoned. However, he could not identify the agent being used, and could not directly accuse the husband for fear of legal action for slander if proved wrong.

He took the train back to Croydon, and by the time he arrived at his destination he became so certain in his mind that arsenic was the poison being used that he sent a telegram to Dr Stoker, telling him to look for the poison. The telegram arrived too late. Maud was dead.

Chapman must have been frightened by Dr Grapnel's visit and evident suspicions, and so had given Maud a much stronger dose and finished her off quickly. She died on October 22nd, 1902. Because of the telegram he had received Dr Stoker refused to sign a death certificate.

Angrily, Chapman asked why the doctor would not issue the certificate. "Because I cannot find out what is the cause of death," the doctor replied.

"It was exhaustion caused by inflammation of the bowels," Chapman told him.

"What caused the inflammation?" the doctor asked.

"Continual vomiting and diarrhoea," said Chapman.

"But what caused the vomiting and diarrhoea?" the doctor persisted.

There was no reply.

Dr Stoker took the unusual step of conducting a private autopsy, without informing the coroner. He discovered what he took to be arsenic in the remains, and then wrote to the coroner, Dr Waldo. He also informed the police.

Chapman was arrested on the morning of Saturday, 25th October, 1902, the day on which the Coronation procession of Edward VII passed through the streets of London. Police searched his premises and found many documents, medicines and powders, and almost £300 in gold and notes. They discovered that his real identity was that of Severin Klosowski, and that evening he was charged under both his names with the murder of Maud Marsh by arsenical poisoning. When she was finally buried, Chapman's wreath was the most prominent of those upon the coffin.

Further tests were carried out. Dr Stevenson, a Home Office analyst, took several organs to Guy's Hospital for detailed examination, and after a few days revealed that it had been antimony, not arsenic, which had killed Maud.

At the first hearing Chapman's solicitor asked for bail for his client. This was opposed by Inspector Godley, who said that he feared that Chapman might flee the country if freed, and so the prisoner was remanded in custody.

Among the items found in Chapman's rooms at the Crown was a copy of hangman Berry's autobiography. When this was revealed by a newspaper, Berry wrote to Inspector Godley asking for all references to his book to be kept out of the case, stating that he had destroyed all copies of the book in his possession, and intended to destroy any other he could find. He gave no reason for this request. The book survives, despite the author's attempts to obliterate his literary creation.

Two separate inquiries investigated the case: the coroner's and the magistrates'. Coroners then had enormous powers and could, in effect, hold a separate trial of the person named as a suspect, and examine all the evidence. These powers were curtailed by the Coroner's (Amendment) Act of 1926.

At the magistrates' court the police suggested that it was necessary to exhume the bodies of Mary Spink and Bessie Taylor. It took many months and many adjournments before all the evidence was assembled. The bodies of both women were found to be remarkably well-preserved (a curious side-effect of antimony) and the tissues were soaked in the poison.

The trial of Chapman began on March 16th, 1903, before Mr Justice Grantham, who often displayed preconception of a prisoner's guilt and took over the role of prosecutor. This trait was to be seen in the course of the trial, his summing-up to the jury being largely a continuation of the speech for the prosecution. Yet the facts were so damning that it is impossible to see how any counsel, judge or jury, could have failed to convict Chapman. Sir Edward Carson, the Solicitor-General, led for the prosecution, while George Elliot KC was defence counsel, assisted by Mr Arthur Hutton, who in 1896 had defended in the Milsom and Fowler murder case.

The trial took place in No. 1 Court of the old Central Criminal Court, adjacent to Newgate Prison. This old courtroom was like an underground basement, badly lit, gloomy and depressing. The prisoner entered the dock via a trap-door, having had to walk along a stone-paved passage called "Birdcage Walk" which connected the prison with the court. Under the flagstones of this passage were those who had been hanged in Newgate, so every man who left the court sentenced to death had to walk over his own imminent grave.

When he appeared in the dock, Chapman looked pale.

He had lost the cocky assurance which had cloaked him at every appearance before the magistrates. Now he looked defeated, as if he had given up all hope.

The Solicitor-General opened by stating that he intended to prove that Severin Klosowski, in his late thirties, alias George Chapman, wilfully murdered Maud Eliza Marsh, and that after his arrest on this charge, he had also been charged with the murders of Mary Isabella Spink and Elizabeth (Bessie) Taylor, by the same method, antimonial poisoning. The defence protested that Chapman was being tried for only one murder, and that any evidence relating to the other two cases was inadmissible. The judge ruled that it was admissible to prove a *system*.

The Solicitor-General said that Maud Marsh's body was "literally saturated with antimony," explaining that antimony was a metal, an irritant poison which, in powder form as a tartar emetic, was easily soluble in water, and odourless and tasteless. The main use of tartar-emetic was to induce vomiting, but one other curious effect of the poison was that it preserved bodies, making them seem newly-interred after years of burial.

Chapman had bought an ounce of tartar emetic on April 3rd, 1897, which contained 146 grains of antimony. A dose of two grains was known to have been fatal, and ten or twelve grains would probably be so. Mrs Spink died in December 1897. On February 13th, 1901, Bessie Taylor died, and in the following year Maud Marsh had passed away in October. In each case the symptoms were identical, and all the women had been poisoned with antimony. Chapman had nursed and fed each victim, thus he had the means and the opportunity to kill them.

Sir Edward Carson told the jury: "Only four people could have administered the poison, and as to two or three of them it is impossible that they would have done so. It was the accused alone who was in very close contact with the girl, and who took it upon himself to introduce into the room the only food and drink she received. It was the accused who purchased a very large quantity of this poison. It is to this man that all the evidence points."

Relating the deaths of Mrs Spink and Bessie Taylor, and emphasising that Chapman was being tried solely for the murder of Maud Marsh, the Solicitor-General said: "I submit that no murder can be more determined and more malicious than that by slow poison. Certainly no murder could be more demonstrative of the cruelty of the person perpetrating it than that of a man standing by the bedside, day after day, of the person he professed to love and seeing her suffering and gradually sinking away from what he had by his own hand administered. . .

The first prosecution witness was Wollf Levisohn, a Pole who came to England in 1862. He had met Chapman in 1888 in a barber's shop in Whitechapel. Chapman had then been using the name Ludwig Zagowski, and had what the witness called "lah di dah ways." As Levisohn was a traveller in barber's supplies, he met Chapman several times between 1888 and 1895. They spoke in Yiddish, and Chapman said he had been a *feldscher* in Warsaw, as had Levisohn himself.

The witness continued: "I talked to the accused about medicine and he asked me if I could get him a certain medicine, but I said no, I did not want to get twelve years."

The chemist from Hastings testified to having sold Chapman an ounce of tartar emetic, producing his poison register as proof.

On the second day of the trial the mother of Maud Marsh went into the witness box. She spoke of nursing her daughter: "Maud was in bed and seemed very bad. She complained of great pain in the lower part of her stomach and of excessive thirst. She kept vomiting. The accused brought her a drink. After she had taken it she vomited, and the vomit was of a greenish colour. . . "

Her daughter's last words had been to Chapman: "I'm going. Goodbye, George." Chapman began crying and seemed greatly upset.

In cross-examination the defence established that

Chapman had made no attempt to hide any medicines; they were in plain view and could have been examined by anyone. Chapman had seemed genuinely fond of Maud, and his conduct towards her had always been that of a caring and devoted husband.

The father, Robert Marsh, testified that he had always been on the best of terms with Chapman, adding: "I thought he treated my daughter very well." But he did recall a peculiar conversation with Chapman. Mr Marsh had been to the pub to see Maud ill in bed. Afterwards he talked to Chapman downstairs at the bar, and said: "Maudie is very bad, is she not, George?" Chapman replied: "Yes." The father asked him if he had ever seen anyone else in the same condition, asking: "Was your other wife like it?" Chapman had replied casually: "Just about in the same way." The father went on: "I think my daughter will pull through now, George." And Chapman replied: "She will never get up no more."

Maud's sister, Mrs Louisa Sarah Morris, told the court that she had talked with Chapman when her sister lay ill, and had said to him that she thought it was odd that despite all the medicines the doctors were prescribing, they could not find out what was the matter with her. Chapman had commented: "I could give her a bit like that" – snapping his fingers – "and fifty doctors would not find out."

Another sister, Alice Marsh, told of going to the pub to see her sister and asking Chapman where Maud was. He had replied: "In bed, dying fast." Later, after her sister had died and her body had been removed to the mortuary, Alice went with her mother to have tea with Chapman, and he said to her: "There is a chance for you as barmaid now. Will you come?" She had declined the offer.

Mrs Jessie Toon told of how Chapman had employed her to nurse his sick wife. She described the various medicines the patient was given, and how Chapman had to inject beef extract up her back passage. "But the injections did not stay with the deceased - they came back again quickly and she was in terrible pain." After Maud died, Mrs Toon went to view the body, but it had been removed. She asked Chapman for a glass of rum, but he refused. Mrs Toon asked him why not and he had replied: "Because you talk, Jessie, when you have rum. . . I don't want you to say anything of what occurred upstairs."

Florence Raynor told of going to work at the Crown as a barmaid, when Maud was still alive. After a fortnight Chapman kissed her and asked her to go to America with him. Florence told him: "You have got your wife downstairs, you don't want me." He said: "If I give her that" – snapping his fingers – "she will be no more Mrs Chapman." Florence claimed that Chapman kissed her constantly – she could not object, could not help herself – and later "fainted from the stuff which the accused had given me."

Defence counsel asked: "Was it not on account of drink that you were discharged?" She insisted that Chapman had tried to enter her bedroom and that she had never been intoxicated, although she admitted she had been arrested and fined the following morning for being drunk.

"What happened when you went to the accused to get a reference?" asked the judge.

"He took me by the throat and threw me out," she said.

On the third day of the trial Dr Stoker testified about treating Maud Marsh. He said her symptoms had been consistent with peritonitis, and he had prescribed bismuth, morphia and ipecacuanha. After five days, with the patient's condition worsening, the doctor prescribed food injections via the rectum – a mixture of egg, milk and beef tea. He admitted having been baffled by the mystery ailment.

In cross-examination the defence tried to establish that the bismuth which he had prescribed might have caused the vomiting and diarrhoea, but the doctor said that an "enormous quantity" would have to be taken to produce that result.

Dr Thomas Stevenson, a Home Office analyst, testified that he had carried out a post mortem on Maud Marsh eight days after her death. Every organ of the body he analysed had antimony in it. He said antimony might be prescribed for bad colds or to produce perspiration, but then only in one twenty-sixth of a grain. Half a grain would be emetic. But Maud Marsh's remains had contained 20.12 grains. Dr Stevenson said he had found antimony in medicine bottles taken from Chapman's premises. He believed that much of the poison had been injected via the anus, and thus quickly absorbed into the body.

Evidence was then heard about the death of Mary Spink and of Bessie Taylor (whose exhumed body had contained 29.12 grains of antimony). One witness described how, as Mary Spink lay dying, she saw Chapman bend over her and heard Spink say: "Pray God go away from me." When Mary died Chapman cried for a while, then went downstairs to open the pub.

The witness said to him: "You are never going to open the house today?" And Chapman replied: "Yes, I am." Another witness testified that Chapman said his wife was suffering from delirium tremens because of her drink problem, and he was giving her medicines to cure her of this.

Dr Stevenson, recalled, said that he had attended the exhumation of Mary Spink. Her body was "altogether remarkable, her face and head were those of a woman who might have been coffined that day." He found 3.83 grains of antimony in her organs, and concluded that death was due to poisoning. There was no physical evidence that she had been a drunkard. The defence established that she had been in an elm coffin, buried eighteen feet deep, with seven coffins above it – the intention being to suggest that the remarkable preservation of the body was because water had not been able to

Thallium poisoner
Graham Young (above)
and the workmates
he murdered:
Bob Egle (left) and
Frederick Biggs

Death of a Gargoyle: see page 227

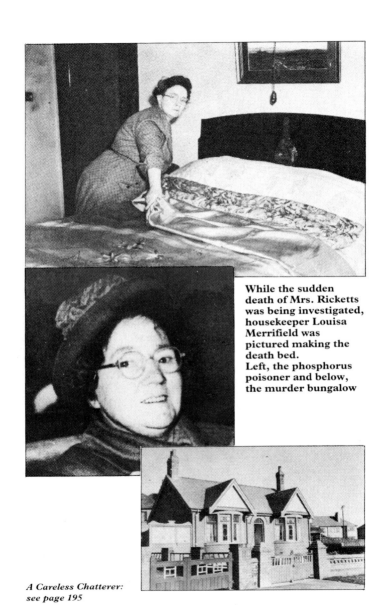

While the sudden death of Mrs. Ricketts was being investigated, housekeeper Louisa Merrifield was pictured making the death bed.
Left, the phosphorus poisoner and below, the murder bungalow

A Careless Chatterer:
see page 195

Dr. Hawley Harvey Crippen and his young mistress and secretary Ethel le Neve

Mrs. Cora Crippen (right) better known by her stage name of Belle Elmore

Dr. Crippen and Miss le Neve in the dock at Bow Street

The Hen-Pecked Husband: see page 128

Florence Maybrick was found guilty of the murder by arsenic of her husband James (below)

Above, bottles of Valentine's meat juice with water

The Cat Woman: see page 46

penetrate that deep. But Dr Stevenson pointed out that the other seven bodies which had to be removed to reach Mary Spink's coffin "had a fearful smell."

Bessie Taylor's brother, William, testified about his sister's relationship with Chapman, and her subsequent death. She had gone from being a healthy woman to being "ill and shrunken, like a little old lady." Chapman appeared to treat her kindly, and when she died "he behaved in every way that I should expect of a man who had just lost his wife."

Mrs Martha Stevens told how she nursed Bessie, who had diarrhoea, vomiting and great pain. Again Chapman had cried after his "wife's" death. She agreed with defence counsel that Dr Stoker treated Bessie, and three consultants were also called in to examine her. Chapman had seemed willing for the consultations to take place, and did everything to look after her "with every possible care."

Dr Stoker, recalled, said that none of the four doctors called in had suspected poisoning and Chapman had paid their fees. He was treating the patient for constipation, and counted the diarrhoea as evidence of success.

Detective Inspector Godley said that when he arrested Chapman for the murder by poison of Maud Marsh, Chapman had replied: "I know nothing about it. I do not know how she got the poison. Can I have bail?" Later, when Inspector Godley charged him under the name of Severin Klosowski, Chapman replied: "I do not know the name of the other fellow." And when charged with the murders of Mary Spink and Bessie Taylor, Chapman had asked: "By what means? Stabbing, shooting, or what?"

Making the closing speech for the defence, Mr Elliot said he did not intend to call any evidence, and complained that there was a "storm of prejudice" surrounding his client because of popular resentment against aliens. He emphasised that Chapman had no motive for murdering his wives. "There was no necessity for the accused to resort to any act of this sort to free himself from one woman so that he might live with another."

Chapman wept throughout the defence speech.

For the prosecution, the Solicitor-General claimed that Chapman had committed murder simply to sleep with three women.

It took the jury only ten minutes to find Chapman guilty. The judge then told him: "Severin Klosowski – for I decline to address you by the English name which you have assumed – the only satisfactory feature in this case which we have just completed is that I am able to address you as a foreigner and not as an Englishman. The jury has come to the only conclusion which I am sure everyone who has heard the case would have come to. It is not necessary for me to go into the harrowing details of the case and refer again to the frightful cruelty you have been guilty of in murdering the women on whom you have gratified your vile lust. I have but one duty to perform. It is the duty of sentencing you to death."

Chapman seemed dumbstruck with terror after the sentence was pronounced, and was driven away through a hostile crowd who hissed at him. No one protested on his behalf or pleaded for clemency, and he was hanged at Wandsworth Prison on April 7th, 1903, having made a will leaving property valued at £140 to Bessie Taylor's relatives.

Chapman's letters from the condemned cell contain spelling errors which invite comparison with the notes allegedly written by Jack the Ripper.

One read: ". . . be careful in your life of other enemis whom are unknow to you. Shall now be starting preparing for my Deth as it is past four-o-clock afternoon." Another declared: "I am an American orphan of good family. I took to erning my own living at the age of ten. I have never been so unlucky since I lost poor Bessie Taylor and therefore I regretted that day ever since I stopped in this country." Chapman went on to accuse witnesses of having committed perjury, and the police of fabricating evidence against him, but his guilt is surely abundantly clear.

Why did this Casanova kill women when he could woo them so easily and without risk? I am convinced that the answer is that he secretly despised women. Time and again it has been noted in studies of promiscuous people that although they engage in abundant sex, they do not really like it. For them, the act is not an expression of love, but a means of expressing contempt for their eager victims.

And psychologists might declare, as they have about the real Casanova, that there was a considerable hidden element of latent homosexuality in Chapman. . .

2
ANTIMONY

Antimony is closely related in toxicology and chemistry to arsenic. Their symptoms and effects are much the same. Both preserve the body after death in an almost embalmed state. Each is an irritant poison which gives rise to an illness which can easily be mistaken for gastroenteritis. Like arsenic, antimony is soluble, colourless, odourless, and practically tasteless. Both poisons can be detected by the Marsh Test.

Yet although arsenic cases can be numbered by the score, antimony has been rarely used. Arsenic was favoured over antimony because it was easy to obtain, being sold in every corner shop as a pesticide. Antimony, a metallic element used to strengthen alloys, was harder to acquire and had one great disadvantage. It caused copious vomiting, which meant that the victim was likely to purge himself of the poison rather than ingest it. For that reason, the antimony poisoner had to rely on small doses given frequently.

Antimony is extracted from the ore stibnite, and the effect of a number of small doses is cumulative. The poison accumulates in the vital internal organs, especially the liver, causing stomach and muscular pains, diarrhoea, skin rashes, and death. Antimony compounds are all toxic, but this poison was most common in Victorian times as tartar emetic (potassium antimonyl tartrate), and used, as its name suggests, as an emetic to induce vomiting and purge the system.

The fatal dose varies according to the individual, but one and a half grains have been known to cause death, although there are recorded cases of four hundred grains being taken without fatal effect. (Over twenty-nine grains were found in the body of one of George Chapman's victims).

The victim of antimony poisoning will experience a loss of appetite which, combined with vomiting, soon leads to an emaciated state. Constriction of the throat and muscle cramps and intense thirst make the effect more violent than arsenic poisoning, and since the poison depresses the heart and respiratory action, death usually occurs from heart failure.

In Roman times, it was common for guests at a feast to overeat so much that they used to make themselves vomit in order to make room for more. For this purpose special cups would be cast out of antimony and filled with wine, which was then left to stand for several days. The acid in the sour wine would dissolve the antimony, producing a drink which induced vomiting. Such cups were also common in monasteries, where greedy monks who had over-indulged were forced by the Abbot to have "one more from the Cup."

Notable poisoners who used antimony include Florence Bravo, Dr William Palmer and Dr Edward William Pritchard. Florence Bravo was never tried, but the facts are these. Charles Bravo, a barrister, lived with his wealthy twenty-five-year-old wife, Florence, at The Priory, Balham. On April 18th, 1876, after a dinner party they had given, Bravo retired to his room. At 9.45 p.m. he was heard calling loudly for his wife to fetch hot water. Mrs Cox, Florence's companion, went into Bravo's room and found him sick. He almost immediately lapsed into unconsciousness.

Florence was awakened and sent for a physician, Doctor Gully. He suspected poisoning but could not identify the agent, and so Florence sent for Sir William Gull, the most esteemed physician in England, to examine her husband. Once Bravo was conscious, Gull asked him what he had taken, saying: "This is not a disease. You are poisoned; pray tell me how you came by it." Bravo mumbled that he had merely rubbed some laudanum on his gums against neuralgia, and might have accidentally swallowed some. Gull told him: "That won't explain your symptoms."

Thirty-year-old Bravo died on April 21st, and a post mortem examination found the cause was antimony poisoning, administered in a single dose of between twenty to thirty grains. His inquest recorded an open verdict, and it was widely felt that he had committed suicide. But as it was known that Florence had had an affair with the elderly Doctor Gully, and that Mrs Cox had quarrelled with Charles Bravo, the case became a Victorian *cause célèbre*.

Dr William Palmer – "The Rugeley Poisoner" – was a notorious rogue who possibly murdered fourteen people, simply to gain the insurance monies due on their lives. He disposed of his mother-in-law; four of his children died in infancy; his wife and brother died after he had insured them; he poisoned his best friend to collect his gambling winnings.

Local prejudice against him was so great that it was felt that he could not get a fair trial in Staffordshire, and the "Palmer Act" was passed by Parliament, making it possible for an accused person in a similar position to be tried in London. Following his Old Bailey trial in May 1856, Palmer was convicted and sentenced to death. He was hanged outside Stafford Gaol on June 14th, 1856, the huge crowd which had gathered to watch him swing hissing "Poisoner!" at him as he mounted the scaffold. He made no last-minute confession.

An inveterate backer of horses, he had in 1853 lost most of his recent winnings of £14,000 by laying them against the horse West Australian in the Derby. "Have you nothing to regret, William?" asked his clergyman brother when Palmer arrived at the gallows. "Yes," said the poisoner. "I have never ceased to reproach myself for opposing West Australian."

3
GEORGE HENRY LAMSON
The Saint who Strayed
"The Doctor died like a gentleman" –
James Marwood, hangman.

Dr George Henry Lamson, born in 1850, had the makings of a great man. Young and idealistic, generous and moral-minded, he spoke French fluently, along with other European languages, and had by hard work and reading attained a level of culture and sophistication well above that of his contemporaries. And he wasn't just a bookworm. In 1876-77 he went out to serve as a volunteer army-surgeon in Serbia and Romania during the Russo-Turkish war, and his humanitarian work brought him decorations from both countries. He gained a wide reputation, and had a wide circle of friends not only in England, but also on the Continent and in America. He seemed a young man destined for distinction.

And distinguished he duly became. . . as a poisoner. He was a would-be saint who strayed, and his actions were to be as shocking as if Mother Theresa of Calcutta were to be exposed as a shop-lifter. . .

It was in 1876, when he was aged twenty-three, that Lamson married Miss John, a ward in Chancery whose small fortune passed by the marriage into his hands. He gained not only wealth, but also two brothers-in-law from his marriage, Herbert and Percy. When Herbert John died suddenly in 1879, he left £700 to his sister – now Mrs Lamson – and with this money Dr Lamson bought a medical practice in Bournemouth. (It was later claimed that the untimely death of Herbert John owed something to Lamson's skill as a poisoner).

The practice failed to flourish, and Lamson had to sell it, together with his home. It seems he had no head for business, and this wasn't helped by another failing: he had become a drug-addict. In 1881 he went to America to try to make his fortune, but met with no greater success. He arrived back in England with only five pounds – and that borrowed from the surgeon on the ship on which he returned. Lamson was in desperate need of cash, not just the few pounds he could count on from friends, but several thousand to settle his debts.

Although this crisis undoubtedly led to what was to come, the seeds of destruction had been planted years before. It was while serving in the Balkans that Lamson had become addicted to morphine, and it was to this that he later attributed his downfall.

The young doctor now had to provide for a wife and child, with no income and creditors pressing for repayment. It never seemed to occur to him to seek work. Instead he began writing cheques which he knew would not be honoured, for his account was overdrawn. He also wrote a cheque for £12 10s upon a bank at which he had never had an account. For a few pounds, this man of promise was risking a hefty prison sentence.

Lamson was to deny having anything to do with the death of Herbert John, but as that death had proved to be so fortunate, gaining him a legacy through his wife, it may have given him the inspiration for the murder he *did* commit and to which he confessed on the gallows.

If his remaining brother-in-law, Percy Malcolm John, were to die unmarried and before reaching the age of twenty-one, half his inheritance of £3,000 would pass to Mrs Lamson. Dr Lamson must have thought long and hard about this. Perhaps he reasoned that as Percy was a cripple with not many years to live as his condition was getting worse, bringing about his death could even be considered an act of mercy. The money he left would bring such relief to his grieving relatives. . .

And so sentence of death was passed on Percy John, aged eighteen and crippled from birth. He suffered from curvature of the spine, his lower limbs being completely paralysed, and spent his days in a wheelchair, having to be carried up and down stairs by fellow-pupils at Blenheim House School, Wimbledon. Yet he had a happy disposition, and his good nature and cheerful courage earned him the respect and friendship of all who knew him.

Lamson had made his first attempt on young Percy's life in the summer of 1881, while on holiday on the Isle of Wight, where the doctor had taken his wife immediately on his return from America. Percy joined them at Shanklin for a brief holiday, and Lamson experimented with aconite by feeding Percy a "quinine pill". Percy recovered from his sudden malady. Perhaps the doctor was just trying to determine the lethal dosage.

After this Lamson made another trip to America, but came home even poorer than before, having to pawn his watch and a case of surgical instruments for five pounds. Now he must have become even more desperate for money, since in November 1881, while staying at Nelson's Hotel in Great Portland Street, London, he attempted to buy aconitine from a chemist in Oxford Street. He was refused because the proprietor did not know him, but he did manage to purchase two grains from a shop in Hanbury. It was later established that this was enough to kill thirty people, the sale subsequently prompting the trial judge to comment on the ease with which lethal poisons could be purchased.

Now Lamson needed some cash to keep him going until he could dispose of Percy, and so he went to the Isle of Wight and got a friend to advance him twenty pounds on a worthless cheque drawn on the Wilts & Dorset Bank.

Lamson next let it be known that he had long intended

to visit Paris, writing to Percy on December 1st: "My Dear Percy, I had intended running down to Wimbledon to see you today, but I have been delayed by various matters until it is now nearly six o'clock, and by the time I should reach Blenheim House you would probably be preparing for bed. I leave for Paris and Florence tomorrow and wish to see you before going, so I propose to run down to your place as early as I can for a few minutes, even if I can accomplish no more. Believe me, my dear boy, your loving brother, George Lamson."

What Lamson really wanted to accomplish was the poisoning of the boy whose death represented £1,500, but the method he employed was so clumsy and contrived that detection was inevitable. Despite his intellectual accomplishments, he was an inept killer. Just as morphine had landed him in this mess, so did it probably cloud his judgement when he planned Percy's poisoning.

On December 2nd, Lamson went to Wimbledon, leaving a friend in a public house before going to visit the school. But he never arrived there. Perhaps his nerve failed him. He was back at the pub twenty minutes later, saying that he had seen Percy, and the poor boy was much weaker.

Returning to London, Lamson cashed yet another fraudulent cheque, and armed with some cash, the following evening just before seven o'clock, he called at Blenheim House and asked to see Percy. Mr Bedbrook, the headmaster, and Lamson waited in the dining room while Percy was carried up to them. Lamson, who had asked the headmaster to remain with them, greeted Percy with the words: "How fat you are looking, Percy, old boy." His brother-in-law, who thought Lamson was looking decidedly unwell, replied: "I wish I could say the same of you, George."

Now came the pantomime, the sleight of hand, the artful conjuring trick which Lamson had devised. When offered a glass of sherry, Lamson asked for sugar to "neutralise the alcohol", spooning it into his glass. The headmaster thought this was odd: he believed that sugar would tend to increase the alcohol's potency, if anything. Lamson then took from his bag a Dundee cake which was already cut into three slices, and placed it on the table, offering one slice to the headmaster, another to Percy, before taking one for himself. Undoubtedly, the poison had been pre-concealed in the slice given to Percy, a slice which Lamson must have carefully marked and noted in order to ensure it went to the right party, perhaps hiding the aconitine in the raisins.

Lamson next remarked to the headmaster: "While in America I did not forget you. I have bought these capsules for you. You will find them very useful to give the boys medicine. I should like you to try one and see how easily they can be swallowed."

He took from his bag a box of capsules, taking one apart to show that it was empty, before filling it with sugar from the bowl and resealing it. "Here you are, Percy," he said, smiling, "You are the champion pill-taker. Let's see you swallow this."

Percy took the capsule and gulped it down. The capsule business was designed to divert attention from the real source of poisoning: the cake. Everyone would suspect the capsule, but Lamson had the headmaster as a witness to say that only sugar had been added to that. Already Lamson was planning how to hoodwink a possible jury, but his scheme backfired. The jurymen were not concerned with *how* Percy had been poisoned, but with the undisputed fact that he had been.

Immediately Percy had taken the capsule, Lamson rose abruptly, looking at his watch. "I must be going now," he said. The headmaster pointed out that he had just missed a train and would have a half-hour wait for the next, and suggested he should stay a little longer. But Lamson was adamant, saying he would miss the boat-train from Victoria unless he went at once. No doubt he was anxious to be off the premises, not knowing how soon the poison would take effect.

Within twenty minutes of the doctor's departure, Percy

began to complain of heartburn, becoming steadily worse as he was carried up to bed. He was obviously in great pain, telling the headmaster, who had asked what his symptoms were: "I feel the same as I did, only worse, after my brother-in-law gave me a pill when we were at Shanklin!"

The school matron was soon at the boy's bedside, to be joined within a minute or so by the school doctor, Dr Berry. By chance there happened to be a second doctor at the school that evening, Dr Edward Little, and he too hurried to the boy's bedside. It was immediately obvious to both doctors that Percy was suffering from the effects of a vegetable poison, and they collected samples of the boy's excreta and vomit. Percy was now writhing about in such agony that he had to be held down on the bed. Meanwhile they tried vainly to save him with hot linseed poultices on his stomach, which had little effect.

Unable to save Percy's life, the doctors tried to make the pain bearable by giving him massive doses of morphine, but within an hour the boy had died. The headmaster immediately informed the police, indicating his suspicions about Lamson.

Lamson, meanwhile, had caught the boat-train to Paris, where he stayed for the next five days, no doubt studying with some interest the London newspapers. They carried extensive reports on the case, with references to the suspicion of Lamson's guilt. He had been the last person to give Percy food, and he stood to gain from the boy's death.

Lamson now decided on bold action. He returned to England on December 8th and went straight to Scotland Yard, demanding to see Inspector Butcher and explaining: "I am Dr Lamson whose name has been mentioned in connection with the death at Wimbledon." His voluntary return, he must have thought, would make a good impression, not being the act of a guilty man.

Inspector Butcher was indeed anxious to see him. He arrested him and took him before magistrates to be remanded to Wandsworth Prison.

Everything now depended upon the outcome of the Old Bailey trial. The police used the time Lamson was on remand to investigate his background, discovering the extent of his debts, his habit of writing dud cheques, the fact that he stood to gain from Percy's death, and more significantly his purchase of two grains of aconitine.

The authorities soon found that Lamson was a morphia addict who sometimes took injections every hour. Denied recourse to the drug in prison, Lamson went through the agonies of "cold turkey", begging for morphia and completely unable to help his defence counsel.

His trial began on March 9th, 1882, before Mr Justice Henry Hawkins. The Solicitor-General, Sir Farrer Herschell, led for the Crown, while Lamson was represented by four defence counsel. (It is traditional for the Solicitor-General to prosecute in poisoning trials, because of their gravity – as will be seen in later cases).

A huge crowd had gathered to see Lamson, whose pale face, lofty forehead, dark intelligent eyes and black spade beard gave him the appearance of a young Charles Dickens. After bowing elaborately to the judge, he pleaded not guilty to the charge of murder.

The prosecution outlined its case in an opening speech which left no doubt of Lamson's guilt. Although there existed no chemical test as yet to detect vegetable poisons, proof would be presented of the presence of aconitine in the victim's organs. Proof would be given that Lamson had fed the boy a capsule and a slice of cake immediately prior to his death. There would also be proof that Lamson had purchased aconitine, and that he stood to benefit from Percy's death. In short, the Crown would establish means, method, opportunity and motive.

Home Office pathologist Dr Thomas Stevenson (Alfred Swaine Taylor's successor at Guy's) gave evidence of having tested the boy's vomit, and of having extracted a substance which could only be aconite. He had a quaint method of identifying poisons: he told the judge that he had between fifty and seventy alkaloid poisons in his possession and he tasted them all, trying to find a match to the suspect substance. He had no trouble diagnosing aconitine: in fact, he suffered from its effects for four hours after his tasting session.

The doctor told the court that from the contents of the bowels he had obtained an alkaloid extract "which was distinctive and produced a very faint sensation like that of aconitia. When placed on the tongue, burning of the lips was produced though the extract did not touch the lips. Burning, tingling – a kind of numbness peculiar but difficult to define; a salivation creating a desire to expectorate, a sensation at the back of the throat of swelling up, and this was followed by a peculiar seared sensation of the tongue, as if a hot iron had been drawn over it."

He had also injected mice with this extract, and in each case the injections produced precisely the same symptoms and results as an injection with Morson's Aconitia. A considerable number of mice were killed in the course of this experiment. In his closing speech, defence counsel condemned the cruelty of these experiments. But it was not the last time mice were to be used in this way – see, for example, the case of Kenneth Barlow.

Drs Little and Berry, who had attended the dying boy, admitted in the witness box that they knew nothing of the properties of aconitine, and could not commit themselves to the defence theory that Percy had died from pressure on the arteries, caused by curvature of the spine. It was possible, but not likely. But Dr Stevenson more than made up for their lack of knowledge, his testimony greatly influencing the jury. And he could not be shaken under cross-examination.

As the Criminal Evidence Act had not then been passed, the prisoner was not allowed to give evidence on his own behalf, and had to watch in silence while others fought for his life.

The jury took just forty-five minutes to return with a verdict of guilty, and Lamson, "protesting his innocence before God", was sentenced to death.

Strenuous efforts were made by his many friends to win him a reprieve, with affidavits being sent to the Home Office stating that Lamson's brain had long been abnormal, his ethical sense having been destroyed by his morphine habit.

A colleague who had served with Lamson during the Balkan War of 1877 wrote that while there, Lamson had "exhibited a mania for the administration of aconitine in almost every case, using it in season and out of season, and in such quantities as to alarm the medical staff and to render his recall to England necessary." Another affidavit told of his conduct at the siege of Paris in 1871, when his reckless use of drugs made him a public danger. From America came an affidavit signed by three prominent physicians who had met him the previous year and were convinced that morphia injections had turned his brain. "He passed the greater part of the day either dozing or attempting to read. He was then using a mixture apparently of morphia and atropine, but said that he preferred aconitine but could not procure it in that section of the country." Dr Winston, the medical director of the New York Mutual Life Assurance Company, wrote that he considered that "he had become a helpless victim of the habit, which had seriously impaired his mental powers and destroyed his moral responsibility." Lamson's defence counsel testified that he "could obtain no assistance from him in the preparation of his defence – that he appeared to have no memory and to be incapable of appreciating the bearing of any of the facts of his case or the gravity of his position."

The Home Secretary, Sir William Harcourt, postponed the date of the execution in order to have time to study these affidavits, but after reading them stated that he found no reason to advise the Queen to exercise her prerogative of mercy, especially in view of the fact that the defence of insanity had not been raised at the trial.

A few days before his execution Lamson, reduced to a terrified wretch, wrote a long, rambling document which appeared to be a confession, and also confessed his guilt to the prison chaplain. But he denied that he had been responsible for the death of Herbert John.

On April 28th, 1882, the broken Dr Lamson, aged only twenty-nine but looking much older, had to be practically carried, almost unconscious, to the gallows at Wandsworth Prison. Unable to stand, he was held on the drop by two warders, and even then tried to snatch another minute of life by begging the chaplain to recite just one more prayer. But the hangman pulled the lever, ending the life of this man who had once seemed to have so much to offer.

Outside the prison the great Victorian executioner, James Marwood, told reporters, without apparent irony: "The doctor died like a gentleman."

There is a footnote to this case, missed by many writers. In 1904 the trial judge, Sir Henry Hawkins, published his *Reminiscences* in which he stated that he was not altogether convinced by the prosecution suggestion that Lamson had inserted poison into the capsule he handed to Percy John. To have poisoned the boy in such a manner would have been a clumsy device for so keen and artful a criminal as Lamson, and I knew that it was conveyed in another manner. . . If the poison had been conveyed in the capsule, its operation would have been almost immediate, and so would the detection of the aconitine. . . A detective would not expect to find the design so foolishly exposed, any more than a spectator would expect to see the actual trick of a conjurer in the manner of its performance.

"I was not able to bring the artifice before the jury; the Crown had not discovered it, and Lamson's deep-laid scheme was nearly successful. His plan, of course, was to lead the prosecution to maintain that he gave the poison in the capsule. and then compel them to show that there was no evidence of it. The jury were satisfied that the boy had been poisoned by Lamson, and little troubled themselves about the way in which it was done."

4
ACONITINE

Aconitine is a drug extracted from the leaves and roots of the family of plants known as aconites. These include monkshood and wolfsbane, "bane" being the cautionary word: one of its meanings is "a fatal poison."

As little as one-fiftieth of a grain of aconitine can stop the heart beating. It is particularly dangerous because, being partially soluble in water and oil, it can be absorbed directly through contact with the skin.

The plant often causes accidental death since it looks so edible, both above and under ground. *Aconitum napellus* is the variety found commonly in Europe and America, and its foliage looks very similar to parsley or watercress. In the last twenty years, several deaths have been reported in California after hungry hikers have nibbled the tops of the plants.

Aconitum columbianum is a larger variety, with a root resembling a young turnip or radish. In 1969 a group of French soldiers on a survival course cooked and ate the roots. They all died. An Indian variety, *Aconitum spicatum*, is even more deadly. During the Nepalese War of 1814–16, Gurkhas extracted this plant's poison, which they called *bikh*, to contaminate wells used for drinking by British troops.

One-fiftieth of a grain (1–2 milligrammes) taken by mouth will almost instantly paralyse the lungs and cause death. As aconitine can penetrate the skin, it is often used in the form of liniments and ointments to treat sciatica and rheumatism, or tinctures to alleviate toothache. A very minute amount rubbed on the skin will produce a warm, tingling glow which acts as a mild anaesthetic. There are still some patent liniments available which use a preparation of about two per cent of the pure drug, but they have fallen into disfavour since the discovery that rubbing these lotions into the skin can produce exactly the same symptoms of aconitine poisoning as if taken orally.

A published warning of this dangerous quality read: ". . . a lethal dose causes diminution in force and frequency of pulse, a cold and clammy skin, a tingling and numbness of the mouth, face, and throat. Somewhat larger doses cause burning of the throat and stomach, increased salivation, nausea, retching and vomiting, grinding of the teeth and extension of the numbness and tingling to other parts of the body. There is difficulty in swallowing and speaking and pain in eyes and head. The fatal period is from eight minutes to three or four hours." (N. Irving Sax, *Dangerous Properties of Industrial Materials,* 1975.)

The ancient Greeks called aconitine the Queen of Poisons – although another Greek term for it was "stepmother's poison." It was used extensively in Greece and Rome for the assassination of political rivals, and the Emperor Trajan had to issue an edict forbidding Romans to grow wolfsbane in their gardens. According to Greek mythology, the poison was created from the saliva of the demon-dog Cerberus, guardian of the underworld, as Hercules carried him towards Mariandyne; the cave where they rested is called Acone. Another version has the sorceress Medea creating aconites, and even the queen of the witches, Hecate, is credited with their genesis. Another name for aconite is hecateis.

Indians used the Himalayan aconite from at least the second century BC, and Japanese whalers used to grind *Aconitum japonicum* between stones to produce a paste with which to tip their harpoons, a practice they continued for centuries. Since not much paste could be smeared on the tip of a harpoon, and the whale is very large, some idea of the potency of the poison can be gained from this.

Nevertheless, aconitine does not figure much in the history of our poisoners. Apart from the notable case of Dr Lamson, the only other candidates who were known to have used aconitine were Dr Alfred Warder and Dr Edward William Pritchard. Both aconitine and antimony were employed by Pritchard to poison his wife and mother-in-law. He was hanged in Glasgow on July 28th, 1865, before a crowd of 100,000.

Dr Alfred Warder was an authority on forensic medicine and toxicology, and in this capacity testified for the defence at the trial of Dr William Palmer in 1856.

Warder had his first practice in London and was married in 1863, but his wife died suddenly. He married again two years later, having heavily insured this wife's life, but she too died suddenly, just eight months after the wedding.

In 1866 Dr Warder moved to Brighton, where he met and married Ethel Branwell, a doctor's sister. Aged thirty-six, she was in excellent health, but became ill not long after her wedding. Although she was being treated for her mysterious ailment by her doctor-husband, her brother insisted that another doctor be called in. Consequently, local practitioner Dr Taafe took care of the patient, who appeared to improve under his treatment. Learning that Dr Warder had been giving his wife Fleming's Tincture of Aconite, Dr Taafe pointed out that this was intended for external application only, and began treating the patient with a mixture of henbane and opium.

However, Dr Warder insisted on once more taking over his wife's case, complaining that she did not like Dr Taafe's remedy and refused to take it any more. Mrs Warder rapidly took a turn for the worse and died. The suspicious Dr Taafe insisted on a post-mortem examination, and the dead woman's intestines were sent to Dr Alfred Swaine Taylor, the leading authority in toxicology, at London's Guy's Hospital.

At a subsequent inquest on the dead woman, Dr Taylor said her death was consistent with aconitine poisoning over a long period. Before the inquest had ended and before police officers could arrive at his home to arrest him, Dr Warder committed suicide with prussic acid.

The final inquest verdict on his wife was that she had died "from the effects of aconite administered wilfully and with malice aforethought by her late husband." But by killing himself, Dr Warder left unanswered the questions about the sudden deaths of his first two wives. As he was a forensic expert, he remains a rare example of a game-keeper turned poacher.

Aconitine was probably chosen by three murderous doctors because no test then existed to detect this particular poison. It was not until the 1920s that a test was devised.

Professor Sir Robert Christison – who had George Lamson as a student and was one of the foremost toxi-cologists of his time – was once giving evidence in a poison case and said to the judge: "My Lord, there is but one deadly agent of this kind which we cannot satisfac-torily trace in the human body after death, and that is. . ." At this point the judge stopped him, "in the public interest," from naming the poison. It was aconitine, and this incident may have influenced Lamson when he planned the murder of his young brother-in-law.

Christison, incidentally, was an expert witness in the trial of Burke and Hare. To discover whether a body would bruise after death, he beat corpses.

5
FLORENCE MAYBRICK
The Cat Woman

*"My daughter Florence is not a woman of great
penetration"* – *Baroness von Roques.*
"Come at once. Strange things going on here" –
telegram received by the victim's brother, Michael Maybrick.
"Oh, Bunny, how could you do it?" –
James Maybrick speaking to his wife, Florence.

Remember *Thelma & Louise*, hit film of 1991, and its
depiction of women as victims of men? There is a French
phrase which translates as "the more things change, the
more they stay the same." Back in 1889, Florence Maybrick was certainly a victim of men: of her husband, and
her judges. Finally, perhaps, she was a victim of her own
nature.

She was born in Mobile, Alabama, USA, the daughter
of a banker who died in her infancy. Her mother believed
that the path to happiness lay through marrying wealthy
men, preferably with titles, and had been married three
times, her last husband being a Prussian baron. It was as
Baroness von Roques that she took her daughter on ocean
cruises, hoping she might meet a suitable match among
the fellow-passengers.

They met an English cotton merchant, James
Maybrick, aboard the White Star liner *Baltic*. Although he

was twenty-four years older than Florence, the mother though him a good catch for her daughter. For although the Baroness talked of the family wealth that Florence would inherit, the fact was that finances were somewhat strained.

The mother thought her eighteen-year-old daughter a dumb little ninny, once saying of her: "My daughter is not a woman of great penetration." She was probably glad to get her off her hands. The attraction for Maybrick was obvious: he was getting a child-bride with wide blue eyes, blonde hair and a voluptuous figure. And Maybrick was guilty of exaggerating his financial position. He was not as wealthy as he made out.

The marriage took place in 1881, after Maybrick had introduced his teenage fiancée to his relatives in Liverpool. Then they spent the first three years of their marriage in Norfolk, Virginia, before returning to England in 1884, to settle in the Liverpool district of Aigburth in a large and ugly mansion called Battlecrease House (which stands to this day, opposite Liverpool Cricket Club).

Five servants were required to manage the twenty-room mansion, but despite his much-vaunted wealth Maybrick had only settled a £2,000 insurance policy on his new bride. However, he did initially manage to keep her in the style to which she had become accustomed. Thanks to her mother, Florence had grown up with a taste for designer-clothes and frequent trips abroad.

At first, life was comfortable. But soon Florence began to find the house a virtual prison. The staff were dour, she had no outside friends, and she would walk the grounds of the house restlessly. After the light and warmth of the American South, Merseyside seemed damp and gloomy. Florence missed not only the sun, but also the traditions of the South: the courtesy and easy friendships, the grand balls and excitement.

Two children were born to the couple: a son in America in 1882, followed by a daughter in England in 1886. At first the couple seemed to be the epitome of marital bliss, going to parties arm-in-arm, or going horse-riding together, Florence gently teasing her husband about his grey hairs.

But she was lonely, and her ever-protective mother was now living in Paris, on a small income from Maybrick. The servants resented Florence's youth and her American origin, and she could never bring herself to give them orders.

Unknown to her, Maybrick's business was in trouble and he was losing capital at an alarming rate. The prospect of becoming poor, or even being thought to be poor, terrified him. For years he had been taking arsenic and other drugs, telling friends "I take this arsenic. . . because I find that it strengthens me. . ." He also believed in the common myth that it was an aphrodisiac. Now, beset by financial worries, he began increasing his daily dosage. On the surface the Maybricks were living a placid life, but behind the façade dangerous currents were beginning to stir.

Maybrick's use of poisons can be traced back to 1877 when, while in the USA, he had been treated successfully for malaria with a mixture of strychnine and arsenic. Now he believed in the poison as a sovereign remedy. He was an addict. This was not uncommon. Many people ate arsenic as a tonic, and women used it as a cosmetic to improve the complexion.

Florence was worried by her husband's use of such a dangerous poison and warned him of its consequences. She was also concerned enough to tell both her own doctor and Maybrick's physician about his habit. The doctors smiled benevolently and dismissed her fears. The wealthy could use what nostrums they chose. . .

The first blow to shake the foundations of the May-brick marriage came when James revealed to her his financial plight. His assets were down to £1,500, and the couple would have to economise drastically. He cut her housekeeping allowance – out of which she had to pay for food and the servants' wages – to a mere £7 a week. She hardly dared confess that unknown to her husband, she had run up debts of £600 in buying clothes and gambling on horses.

Florence wrote at this time to her mother: "Is life worth living? I would gladly give up the house tomorrow and move somewhere else, but Jim says it would ruin him outright. For one has to keep up appearances. . ."

The second blow fell when Florence discovered that her husband had been keeping a mistress for years, whom he was still seeing, and by whom he had five children. He was paying her an allowance of £100 a year.

In retaliation, Florence began flirting openly at the dinner-table with Maybrick's brother, Edwin, telling him that she wished she had married him instead. A serious affair then developed between her and a friend of Maybrick's, Alfred Brierley, a tall dashing man who was also a cotton merchant. She first met him at a dance at Battlecrease House, and thereafter pursued him recklessly.

In March 1889 she arranged to meet him in London, telegraphing Flatman's Hotel in Covent Garden to reserve rooms in the name of "Mr and Mrs Thomas Maybrick". Thomas was another of her husband's four brothers. Telling her husband she had to visit a sick aunt, Florence spent three days – from March 22nd to 24th – with her lover as man and wife at the hotel. When she left on the 24th, she stayed at a friend's house in London, before returning to Liverpool on the 28th.

She took no precautions to keep her affair secret, and staff at the hotel could testify to her presence there with Brierley for three full days. At the end of that time, Brierley told her that their relationship must cease. She was later to tell her lawyer: "Before we parted he gave me to understand that he cared for somebody else and could not marry me, and that rather than face the disgrace of discovery he would blow his brains out." Brierley booked himself a two-month sea cruise soon afterwards.

The day after Florence's return the Maybricks went with a group of friends to watch the Grand National. By accident they bumped into Brierley. It must have been an uncomfortable encounter. Defiantly, Florence went to stand alone with Brierley at the rail, infuriating her husband, who suspected the liaison.

The Maybricks had been sleeping apart for some time, and this incident provoked an explosion. When he got her home, the enraged Maybrick blacked Florence's eye and tore her clothes, shouting at her: "This scandal will be all over town tomorrow!" He ordered the housemaid, Bessie, to call a cab and turn Mrs Maybrick out of the house.

The cook, Elizabeth Humphreys, later testified that Maybrick "ranted and stamped like a madman." But she was brave enough to argue with her employer and get him to relent. Florence could stay the night. . .

The following morning Florence made a fatal mistake. She confided her marital problems to a neighbour, Mrs Briggs, who was herself divorced. Mrs Briggs pretended to be a sympathetic and concerned listener, but in reality she was a mischievous and malicious woman who delighted in provoking trouble. She advised Florence to seek a separation and took her to see her own solicitor and doctor. The physician went to Battlecrease House and persuaded Maybrick not only to take his wife back, but also to settle her debts.

Meanwhile, the servants, regarding Florence as an American upstart, had began spying on their mistress. In the month that followed, both the maid and the nanny, aptly named Alice Yapp, saw Florence soaking flypapers in a water-filled basin in her bedroom: flypapers which everyone knew contained arsenic. . .

Florence did this quite openly, and was later to say that she had for many years used a facewash prescribed by her doctor in America, a lotion with arsenic and elderflower among its ingredients. There was a fancy-dress ball due, and since she had a boil coming up on her face, she had soaked the flypapers to get the arsenic for her facewash. Apparently it worked, for she attended the ball, escorted by Edwin Maybrick.

James Maybrick fell ill on April 27th, vomiting after taking medicine prescribed by his London doctor. He commented that it must have contained too much strychnine. He recovered sufficiently to go to the Wirral races, where he got soaking wet and caught a chill. The following morning he again vomited, having taken brandy to ease his stomach. Florence gave him a mustard emetic and sent for Dr Humphreys.

Maybrick told the doctor he feared he was becoming paralysed, complaining of numbness in his legs, but the doctor thought the symptoms were due to the strychnine prescribed by Dr Fuller. In March Florence had told him about a white powder her husband was in the habit of taking and which she thought might be responsible for his pains, but Dr Humphreys responded comfortingly and with an odd lightness: "Well, if he should die suddenly, call me and I can say we had some conversation about it."

Florence had also written to Maybrick's brother, Michael, telling him about the white powder she had found her husband taking. When Maybrick visited London, his brother asked him about his habit of arsenic-eating, and James replied angrily: "Whoever told you that? It is a damned lie!"

By the evening Maybrick was well again, and the doctor concluded that he was a chronic dyspeptic and put him on a diet. He had questioned Maybrick about his drugs habit, but Maybrick denied ever taking arsenic or strychnine. On May 1st the doctor found Maybrick so well that he thought he would not have to call again.

A week before this, Florence had bought a dozen flypapers. Shortly afterwards, Maybrick made a new will, excluding his wife. On April 29th, she bought another two dozen flypapers. The following day she attended the fancy-dress ball, and her husband felt fit enough to return to his office. The servants were by now openly whispering that Florence was poisoning her husband, even though she had nothing to do with the preparation of food or drink. The meddlesome neighbour, Mrs Briggs, took care of that. She had taken to having her meals in the house, and even took over choosing the menu.

On May 1st Maybrick went to his office, taking with him a meat juice extract prepared by the cook and placed in a jug supplied by Florence. Over the next two days Maybrick took the same meat extract and complained of sickness afterwards. Captain Irving, a friend of his who happened to be in the office, testified that Maybrick complained of feeling unwell after drinking the preparation. But he had taken a packet of powder from his pocket, mixed it with a glass of water and drunk it, saying soon afterwards that he felt much better. This did not surprise Irving because, as he said, Maybrick's office "was more like a chemist's shop than anything else. . . It was well known that James Maybrick had been in the habit of taking strychnine for years."

On May 3rd Florence sent urgently for Dr Humphreys at midnight, saying that her husband was very ill and was suffering from "a gnawing pain from the hips down to the knees." The doctor tended his patient over the next few days, nursing him through bouts of severe vomiting and diarrhoea. He gave Maybrick a morphia suppository. By the 4th the pain had gone although the vomiting continued. On the 5th he seemed better, and remained in this condition on the 6th. The doctor now stopped him taking the meat extract, and prescribed for him Fowler's solution of arsenic, of which Maybrick took three doses, amounting to 1/250th of a grain of arsenic in all.

Florence was not satisfied with the medical care. She had told Alice Yapp early on that Dr Humphreys said her husband's illness was due to his liver – "But all doctors are fools," she said. "They say the liver because that covers a multitude of sins." At her suggestion another physician, Dr Carter, was called in and Florence arranged to hire a nurse. Dr Carter prescribed a sedative, diagnosing Maybrick as suffering from acute dyspepsia.

Dr Humphreys called again on May 8th and found Maybrick's condition unchanged. He was hopeful of a recovery soon. But that same day Alice Yapp told Mrs Briggs about the soaking of the flypapers, and Mrs Briggs immediately sent a telegram to Michael Maybrick in London. It read: "Come at once. Strange things going on here." She also told Edwin Maybrick, who was living in the house, about Alice Yapp's statement.

When Nurse Gore arrived that afternoon to begin her duties, Edwin instructed her that no one else should be allowed to attend to his brother, who had taken a turn for the worse. Florence, meanwhile, decided to write a letter in answer to one she had received from Brierley, in which he said he feared Maybrick might be trying to find out about their affair, and he was going away to try and forget "this unhappy business", but hoped to see her in the autumn.

Florence's reply began "Dearest, Since my return I have been nursing M day and night. He is sick unto death." She said her lover need have no fear of discovery, since Maybrick knew nothing, and begged him not to leave England before seeing her first. At three o'clock that afternoon Florence gave the letter to Alice Yapp to post. Instead of posting the letter, Alice Yapp opened it and read the contents, which she immediately showed to Edwin Maybrick and Mrs Briggs.

When Miss Yapp was asked in court why she had opened her employer's mail, she said she had dropped it in the mud and opened it merely to put it in a fresh envelope, but her eyes fell accidentally on its contents. She was asked: "Did it not occur to you that you could get a clean envelope and put it unopened into that?" Miss Yapp replied: "Oh, I never thought of that!"

Michael Maybrick arrived at the house that evening, and was immediately shown the letter and told about Florence's flypaper soaking. The next morning he told Drs Humphrey and Carter of his suspicion, telling them that Florence's infidelity was proved by her letter, her intent to poison by her purchase of flypapers.

Bottles of medicine and a jar of Valentine's Meat Juice

were removed from the sickroom and sent for analysis. The meat juice was found to contain half a grain of arsenic. . .

Florence later explained this by saying that on the evening of May 9th she was sitting at her husband's bedside when he begged her to give him some of his "white powder." She at first refused. She was to tell the court: "I was overwrought, terribly anxious, miserably unhappy, and his evident distress utterly unnerved me. He told me the powder would not harm him. I then consented." She said that by the time she returned to the room, he had fallen asleep, and she left the bottle at his bedside without giving him any.

On Friday, May 10th, Michael Maybrick saw Florence emptying one medicine bottle into a larger one. He remonstrated with her, saying: "Florrie, how dare you tamper with the medicine?" Florence explained that she was unable to shake the larger bottle to stir up the sediment. Tests on the smaller bottle revealed no arsenic traces. A nurse also heard Maybrick say to his wife: "Oh, Bunny – how could you do it?" It sounded ominous, but he was probably referring to her adultery, since Florence replied: "You silly old darling, don't trouble your head about things."

By that evening Maybrick's condition had worsened, and by May 11th the doctors had given up all hope of saving his life. By mid-morning, worn out by the constant strain, Florence fell into a swoon which lasted twenty-four hours. By the time she came round James Maybrick had died, aged fifty.

With Florence a virtual prisoner in her bedroom, Mrs Briggs, Alice Yapp and Maybrick's brothers made use of her absence to search the house. In cupboards and drawers, stored away like provisions for a rainy day, they found enough arsenic to kill fifty people. It had been the private store of James Maybrick, who was always fearful that he would run short of his favourite poison. And in Florence's room Alice Yapp found a packet labelled: "Arsenic. Poison For Cats".

The point everyone missed was this: if Florence knew about this vast store of arsenic in the house, why would she have needed to buy flypapers?

On May 14th, while Florence was still semi-conscious in her bed, Police Superintendent Isaac Bryning came into the room. He told her: "Mrs Maybrick, I am about to say something to you. After I have said what I intend to say, if you reply, be careful how you do reply, because whatever you say may be used in evidence against you. Mrs Maybrick, you are in custody on suspicion of causing the death of your late husband, James Maybrick, on the 11th instant."

She said nothing. In the days which followed she remained in her bed, guarded by a succession of policemen. She was to write later: ". . . I heard the tramp of many feet coming up the stairs. . . a crowd of men entered. . . 'Mrs Maybrick, you are in custody on suspicion of causing the death of your late husband.' I made no reply, and the crowd passed out."

She told Mrs Briggs that since she had no money for stamps, she could not communicate her situation to her friends. Mrs Briggs suggested that she should write to Mr Brierley for money. Florence took this sarcastic suggestion seriously, and penned a letter to him which, after detailing the cause of her being in custody, went on: "Your last letter is in the hands of the police. Appearances may be against me, but before God I swear I am innocent." Mrs Briggs ensured that this letter passed into police hands.

Three days later the Baroness came to her daughter's assistance, brushing aside policemen to enter the house. She demanded of Michael Maybrick: "How could you have delivered her up to the police in this way and not a friend by her?" He replied: "I assure you we had no idea matters would result in this way. I would never have believed anything wrong of her. I would have stood by her, and I did – until the letter to a man was found."

The Baroness retorted acidly that in her country, a man would meet the other man face to face and thrash him, sooner than call in the police. She forced her way into her daughter's bedroom, treating the police with contempt, and demanding to know what was going on. "They think I have poisoned Jim," Florence said.

"Poisoned Jim!" the mother retorted. "Why, if he is poisoned, he poisoned himself. He made a positive apothecary's shop of himself, as we all know." Catching sight of Alice Yapp, the Baroness told her: "You are an ungrateful and disloyal servant!" The police had to lock the mother in a bedroom when they removed Florence to Walton Jail, to prevent her from interfering.

On May 13th, a post-mortem examination had found only one-half of a grain of arsenic in Maybrick's body – a fatal dose being two grains. There were also traces of hyoscine, prussic acid, strychnine and morphia. Doctors concluded that death had been caused by inflammation of the stomach due to an irritant poison.

At the inquest, the jury had found the cause of death to be poisoning by Florence Maybrick, which amounted to a verdict of wilful murder against her, and she was committed for trial.

So it was that, at the age of twenty-six, Florence Maybrick faced judge and jury at Liverpool Assizes, defended by Sir Charles Russell QC, who sixteen years earlier had prosecuted Mary Ann Cotton, the queen of arsenic poisoners. He had got her hanged; his task now was to save the life of Florence Maybrick.

The trial had to address itself to two vital questions: did James Maybrick die of arsenic poisoning? And if he did, was it administered to him by Florence with intent to murder?

Medical witnesses for both the prosecution and the defence agreed that Maybrick's death might have been caused by gastro-enteritis; where they differed was in whether this had been brought on by doses of arsenic administered between April 27th and May 8th, or by the chill Maybrick caught at the Wirral Races.

Both sides agreed that the amount of arsenic found in

the dead man's liver, kidneys and intestines amounted to less than half a grain of the poison – far from a fatal amount – which could be explained by the Fowler's solution prescribed by his doctor, or by the victim's habit of arsenic-eating.

The defence expert pointed out that Maybrick had exhibited none of the classic symptoms of arsenic poisoning, apart from vomiting and abdominal pains, but the principal prosecution medical witness said bluntly that he had "no doubt that Maybrick had died from the effects of a poisonous dose of arsenic." Two defence medical experts, however, were equally certain that death had not been from arsenic poisoning. Sir Charles Russell emphasised this lack of proof. There was doubt, he said, and the jury must acquit.

The defence claimed that Maybrick, a known arsenic-eater, had died from natural causes. Three witnesses from America testified to Maybrick's habit of taking arsenic, while a Liverpool chemist testified that Maybrick had been calling at his establishment for eighteen months prior to his death, buying increasing amounts of arsenic, averaging one-third of a grain a day. Sir James Poole, an ex-Mayor of Liverpool, stated that Maybrick had admitted to him his habit of taking "poisonous medicines," and Sir James had admonished him, saying: "How horrid! Don't you know, my dear friend, that the more you take of these things the more you require, and you will go on until they carry you off?"

At the end of his opening speech, Sir Charles Russell said Mrs Maybrick wished to make a statement, and he asked permission for her to do so now. It proved to be a mistake. Defendants did not then have the right to go into the witness box to give evidence and be cross-examined. With the permission of the judge, they could make an unsworn statement *at the conclusion of the defence case*, which meant that no witnesses could be brought forward to corroborate it. Florence Maybrick had nothing to gain from making her statement, and everything to lose.

She began by saying she wished to defend herself against the "dreadfully crushing charge" brought against her, and she explained the facewash, referring also to her husband's habit of taking arsenic. She talked of the pressure her husband had put her under to add a small amount of the white powder to the meat juice. She then said: "My lord, I had not one true or honest friend in that house. I had no one to consult and no one to advise me. I was deposed from my position as mistress in my own house, and from the position of attending to my husband, notwithstanding that he was so ill." She added: "For the love of my children and for the sake of their future, a complete reconciliation had taken place between myself and my husband. The day before he died I made a full and free confession to him and received his entire forgiveness."

The judge criticised this statement, as did the prosecutor. Why had she not told the shopkeeper the real reason why she bought so many flypapers? With her husband so ill, why did she not tell the attending doctors about what she had done with the "white powder"?

In the closing speeches, Sir Charles Russell stressed the failure of the prosecution to establish the exact cause of death, pointing to the contradictory medical evidence. The prosecution concentrated on the fact that Mrs Maybrick had administered arsenic to her husband. Admitting that her adultery amounted to "a grave moral guilt," Sir Charles referred to the notorious double standard between the sexes, saying: "In a man such faults are too often regarded with toleration, and they bring him often but a few penal consequences. But, in the case of a wife, in the case of a woman, it is with her sex the unforgivable sin."

The judge, Mr Justice Fitzjames Stephen (who had suffered a stroke in 1885 and who became insane a year after the trial), seemed to falter and stumble over words at times during his two-day summing-up.

Although he began by warning the jury "It is essential

to this charge to prove that a man died of poison, and that the poison suggested is arsenic," he failed to point out that if Maybrick did not die from arsenic poisoning, then no crime had been committed.

He told the jury: "For a person to go on deliberately administering poison to a poor, helpless, sick man upon whom she had already inflicted a dreadful injury – an injury fatal to married life – the person who could do such a thing as that must indeed be destitute of the least traces of human feeling."

The jury took just thirty-eight minutes to find Florence Maybrick guilty of murder. On hearing the verdict Florence told the court: "Although I have been found guilty, with the exception of my intimacy with Mr Brierley, I am not guilty of this crime." On August 7th the judge sentenced her to hang, and as he left the court, he was booed by the large crowd waiting outside.

The verdict was greeted by the nation with astonishment, *The Times* commenting: "It is useless to disguise the fact that the public are not thoroughly convinced of the prisoner's guilt."

Petitions for a reprieve poured in from all over the country, and Florence's solicitor forwarded his own affidavit to the Home Office, pointing out that Maybrick had been an habitual arsenic-eater, and had been guilty of adultery himself – a fact not brought out in court, out of a sense of delicacy and respect for the dead man by the widow on trial.

In the condemned cell in Walton Prison, Florence heard her gallows being constructed. Then, on August 22nd, it was announced that the Home Secretary had "advised Her Majesty to commute the punishment to penal servitude for life, inasmuch as, although the evidence leads clearly to the conclusion that the prisoner administered arsenic to her husband with intent to murder, yet it does not wholly exclude a reasonable doubt whether in fact his death was caused by the administration of arsenic."

In other words, as Sir Charles Russell pointed out acidly, "Mrs Maybrick is to suffer imprisonment on the assumption of the Home Secretary that she had committed an offence, for which she was never tried by the constitutional authority, and of which she has never been adjudged guilty." Florence had never been charged with *attempted* murder.

In 1892, following a change of Government, her solicitors made an approach to the new Home Secretary to get Florence released, pointing out that there was no proof that Maybrick died from arsenic poisoning, or that Florence administered poison to him with intent to murder.

It was futile. It was well-known that Queen Victoria had been particularly incensed by the case, offended by Florence's adultery, and would never agree to any Royal mercy. And there was as yet no Court of Criminal Appeal. That had to wait for another case, some fifteen years later.

The American people took up the cause of Florence, the Secretary of State urging the ambassador to Britain to make representations at the highest level for her release. A petition signed by the US Vice-President, among other prominent men, urged her release, stating that "the conduct of her trial has resulted in a profound impression of a miscarriage of justice."

Shortly after he became Lord Chief Justice, Lord Russell wrote to Florence to assure her of his continuing efforts to secure her release. He had always believed fervently in her innocence, and he now wrote to the Home Secretary: "The foundation on which the whole case for the Crown rested was rotten, *for there was in fact no murder*; on the contrary, the deceased had died from natural causes." His appeal fell on deaf ears. In 1900 – the year in which he died – Lord Russell visited Florence in Aylesbury Prison and spent some time alone with her in her cell, offering what comfort he could. He found her to be "looking wretched".

In 1901, following the Queen's death, the Government announced that Florence Maybrick would be released in three years time. On January 25th 1904, now a middle-aged woman with grey hair, she left prison to cross the Atlantic for the last time, with an escort provided by the American ambassador. She went first to France, to be re-united with her aged mother, who died soon afterwards in penury. There was nothing left for Florence: both her children, whom she had not seen since the death of her husband, had died while she was in prison.

On her return to the United States, Florence found herself a media celebrity, giving interviews and going on a lecture tour. She also wrote and published her autobiography, *My Fifteen Lost Years*, and *Mrs Maybrick's Own Story* was published in a magazine. But her fame did not last long.

She tried living in Florida for a time, and later Highland Park, in Illinois, sticking to her married name. But twenty years before her death she reverted to her maiden name of Chandler, going to live in virtual solitude in a tiny three-room shack. Regarded as an eccentric old lady, she was known by the local children as The Cat Woman.

In 1941, she died in poverty and squalor, aged seventy-six and surrounded by her innumerable cats in her shack in the village of South Kent, Connecticut.

At her trial, she had been unable to produce the recipe for the cosmetic for which she claimed to have needed the arsenic from all those flypapers. Years later, it turned up. . . discovered tucked between the pages of her Bible. And yes, the recipe included arsenic, which if it didn't kill her husband certainly poisoned the life of Florence Maybrick.

6
ARSENIC
Some Notable Cases of Murder by Arsenic
(in chronological order)

Marquise de Brinvilliers. France. 1676.Victims: 100-plus. Beheaded.

Mary Blandy. England. 1752. Victim: 1 (father). Hanged.

Anne Marie Zwanziger. Germany. 1811. Victims: 11. Beheaded.

Marie Lafarge. France. 1840. Victim: 1 (husband). Imprisoned.

Christina Gilmour. Scotland. 1844. Victim: 1 (husband). Not proven.

Hélène Jagado. France. 1851. Victims: 23. Guillotined.

Madeleine Smith. Scotland. 1857. Victim: 1 (lover). Not proven.

Dr William King. Canada. 1859. Victim: 1 (wife). Hanged.

Dr Thomas Smethurst. England. 1859. Victim: 1 (lodger). Pardoned.

Mary Ann Cotton. England. 1873. Victims: 20. Hanged.

Dr Philip Cross. Ireland. 1887. Victim: 1 (wife). Hanged.

Florence Maybrick. England. 1889. Victim: 1 (husband). Imprisoned.

Edith Carew. Japan. 1896. Victim: 1 (husband). Imprisoned.

Cordelia Botkin. USA. 1898. Victims: 2. Imprisoned.

Johann Hoch. USA. 1905. Victims: 15 (wives). Hanged.

Henry Clark & Augusta Fullam. India. 1911. Victims: 2. He hanged, she was imprisoned.

Bingham Family. England. 1911. Victims: 3 in family. Unsolved.

Frederick Seddon. England. 1912. Victim: 1 (lodger). Hanged.

Dr Arthur Warren Waite. USA. 1915. Victims: 2 (in-laws). Electrocuted.

Amy Archer-Gilligan. USA. 1917. Victims: 5-50 (patients). Imprisoned.

Harold Greenwood. England. 1920. Victim: 1 (wife). Acquitted.

Herbert Rowse Armstrong. England. 1922. Victim: 1 (wife). Hanged.

Edward Ernest Black. England. 1922. Victim: 1 (wife). Hanged.

Ronald Geeves Griggs. Australia. 1928. Victim: 1 (wife). Acquitted.

Croydon Poisonings. England. 1928/9. Victims: 3 in family. Unsolved.

Annie Hearn. England. 1931. Victim: 1 (neighbour). Acquitted.

Daisy de Melker. South Africa. 1932. Victims: 3 (2 husbands and son). Hanged.

Charlotte Bryant. England. 1936. Victim: 1 (husband). Hanged.

Mary Creighton & Everett Appelgate. USA. 1936. Victim: 1 (wife). Electrocuted.

Frederick Radford. UK. 1949. Victim: 1 (wife) Suicide.

Marcus Marymont. UK. 1958. Victim: 1 (wife). Imprisoned.

Marie Besnard. France. 1961. Victims: 12. Acquitted.

Maria Groesbeek. South Africa. 1969. Victim: 1 (husband). Hanged.

This is by no means a comprehensive list. Indeed, it would be easy to fill three volumes just with arsenical poisoning cases. Poisoning by arsenic did not end in 1969; there have been more cases since.

The above list, incidentally, contains the names of two solicitors (Armstrong and Greenwood) and four doctors (Cross, King, Smethurst and Waite).

Arsenic is a metallic poison, occurring naturally in an ore called realgar, found in lead and iron mining. As early as the eighth century an Arab alchemist had devised a method of producing arsenious oxide, a white, odourless powder, from this ore, and it became the most common poison to be employed by those with homicidal intentions. However, a form of arsenic had been long in use in Imperial Rome.

Arsenic remained the favourite among all poisons principally because it was so easy to obtain – it was sold openly to keep down vermin, as a form of rat-poison. As well as in pesticides, arsenic was also used extensively in glassmaking and dyeing, and in the manufacture of wallpaper printing inks (Paris green and Scheele's green.) It has only recently been established that Napoleon's quarters in exile on St Helena were decorated with green wallpaper, thus accounting for the large amount of arsenic found in his body after death. The arsenic in the wallpaper would have escaped very slowly as arsine gas, thus accidentally killing the Emperor, who rarely left his room.

Arsenic reigned so long as the king of poisons because, being white, odourless and virtually tasteless (it has a sweetish flavour), it can easily be disguised in flour or sugar, or given in drinks. Moreover, the effects of arsenic are very similar to those of many ordinary gastric complaints, and there is little doubt that hundreds of arsenic poisoners escaped detection because doctors failed to diagnose the condition of their patients correctly, treating them for dysentery or cholera, when they were in fact being slowly murdered.

The symptoms include vomiting and diarrhoea, stomach upset, dermatitis and discolouration of the body – all of which can readily be attributed to other causes. Another advantage of this poison is that one dose is not usually fatal, but the effects of several doses are cumulative, concentrating in the liver and kidneys and other internal organs to cause eventual death. And for centuries, there was no means of detecting arsenic in the body.

The Marsh Test put an end to the free reign of the poisoner, being first used in 1840 to convict Marie Lafarge of the murder of her husband, Charles, a French industrialist. It was proved that Marie had bought arsenic as rat-poison; the Marsh test established that the arsenic was now in her husband's body. The great toxicologist, Dr Mathieu Orfila, was asked by the court to examine the exhibits and carry out the Marsh Test. In his report Orfila stated confidently: "I shall prove first, that there is arsenic in the body of Lafarge; second, that this arsenic comes neither from the reagents with which we worked nor from the earth surrounding the coffin; also that the arsenic we found is not the arsenic component which is naturally found in every human body." The court had no hesitation in finding Marie Lafarge guilty.

Yet despite this, in 1931, at the trial of Annie Hearn for poisoning her friend and neighbour, Alice Thomas, with an arsenic-laced tinned-salmon sandwich, the great advocate Norman Birkett managed to get the defendant acquitted by proving that the graveyard soil around the coffin of the exhumed victim had heavy concentrations of arsenic. Marie Besnard was acquitted in France in 1961 on the same grounds.

There were no such doubts in the case of Herbert Rowse Armstrong, a solicitor in Hay-on-Wye. He murdered his nagging wife, Katherine, with arsenic, and when she died on February 22nd, 1921, her death was attributed to gastritis and she was duly buried. It was only later, when Armstrong attempted to poison a rival solicitor, that the truth came out. He was arrested with packets of arsenic in his clothing, and the court did not believe his claim that he had bought the poison as a weed-killer. In May 1922 he became the only solicitor to be hanged for murder in Britain.

Before turning to the main cases in this section, there

are a couple of "small" arsenic cases which I cannot resist mentioning.

The murder committed by Frederick Radford was described by Professor Keith Simpson as "one of the coolest murders by arsenic that ever came to lie in my crime files."

Radford's wife, Margery, had suffered from tuberculosis for many years, and in 1949 she lay close to death in a Surrey sanatorium. Her husband was in the habit of taking her food when he visited, and after the last meal Mrs Radford was very ill with vomiting. She immediately suspected poisoning – she had found out that her husband was associating with another woman – and when Radford visited again, bringing her a fruit pie, she asked for it to be analysed. (In fact, the superintendent of the sanatorium unsuspectingly ate a slice and was extremely ill).

Analysis of the pie showed it to be laced with 3.25 grains of arsenic, and as Mrs Radford had now died, her body was examined and was found to contain more than six grains of arsenic. Arsenic permeates the roots of its victim's hair, providing a useful calendar of how long the poisoning has gone on. The hair of Mrs Radford had arsenic extending for a distance of five centimetres from the base, and as hair grows at the rate of 0.44 millimetres per day, it was easy to establish that Mrs Radford had received her first dose of arsenic between a hundred and a hundred and twenty days prior to her death.

The husband was naturally questioned, but although admitting having bought the pie, insisted he had no wish to kill Margery. "Why should I want to kill my wife? I knew she was going to die anyway," was his response. But the day after his first questioning by the police, Radford was found dead at his home, having taken his life with cyanide.

In both this case and that of Dr Warder, mentioned in the Aconite section, the suspects chose a quick-acting poison to commit suicide, rather than endure the long agony of the slow poisons they had used on their victims.

Chronicles of arsenical poisoning cases contain some fascinating stories, particularly that of Dr Philip Cross. He was a former British Army surgeon living at Shandy Hall, Coachford, Co. Cork, Ireland. Aged sixty-two, he still had an eye for the ladies, despite being married to a woman twenty-two years his junior. They lived in some disharmony, with her six children.

In the autumn of 1886 they engaged pretty Effie Skinner as a governess for the children, and within a few weeks the doctor and the governess were having an affair which became the talk of the neighbourhood – especially when during a violent row his wife shouted at the doctor: "Effie Skinner's got to get out of this house!"

Effie Skinner did leave, the doctor giving her a handsome cheque in lieu of notice. But she only went as far as Dublin, where the doctor joined her the following day, booking them into a hotel as "Mr and Mrs Osborne."

The doctor eventually returned home, after Effie went back home to London to live, and he found his wife ill. He began caring for her himself, and as a doctor prescribed medicines for her. Those medicines included arsenic. Laura Cross grew steadily worse – "a touch of fever", the doctor told friends – and she died on the morning of June 2nd, 1887. What caused tongues to wag was the doctor's marriage to Effie Skinner in London just fifteen days after the funeral. . .

Exhumation was ordered, and when an autopsy found traces of arsenic in Laura's stomach, the doctor was arrested and charged with wilful murder. He protested: "There is a God above who will see the villainy of such a charge!" But when his house was searched, the police discovered two medicine bottles containing arsenic.

At his trial it was proved that he had bought arsenic from a chemist, and the jury had no hesitation in finding him guilty. The English hangman, James Berry, was sent over to hang him at Cork Prison. Afterwards, the poetical Berry told a journalist: "Quite a good job. I give you my word – Dr Cross passed away as peaceful as a summer's eve."

To illustrate the fact that arsenical poisoning is by no means a thing of the past, we have the case of Sandy Coulthard who at 5.30 am on July 9th, 1988, died in the intensive care unit of Duke University Medical Center in Durham, North Carolina, USA. She had been ill for many months, with symptoms which included nausea, vomiting, diarrhoea and tingling sensations in her hands and fingers. Doctors at first diagnosed these as being consistent with Guillan-Barré Syndrome – a spinal virus infection.

However, as the thirty-year-old attractive woman lay dying in agony, terrified, and with her family kneeling in prayer at her bedside, she cried out in delirium: "They are trying to kill me! Help me!" Perhaps the doctors listened. . .

She had been ill for about a year, the ailment going into remission at times. It allowed her to go on a cruise, but it returned when she arrived back home. Her husband, Rob, was vice-president of a furniture company, and nurses noted that he was surprisingly knowledgeable on medical terminology. He also seemed oddly detached about his wife's illness. This seemed suspicious when the autopsy results revealed that Sandy had died as a result of arsenic poisoning over a long period.

Detectives questioned Rob Coulthard at his home, finding him devoid of any emotion – including the natural anger a husband might display when accused of murdering his wife. Detectives traced a purchase of arsenic by Rob in the autumn of 1986, and found a cheque dated December 1st, 1986, which had been used to pay for the purchase. There had been enough arsenic to kill 2,500 people. Rob admitted to gambling debts, and to two large insurance policies on his wife's life. But he refused to take a lie detector test. Detectives reasoned that Rob had taken so long to poison his wife because he had wanted to establish a pattern in her illness.

Indicted by a grand jury, he was due to stand trial on November 28th, 1988. But when he appeared in court that day, the prosecution admitted that there was insufficient evidence to ask for the death penalty. Some kind of plea-bargaining had taken place. Rob Coulthard pleaded guilty to first-degree murder, and the judge sentenced him to life in prison. He will be eligible for parole in seventeen years.

While the Marsh test is still used in our forensic laboratories, most scientists now prefer to use the Reinsch and Gutzeit Tests, which employ the same principle of reducing arsenic to arsine gas, but are easier to conduct. Hugo Reinsch devised his test in 1842, but although easier to use than the Marsh test, it has one serious drawback. The reagents employed must be carefully checked to make sure they are arsenic-free. Dr Alfred Swaine Taylor failed to ensure this in the Smethurst case of 1859, as a result of which Smethurst, who had been found guilty and sentenced to death, was pardoned. Dr Taylor was acutely embarrassed. . .

7
ARTHUR WARREN WAITE
The Man from Egypt

"This other fellow. He's been inside me ever since I can remember" – Arthur Waite answering a question from the New York District Attorney

A young dentist, Doctor Waite might almost have served as a model for the Jekyll and Hyde story. Good-looking, athletic, attractive to both sexes and oozing charm, he had a wife who was the daughter of a millionaire, and a plush home in New York's exclusive Riverside Drive. But he also had an inclination to kill.

Waite was a native of Grand Rapids, Michigan, as was his father-in-law, retired millionaire druggist John E. Peck. Waite, however, had come from a poorer family, who struggled hard to put their son through a dental course at the University of Michigan. He then came to Britain and qualified in Glasgow, afterwards moving on to South Africa before returning home at the outbreak of the Great War.

There, in Great Rapids, Waite met Miss Clara Peck, who was swept off her feet by the sophisticated and handsome young dentist. They soon became engaged, marrying in September 1915. Waite did not set up his practice in that town, however, but moved with his wife to New York, where he claimed professional opportunities were much better, and his wife would find more entertainment to keep her amused.

Waite seemed in no hurry to set up his practice. Instead he was to be found in the company of doctors, persuading them to believe that he was also a qualified physician, with a special interest in bacteriology. They knew Waite to be a good tennis player – he had recently won tournaments at Palm Beach, in Florida – and he had a good smattering of medical terms.

Using his new contacts, Waite insinuated himself into the bacteriological laboratory of the Flower Hospital in New York, persuading Dr Nyce, the doctor in charge, that he wanted to become a pupil. Dr Nyce was impressed by the young man's keenness. But there was one odd thing about him: he only wanted to study the more virulent germs, and complained that they were not deadly enough for his experiments. He also researched germ culture at the Cornell Medical School.

Waite's wife thought her husband was employed as a doctor. Sometimes he took her to the hospital, leaving her in the waiting room while he conducted an "important operation." It was necessary for Waite to convince his wife that he was a successful doctor, because he had to account for the income required for his expensive life-style.

Waite was actually getting the money from the Peck family. Mr Peck had provided his daughter not only with a handsome dowry, but also with an allowance that was the dollar equivalent of £60 a month. Waite's wife's aunt, Catherine, impressed by the brilliant new addition to the family, had given the couple a thousand pounds as a wedding present, subsequently handing Waite £10,000 to invest for her. He could count on a substantial legacy from her will on her death, she told him, and Waite knew that Mr Peck would leave half his fortune to his daughter.

To Waite the equation was simple. If Mr and Mrs Peck died, and then Aunt Catherine, followed by his wife Clara, then he would be a very wealthy widower. . .

A few weeks after settling in New York, Waite invited

his wife's parents to visit. They did so, but the father-in-law complained of feeling run down and Waite diagnosed the onset of a cold and gave him a throat spray every evening, which didn't seem to help. When Mr Peck returned to Grand Rapids, his health rapidly improved.

Mrs Peck felt that her trip to see the son-in-law she adored had been cut all too short by her husband's illness, and soon visited again, this time on her own. Soon after her arrival she fell ill and a Dr Porter was called who examined her and said he could find nothing wrong. But one night, when Waite was out – "visiting his patients", he said – his wife found the gas tap in her mother's room turned full on and the room filled with deadly fumes. She turned the gas off and opened the windows – saving her mother's life.

But Waite was set on ending that life, and Mrs Peck went rapidly downhill, finally dying on January 30th, 1916. Dr Porter signed the death certificate, and a grief-stricken Dr Waite escorted the body back to Grand Rapids, telling relatives that it was his mother-in-law's dying wish to be cremated. This was duly done.

Mr Peck, lonely following the loss of his wife, readily accepted another invitation to come to New York to visit his daughter. He arrived in February and was made to feel very welcome by his son-in-law. He didn't actually see much of Arthur, since the young man was always late home, ostensibly visiting patients and performing life-saving operations, but in reality entertaining women in nightclubs.

It was while dining with Margaret Horton, a beautiful young widow, in an expensive restaurant, that Waite was spotted by a Dr Cornell, a relative of the Peck family. When Waite saw Cornell, he calmly walked over to the other man's table and explained that his companion was his theatre nurse, who had been so efficient and tireless during an hours-long operation that he had bought her a meal as a reward for her dedication. All at the table, except a certain Miss Hardwicke, accepted this explanation.

The truth was that Waite, who had met Mrs Horton at the Berlitz School of Languages, was entranced with her and had set her up in a suite at the Hotel Plaza. She was ambitious to become an opera singer, and Waite himself was very fond of music.

She was to say of her benefactor later: "Dr Waite had an extraordinary kind heart. He loved all the fine sentiments and the beautiful things of life. He used to say to me: "Margaret, when you sing you make me weep, because you make me think of beautiful things."

A few days after this sighting in the restaurant, Mr Peck was taken seriously ill and a Dr Moore was summoned. He thought the cause was digestive trouble and prescribed antacid medicine. Mr Peck didn't like the taste of this, and his thoughtful son-in-law soon found a way to make it more palatable. In the kitchen, without attempting to hide his actions, he would pour some of the medicine into the sick man's soup. He put more medicine into the teapot. That way Mr Peck would get his medicine without realising it. Only it wasn't just medicine.

Dr Moore called again, remarking that he didn't think there was much wrong with Mr Peck. Dr Waite disagreed with him. "He hasn't a very strong constitution," he said, "and I should not be surprised if he did not live for long."

On March 12th, just six weeks after his wife's death, Mr Peck followed her. Once again Waite said that the dying request of his relative had been to be cremated, but before he could take the body to Grand Rapids, it had been embalmed.

When Waite arrived at Grand Rapids it was to find a family firmly opposed to cremation, and Waite wisely made no objections and attended the burial service. He then hurried back to Mrs Horton in New York, confident that he could now support her in style with the money due under his in-laws' wills.

But one member of the Peck family had always disliked and distrusted him. This was Percival Peck, Clara's only brother. It was he who had objected to his father being cremated, and the reason for this was a mysterious telegram from New York which read: "Suspicions aroused. Demand autopsy. Keep telegram secret. – K. Adams." Percival did not know anyone named Adams – it later transpired that the sender was Miss Hardwicke, using a pseudonym – but the telegram had its intended effect.

Percival had a private examination carried out on his father's body and hired private detectives to report on Waite's movements. Waite, who had returned to New York alone, leaving his grieving wife behind, had intended going on a spending spree, but then the undertaker called to demand the embalming fee.

"What's the hurry?" Waite demanded. "You know I'm good for the money."

"It's Kane, sir, the embalmer," explained the undertaker. "He thinks he might not get his money."

"Why?" Waite asked, puzzled by the uneasy look on the other man's face.

"There's some idea that arsenic has been used. . ."

Waite hurried to see Kane and asked him abruptly: "How much is it worth to you to say that you used arsenic in the embalming fluid?"

After some haggling a fee of $9,000 was agreed, but before this could be paid Kane lost his nerve and went to the police with the full story: "Waite told me he was in a hole and asked me to put arsenic in the sample of embalming fluid I was to give to the district attorney. He said he would make me independent for life if I did what I was asked."

An investigation began, with Waite being put under observation. Professor Vaughan of the University of Michigan had carried out a post mortem on Mr Peck's body and had reported that the millionaire had died as a result of arsenical poisoning, although, he added, there was just an outside chance that the embalming fluid had been contaminated with arsenic. Now, armed with Kane's statement, the district attorney obtained a warrant for Waite's arrest.

Aware that he was under suspicion and was being followed, Waite attempted suicide. When police called at his home to arrest him, they found him unconscious in his bedroom. He had taken a drugs overdose, but swift medical attention saved his life. When he recovered consciousness, Waite considered how best to defend himself, and came up with the idea of Jekyll and Hyde. Madness would be his defence.

Questioned by the district attorney in hospital, Waite admitted giving his father-in-law arsenic.

"Have you any accomplices?" he was asked.

"Only this other fellow," Waite replied casually.

"What other fellow?"

"The Man from Egypt. He's been inside me ever since I can remember. He has made me do things against my will. He made me take up the study of germs, as if I used them I wouldn't be detected. I was compelled against my will to put them in my father-in-law's food. Try as I would, I could not get rid of my murderous other self. Often I have gone for long walks and fought against the evil one, and tried to run away from him, but he was so fleet of foot that he always caught me up."

Perhaps neither Waite nor the district attorney had read James Hogg's *Confessions of a Justified Sinner* (1824), in which a killer tells a similar story, but the district attorney was sceptical about the "Man from Egypt", who first forced Waite to spray his father-in-law's throat with germs, and when that didn't work, resort to good old-fashioned arsenic. However, leading psychiatrists were called to testify at Waite's trial, some for the prosecution, others for the defence.

Dr Jeliffe said at the trial: "In my opinion the prisoner was sane and knew the nature and quality of his act. He was fully aware of all the phases of his crime. In my opinion he is an average man, somewhat superficial, inclined to be snobbish and of no great intellectual attainments." Other doctors testified just as forcefully that Waite was mad.

The jury were perhaps more impressed by what was found at Waite's apartment when it was searched by the police. They discovered hundreds of slides containing the germs of tetanus, typhoid, diphtheria and cholera, together with dozens of books on poisons.

Those who knew Waite were astonished by his arrest, convinced that he was either innocent or insane. His wife's reaction to the allegations was to declare: "I was so shocked and amazed that I could not believe them true. It seems impossible that a man who has been so uniformly gentle and kind to me and apparently so loyal, could be guilty of the crime with which he is charged."

But Percival Peck had seen through to the real Waite. He said: "I know that Arthur is guilty. The electric chair would be too good for him. . . I will do all in my power to see that he is found guilty and executed."

Convinced that Waite was a fortune-hunter who had married Clara Peck with the sole idea of destroying her family to gain their money, he approached the prosecutor before the trial.

"I have only one favour to ask," he said, "and that is that I have a seat through every minute of the trial near that man, so that I can see the last gleam of hope gradually fade from his face."

In the witness box Waite acted the part of a madman to the best of his ability, knowing that only an insanity verdict could save him. The more coolly he spoke about his terrible crimes, the more the jury would be persuaded that only a madman could have acted as he did.

"What did you do after giving your mother-in-law that fatal dose of poison?" his counsel asked him.

"Why, I went to sleep, of course," Waite replied, adding that he had allowed his wife to discover the dead body. Asked how he had killed Mr Peck, he said: "I gave him a throat spray and a nasal spray containing germs, backed with tuberculosis bacteria, and when that didn't work I got a lot of calomel which I administered to him in order to weaken him so that he could not resist the germs, but it failed. The man recovered every time. I would get him to go out and expose himself to draughts in the hope that he would catch cold, and I dampened his sheets for the same reason. Once I got some hydrochloric acid and put it on the radiator in his room, expecting the fumes would affect him. Finally I gave him eighteen grains of arsenic. I sat up with him that night, as my wife was so tired. He was in great pain, groaning. I gave him some chloroform and when he was unconscious I placed a pillow over his face and kept it there until he died."

Asked if he was crazy, he replied: "I think not – unless it is crazy to want money."

In his final speech, the defence counsel asked: "Is that the evidence of a sane man? Waite has told you the truth. He has no moral sense whatsoever. What are we going to do with such a man as this? You would not send to the electric chair an idiot, a lunatic or a child. On the other hand, we cannot permit such a man as Waite to be at large. We must remove him from society by placing him in an institution."

The judge told the jury: "You are not concerned at all with the question of the punishment of this man. The law determines what shall be done. Your function is to determine the facts so that the law may operate. . . The question is not whether he is sane, but whether he is responsible under the tests prescribed by the law – that is, did he know the nature and quality of the act and know it was wrong? That's not a test for experts but for men of common sense. Moral indifference is not insanity."

At the end of the five-day trial the jury took just an hour to find Waite guilty. He was sentenced to death in the electric chair, and to the end he talked interminably about his double personality, saying: "My life consisted of lying, cheating, stealing and killing. Yet my personality was that of a gentleman and I went for music, art and poetry."

Just days before his execution he was reading the Bible when he remarked to his jailers with a smile: "I have just read the Ten Commandments and found I have broken them all but one – the one about profanity."

He went to the electric chair at Sing Sing Prison on May 24th, 1917. As the warders strapped on the electrodes, Waite asked curiously: "Is this all there is to it?"

Presumably the "Man from Egypt" died with him. . .

8
BACTERIA

The idea of using deadly bacteria as a killing agent is by
no means new. In the American Civil War, for example, it
was common practice for soldiers on both sides to poison
drinking wells with corpses. In July 1863, General
Johnston was in retreat from General Sherman at
Vicksburg, Mississippi. He ordered all the ponds and
lakes in the area to be contaminated with dead sheep and
pigs, compelling opposing troops to carry large supplies of
drinking water and thus slowing them down.

In the First World War poison gases were used, and
deadly bacteria, including typhoid germs, were cultivated
as possible weapons. The Japanese experimented with
bacteria between the wars, mainly on captured Chinese
victims. In the Second World War nerve gases were used
– especially Tabun by the Germans – and Churchill
authorised the breeding of anthrax spores on an off-shore
British island, Gruinard, with the intention of having
anthrax dropped on Germany. That island remains un-
inhabitable to this day.

In the event, it was not necessary to resort to such
measures, but by the end of the war British scientists had
developed various "V agents" or deadly nerve agents, a
single drop of which on the skin can prove fatal. Now,
every major power had stockpiles of nerve gases, such as
Sarin. But the line of descent from the simple tactics of
American generals in the Civil War is clear.

In relatively modern times, it was a Frenchman, Henri Girard, who first used bacteria to kill. For that reason he is remembered as the first "scientific murderer." He was motivated by the old idea of insuring the lives of various people, and then murdering them for profit. In 1912 he insured a friend, Louis Pernotte, for 300,000 francs, and then contaminated his food-supplies with typhoid germs. In the process the entire Pernotte family fell ill. Girard then gave his victim injections to "cure" him, which killed him off.

Girard also experimented with poisonous mushrooms, and devised a cocktail laced with a fungi-derived poison, which he fed to a rich old widow in 1918. However, by now the insurance companies had become suspicious of Girard and he was arrested. He told the police: "Yes, I have always been unhappy, no one has ever tried to understand me: I will always be misunderstood – abnormal, as I have been called – and for all that I am good, with a very warm heart." Claiming to be a misunderstood genius, Girard swallowed one of his own deadly cocktails while in custody in May 1921 and so cheated the guillotine.

But there is an earlier case than that of Girard. Dr Bennet Clarke Hyde was a forty-year-old doctor who married the niece of a Kansas City millionaire, Thomas Swope, and in the process became his medical adviser. Swope had a complicated will which meant that his fortune was to be divided among his nephews and nieces, and if any of them died, his or her share would be added to that of the others. In order for his own wife – and ultimately himself – to benefit, Dr Hyde began killing off the relatives. In September 1909 Hunton, a friend of Swope and administrator of his estate, became ill and died while being attended by Dr Hyde. Mr Swope followed soon after. Hyde tried to have himself appointed administrator of the estate, but was rejected.

Swope's will was duly carried out and his fortune divided among his relatives. Within weeks five of the inheritors succumbed to typhoid fever, one of them dying. This was too much for the authorities, and Hunton and Swope were exhumed, traces of strychnine being found in their remains. In 1910 a coroner's jury returned a verdict of murder and Hyde was sent for trial. The prosecution claimed that Hyde had used a mixture of strychnine and cyanide to kill Hunton and Swope, and had injected Swope's nephew with typhoid germs. Hyde admitted possession of typhoid germs but said he needed them for bacteriological studies.

Found guilty of first-degree murder, Hyde was sentenced to life imprisonment, but on appeal was granted a second trial. This time the jury failed to agree a verdict, as did a third jury, and charges against Hyde were dismissed.

Another, more recent, case of poisoning by bacteria was that of John Hill, a plastic surgeon from Houston, Texas. In 1969 his wife, Joan Robinson Hill, died as a result of "a massive infection of unknown origin." Police inquiries led to Hill being accused of her murder – with the rare charge of "murder by omission", which alleged that he had caused his wife's death by deliberately withholding medical treatment.

Mrs Hill, daughter of a wealthy oilman, had become ill and had been treated at home for four days by Dr Hill, who then took her to hospital where she died. A hurried post mortem found nothing suspicious. However, the dead woman's father publicly accused his son-in-law of having brought about her death, and Hill sued him for slander. As a result, Mrs Hill's body was exhumed and doctors found signs of meningitis in the brain.

Dr Hill was tried in 1971 after his second wife had alleged that he had attempted to kill her. She revealed that he had confided to her that he had killed his first wife with an injection of a bacterial culture made from "every form of human excretion, urine, faeces, and even pus taken from a boil on a patient's back."

The first trial ended up in a mistrial, but before Hill could be tried again, he was shot dead in his home by a hired gunman, who was in turn shot dead by a passing police officer.

It is significant that the three murderers known to have used bacteria to kill were doctors: physicians knowing the lethal qualities of certain germs, and with the means to inject them. But it is an odd method of killing, and there was no one more odd that Dr Arthur Warren Waite.

9
ARTHUR KENDRICK FORD
A Foolish Dreamer
"My mother always told me to tell the truth" –
the start of Arthur Ford's confession.

Arthur Kendrick Ford was an office manager at a firm of wholesale chemists in Euston Road, London. The firm manufactured products for retail chemists around the country and provided all manner of drugs and medical supplies. They also stocked cantharides, which was sometimes in demand by animal breeders, although it is a scheduled poison.

Ford had worked for the firm for thirty years, but knew practically nothing about the chemical properties of drugs. He was simply an administrator, responsible for sending out invoices, paying bills and making sure the general accounts of the business were kept in order.

His service with the firm had been interrupted by the war, when he joined up and became a soldier, serving in the Far East. It was in Singapore, shortly before he was demobilised in 1947, that he first heard old soldiers' stories about the aphrodisiac properties of Spanish Fly.

After the war he returned to his office job and to his wife. He was happily married and a good father, but he succumbed to an overwhelming passion for one of the girls in the office, Elizabeth Grant, aged twenty-seven. Although she responded to some extent to his advances, this never proceeded beyond a quick kiss and fumble. She resolutely refused him sexual intercourse. It was this situation which gave the frustrated Ford his mad idea: that if he could trick Betty into consuming some Spanish Fly, she might be so overcome with lust that she would practically rape him. That was his dream.

On April 27th, 1954, Ford came into the office carrying a bag of sweets – coconut ice. The bag they were in bore the name of a local sweetshop.

Ford did not hand the bag around his staff, who numbered twenty-two women and four men. Instead, he took out a piece of coconut ice with his fingers and gave it to Betty Grant. He then took out other pieces and gave them to a Miss Glover and a Miss Dodds. He was not seen to give any to a Miss June Malins, aged twenty-one, although she was seen eating a piece of the confectionery soon afterwards, which had apparently come from the same packet.

Ford gave the girls the sweets at 2.30 p.m. About an hour later Miss Malins became ill. Betty Grant took her up to the sickroom. By 4.00 p.m. Betty herself was feeling ill, with severe stomach pains. Soon afterwards Ford himself complained of illness. He was very pale and seemed on the verge of fainting.

A doctor was called, but he could find nothing to account for the odd symptoms of the sick women, and had them taken to University College Hospital. Taken to the infirmary with them, Ford soon made a good recovery and was able to be interviewed by the police the following day. By then the two girls had died. . .

As poisoning was suspected, the police grilled Ford thoroughly, and he told Detective Superintendent Jamieson that he thought the coconut ice must have been "off". But once post mortems had been carried out on both girls, the presence of cantharides was detected and Ford was questioned even more intensively.

On the way to a police station, Ford blurted out: "I am to blame. I do not know what made me do it." At the station he made a full statement, telling of how he had first heard about Spanish Fly in Singapore. "It was not until three weeks ago that a query arose about cantharides," he went on, "and although I had worked for the firm for thirty years, it was the first indication I had that the medical term for Spanish Fly was cantharidin."

He said he had noticed the name on a drug in the warehouse while stock-taking and became curious about it. He decided to get hold of some, although at this stage it was pure curiosity which drove him, and he had no idea of what he was going to do with it.

On the morning of April 26th – the day before he gave the drug to the two girls – he had a chat with a Mr Lushington, a chemist with the firm. He asked him if he had any cantharides as he had a neighbour who was breeding rabbits and wanted some to improve their potency. Mr Lushington showed him one or two bottles, Ford said, adding: "You know this is a number one poison?" Ford replied: "In that case I had better not have it," and left the stockroom.

Pointing out that his story about a neighbour breeding rabbits had been a lie, the police demanded the truth, and Ford confessed to taking some cantharides from the poison cupboard, once he was sure that Mr Lushington was out of the way. But he still insisted he had taken it with no intention of using it, and had not given any of it to the dead girls. The police pressed him further, wondering if they were dealing with a murder case or one of manslaughter.

Ford finally cracked. "I have been thinking a great deal about this," he told officers, "and my mother always told me to tell the truth." In a new statement he said: "I now wish to say that I took a little of the cantharidin and put it on the desk. I then used the pair of scissors you have shown me, picked it up on the scissors' blades, and put it into two of the pieces of coconut ice. I pushed it into the coconut ice with the scissors. I gave one of the pieces to Miss Grant. . . We were very fond of each other and she kept putting me off, and I made up my mind to give her cantharidin to stimulate her desire for me. It seemed to me that this was the best way to give it to her."

The police were now satisfied. Ford had given Betty Grant a fatal dose inadvertently because he was ignorant of the toxic effects. But how had Miss Malins been given the same poison?

Asked about this, Ford replied: "I cannot say how Miss Malins got the other piece, except that it must have been by accident. The only girl I was interested in was Miss Grant. I am deeply sorry I gave Betty Grant the drug. I now realise I have caused the death of these two girls in doing this crazy thing, at the expense of losing my dear wife and children."

In June 1954 Ford was tried for manslaughter at the Old Bailey, before the Lord Chief Justice, Lord Goddard. Mr Richard Elwes, defending, said that it was obvious that Ford had not intended to kill anyone, and he had admitted manslaughter. Despite Ford's guilty plea, the full evidence was heard.

Mr Lushington testified that he had found thirty-nine grains of cantharidin missing from the poison cupboard – a safe dose given by medical men was two-hundredths of a grain at most. Lewis Nickolls of the Metropolitan Police Laboratory, an authority on poisons, said that cantharidin had been found in the digestive tracts of both dead girls, and he did not think there had been any possibility of either girl recovering once they had consumed the substance. There was no effective antidote to the poison and they had been beyond medical aid.

Mr Elwes stressed that Ford had been in charge of a large staff of women for many years without any complaint about his conduct towards them. Although his client had instructed him to make no reference to his relationship with Betty Grant, Mr Elwes said that Ford had not given his victim the poison by subterfuge in order to have sexual relations with her.

Lord Goddard would not have this. Fixing counsel

with a fierce glance, Goddard said: "He gave this stuff to her in the hope that she would be sexually inclined to him. Whether she was sexually inclined or not is another matter. Evidently, at the time she was not."

Mr Elwes persisted: "Those instructing me have failed to get any coherent instructions out of him. The result of this case is that he is physically and mentally something like a wreck. . . One thing which emerges clearly is that what he did was certainly not a considered thing. . ."

Goddard interrupted: "Of course he did not intend to murder – everybody understands that. But I do not understand how you can say it was not considered."

Sentencing Ford, Goddard told him: "You were determined to administer to Miss Grant an aphrodisiac, or what you believed to be an aphrodisiac. You asked a qualified chemist to give you some of this substance, giving him an untrue reason why you wanted it. He gave you a serious warning that it was a deadly poison. Nevertheless, after that warning, you went out to a shop and bought a sweetmeat and treacherously administered this poison in the sweetmeat to the young woman. You put the poison in the coconut ice and did not take the precaution to see that no one else got it. The death of these two girls is at your door, and I have no doubt that you bitterly regret it. I have not the slightest doubt that the last thing you intended was to kill these girls."

He sentenced Ford to five years imprisonment.

Ford was not a true poisoner in the sense of all the other criminals in this book, but he illustrates the danger of people meddling with drugs they do not understand. . .

10
CANTHARIDES

The notion of a "love-potion" or aphrodisiac is one of man's most enduring myths. But as any doctor will confirm, there is no substance, medicine or drug which will increase sexual ability or stimulate sexual desire.

Yet for centuries various peoples have sworn by certain substances. Even today, in the Far East powdered rhino-ceros horn is valued at more, weight for weight, than gold, because of a belief that it ensures sexual virility. It does no such thing, but it has led to a decline in the rhinoceros population. . .

Oysters, champagne, various herbs and spices – all have had some sexual quality attributed to them, all falsely. Perhaps the most celebrated of these sexual stimuli has been Spanish Fly, which is in reality cantharides, derived from a beetle called *Cantharis vesicatoria*. This is one of the many varieties of blistering beetles which produce an irritant liquid as a form of self-protection against birds and predators. The species *Mylabris cichorii*, or Indian blistering beetle, is another insect which contains this irritant liquid, while others, like the devil's coach horse, ooze it out, and the bombardier beetle actually squirts it at enemies. Contact with this liquid produces a burning, irritant sensation.

The infamous Madame de Montespan, one of France's most indefatigable poisoners in the seventeenth century,

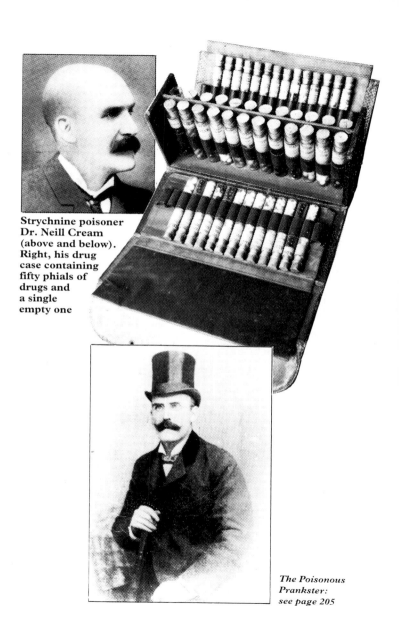

Strychnine poisoner Dr. Neill Cream (above and below). Right, his drug case containing fifty phials of drugs and a single empty one

The Poisonous Prankster: see page 205

George Chapman photographed with two of the women he murdered. Above, Bessie Taylor and below, Maud Marsh

The Cruel Casanova: see page 10

"I have never seen such a villain. He looked like some wild beast," Sir Edward Carson, who prosecuted at the trial, said of Chapman

Adelaide Bartlett. She was
accused of murdering her
husband Edwin (left) with
chloroform

The Lucky Lady: see page 90

One of the bodies being removed from the fashionable house on New York's Riverside Drive

Millionaire drug manufacturer John Peck and his wife Clara

Dr. Arthur Warren Waite

The Man From Egypt: see page 70

was alleged to have bought several items for preparing a cocktail to increase male potency, including rooster's testicles and Spanish Fly.

The active agent in this liquid is cantharadin, which is colourless and produces an instant blister or inflammation if it touches the skin. It has been used in the form of a hair restorer, in the belief that anything which irritates the skin might stimulate growth. It was known to physicians in ancient India, Arabia and Greece, who first promoted it as a sex stimulant.

The thinking behind this is that if it inflames the penis or vagina, sexual intercourse may be demanded as a way of getting rid of the itching. But in fact, if swallowed, just one-third of a grain can cause massive internal damage to the mouth and throat, kidneys and bladder, with the victim usually dying of shock.

11
ADELAIDE BARTLETT
The Lucky Lady

"I only saw my husband once before my wedding day" –
Adelaide Bartlett.
"Now she has been acquitted, she should tell us,
in the interests of science, how she did it" –
Sir James Paget, Queen Victoria's surgeon.

No survey of poisoning crimes would be complete without an examination of one of the classic cases – that of Adelaide Bartlett, tried for the murder of her husband, Thomas. It was the sensation of London in 1886, with the Old Bailey trial becoming a national drama.

It was quickly referred to by the Press as the "Pimlico Mystery" – and a mystery it remains to this day. The alleged poison was then unique in the annals of murder – chloroform. There was no recorded case of it having been used as an instrument of homicide, although the fiery liquid that burns the mouth and throat was known to have been used in suicide cases. The trial was to revolve around the central question of whether it was possible for a lethal dose of this substance to be poured down the throat of an unconscious man.

Even more bizarre were the details of the domestic habits of the Bartletts, as revealed during the trial. There appeared to be something of a *ménage à trois*, with husband and wife enjoying a close relationship with a Methodist minister. Was the husband actively pushing the wife into the arms of the minister? Was there an element of kinky sex in the relationship? Why did the husband carry contraceptives in his pockets?

Thomas Edwin Bartlett had a string of grocery shops in the suburbs of London. In 1875, thirty and prosperous, he married a sixteen-year-old French girl, Adelaide Blanche de la Tremouille born in Orlèans in 1855. After the wedding ceremony at Croydon, Surrey, he sent his child-bride to a boarding-school at Stoke Newington for two years.

Thomas Bartlett may have had oddly progressive views about sex, but he had a very determined and conservative outlook on education. When his wife had completed her two years at boarding-school, he sent her to a convent in Belgium for twelve months to put the finishing touches to her grooming. Only then was she permitted to return to London to live with her husband.

Their first three years were spent living above one of his shops in Station Road, Herne Hill. Apparently the couple were happy, until Bartlett invited his father, a widower, to live with them. The elder Bartlett had not approved of the marriage, and close proximity to the wife did not alter his opinion that she wasn't good enough for his son. When she gave birth to a stillborn child in 1881, it probably confirmed him in his opinion.

The couple had engaged Annie Walker, a nurse, to live with them while Adelaide was expecting the child. They took a great liking to Annie, who became a family friend. After she left, she would visit them from time to time. Annie was to have a role in the drama which was to follow, for Adelaide Bartlett was to claim that it was Annie who first advised her to use chloroform to ease her husband's "internal complaint".

In 1884 the couple moved to The Cottage at Merton Abbey, near Wimbledon, and Bartlett's father departed, setting up home alone. Merton was to have importance in the destiny of the Bartletts. In the autumn of 1885 they went to Sunday service at the nearby Methodist chapel, where they met the Rev. George Dyson, a principal character in the Bartlett saga.

A few days later he called at The Cottage to pay a pastoral visit. The couple were charmed by the well-educated young minister, who was aged twenty-seven, and Bartlett invited him to call at the cottage daily to tutor Adelaide in Latin, history and mathematics. A strong bond developed between all three.

When the tenancy of The Cottage expired and the Bartletts moved to Dover for a month, Dyson visited them there twice. During this period, Bartlett went to London daily to visit his shops, and at one of these he got two assistants to witness his will. He left all his property to Adelaide, with the Rev. George Dyson being appointed one of the executors.

In October the Bartletts returned to London, taking a first-floor furnished apartment at 85, Claverton Street, Pimlico. Dyson was a frequent visitor – so frequent that Bartlett supplied him with a railway season ticket between Putney and Waterloo. And it was at Claverton Street, in the December, that Bartlett first became ill. His wife called in a Dr. Leach, who found the patient to be suffering from sickness, diarrhoea and haemorrhage of the bowels. His pulse was weak and he seemed extremely nervous. When the doctor examined the patient's mouth, he observed a thin blue line around the gums, suggesting that he had been taking mercury. But when he asked Bartlett if this were so, the patient denied it. The doctor recommended rest and nursing.

Adelaide had a bed placed in the drawing-room for her husband to use, and he remained in that drawing-room until his death. While Adelaide acted as the devoted nurse, Dyson continued to be a frequent visitor, and one of Barlett's business partners called every Sunday. Bartlett's father, told that his son was too ill to receive visitors, saw him on only three occasions during his illness, and strongly suggested that Adelaide should get another medical opinion.

She mentioned this to her husband in the presence of Dr Leach. The doctor offered to consult with any other medical practitioner, but Bartlett declined, saying that he was getting better. But he added: "I will see anyone they care to call in, for the protection of my wife." Adelaide joked: "Mr Bartlett's friends will accuse me of poisoning him if he does not come out soon."

Dr Leach then called in a Dr Dudley, and they made a joint examination of Bartlett. Their findings were that Bartlett was in perfectly good health, but was suffering from some kind of hysteria which made him afraid to go out, or to leave his wife's side.

On December 26th, 1885, Dyson returned from a Christmas visit and spent the afternoon with Bartlett, who seemed much recovered and in good spirits. The next day, a Sunday, Dyson called again at nine o'clock in the evening. He met Adelaide at the door as she was just leaving to post a letter, and he offered to walk with her to the postbox. On the way, Adelaide mentioned that she wanted to obtain some chloroform to soothe her husband and help him sleep. She said he was suffering spasms of pain from "an internal complaint," so she needed quite a large quantity.

She also mentioned that Nurse Walker at one time used to get it for her, but she now wanted Dyson to procure it. When Dyson asked her why she couldn't ask the doctor for it, she told him that no doctor would entrust an unskilled person with chloroform. After Dyson agreed to obtain the chloroform, Adelaide gave him a sovereign to cover the cost.

On the Monday morning Dyson called at three chemists' shops in Putney and Wimbledon, obtaining small bottles of chloroform at each, which he then transferred into a larger bottle. He told the staff at each shop that he needed the chloroform for removing grease-spots from clothing. He later handed the large bottle of chloroform to Adelaide during a stroll by the river at Putney.

Thomas Bartlett was now making such a recovery that while Dyson was going from chemist to chemist, he went for a drive in a hansom. Moreover, Dr Leach announced that he intended to discontinue visiting him. But on the following Thursday, New Year's Eve, Bartlett asked his doctor to accompany him to his dentist's. When they returned to Claverton Street, a sort of party took place, with the landlady, Mrs Doggett, coming in to see Bartlett. In good spirits, he talked of going to Torquay for a holiday. It was then, in the course of general conversation, that Adelaide casually asked Mrs Doggett if she had ever taken chloroform – and didn't she agree that it was very nice and pleasant? Adelaide revealed that she was in the habit of giving it as sleeping-drops to her husband, as many as twelve drops at a time. . .

That evening, Bartlett had oysters, cake and tea for his supper. He then told the maid that he would like a large haddock for his breakfast. After he retired to bed in the drawing-room, the maid brought in coals for the night at about ten-thirty. Adelaide Bartlett came out of the sick-room and told her to leave a basin for her husband's beef-tea on the table on the landing.

At 4 a.m. Mr Doggett was awakened by a knocking at his door. It was Adelaide Bartlett. In a hushed voice she told him that she thought her husband was dead. Doggett threw on a dressing-gown, and then went and roused the maid, telling her to fetch Dr Leach. He went into the drawing-room, where he saw Bartlett on his back in bed, his left hand across his chest. He was very cold, and must have been dead for two or three hours. Adelaide explained that she had gone to sleep with her hand around his foot. She had awakened because of a pain in her hand, then found her husband lying on his face. She had turned him over, then tried to force brandy down his throat in a vain effort to revive him.

When Doggett first entered the room he noticed a strong smell of ether. On the mantelpiece, within reach of the bed, was a tumbler half full of brandy, which also smelled of ether. It was 4.30 a.m. before Dr Leach arrived, and he was astounded that a man he had seen the previous day in perfect health should now be dead. He questioned Adelaide about the circumstances, and she burst out crying, repeating what she had already told the landlord.

Dr Leach immediately suspected poisoning, but Adelaide said that it would have been impossible for her husband to have taken anything without her noticing. The doctor searched the room, but found nothing suspicious, except an almost empty bottle of a disinfectant, which Adelaide said her husband had used to rub on his gums to relieve pain. Dr Leach told Adelaide that he could not issue a death certificate – there would have to be a post-mortem examination. Adelaide readily agreed to this, saying: "Spare no expense!"

Adelaide sent telegrams to her husband's father and his business partner, informing them of the death. She requested them to come to Claverton Street immediately. When the elder Bartlett arrived, he made no effort to disguise the fact that he thought his son had been the victim of foul play. He told Dr Leach: "We must have a post mortem. This cannot pass." He also insisted that the doctors who performed the autopsy should be independent, having no connection with his son's treatment. After this was agreed to, it was decided that Dr Green of Charing Cross Hospital, and his assistant, Dr Murray, would perform the post mortem, with Dr Leach in attendance.

The following morning, Dyson called at Claverton Street at 11.30 a.m, staying to hear the result of the post-mortem, which took place at two o'clock. Having finished their examination, the doctors gathered in the drawing-room. Dr Leach, as their spokesman, gave their findings. They had found no natural cause of death. The stomach contents gave rise to suspicion, indicating a large dose of chloroform had been swallowed, and they had been prepared for further tests.

The rooms were then sealed up and the coroner informed. Adelaide, having arranged to stay with a friend, left the house with Dyson. Just before they left, Dr Leach mentioned that when the body had been opened, the doctors had noted a pungent smell of chloroform in the stomach. . .

The moment they were alone, George Dyson anxiously questioned Adelaide about the bottle of chloroform he had obtained for her. She replied that she had not had occasion to use it – the bottle remained still full. Dyson, not entirely satisfied, questioned her further. Adelaide told him firmly not to worry about it.

Dyson remained uneasy. He still had the small bottles in which he had bought the chloroform before transferring it to the larger bottle. What, he wondered, should he do with them? The next day, Sunday, he was due to preach at Tooting. Before he left his lodgings in Putney, he put the small bottles in his pocket. During his journey, he threw them into some gorse bushes on Wandsworth Common.

The day after that, he waited grimly at Claverton Street for Adelaide to return home. When she did, in the company of her friend, Mrs Matthews, Dyson waited until he and Adelaide were alone in the kitchen before once again broaching the subject of the chloroform. But Mrs Matthews overheard part of the conversation.

Dyson said loudly: "You did tell me that Edwin was going to die soon!" And when Adelaide denied this, he groaned aloud, crying out: "Oh, my God! I am a ruined man!"

When he left, Mrs Matthews found Adelaide in a state of fury, stamping her feet on the floor. Asked why she was so upset, she replied that Dyson had been "bothering her about a piece of paper." That piece of paper was a poem Dyson had written to her, which he wanted returned and which she contemptuously handed back to him. It read:

"Who is it that hath burst the door,
Unclosed the heart that shut before,
And set her queen-like on her throne,
And made its homage all her own?
My Birdie."

That same evening, Dyson again visited Adelaide. She begged him not to say anything about the chloroform at the inquest, but he flatly refused, saying he intended to tell all.

The inquest opened the next day, but was adjourned until February 4th, when the report of Dr Stevenson, analyst to the Home Office, would be ready. In the local tea-shop, George Dyson and Adelaide Bartlett sat in guilty solitude. She tried to reassure him that he was worrying himself unnecessarily about the chloroform, but he replied that he had plenty to be worried about. Adelaide then said: "If you do not incriminate yourself, you will not incriminate me."

The last conversation between the couple took place two days later, this time in the presence of Mr and Mrs Matthews. Again, chloroform was the main topic of conversation. With great emotion, Dyson said that his career was at an end, and he would be forced to resign his ministry. To Adelaide Bartlett he said: "Supposing it was proved that you. . .?"

"Do not mince matters!" Adelaide interrupted angrily. "Say that I gave it to him!" She said that she had poured the contents of the large bottle of chloroform out of a railway carriage window on the evening of Wednesday, January 6th, and had then thrown the bottle into a pond on Peckham Rye.

A little later, Adelaide found it necessary to consult Dr Leach about her own health. She learned from him that Dr Stevenson had sent in his report to the Home Office – and had concluded that chloroform had been the cause of death. "That should set your mind at rest," said Dr Leach. "Had it been one of those secret poisons which can be administered without the patient knowing it, you would most certainly have been accused by some people of poisoning him." Adelaide sighed heavily, saying that she wished it was anything but chloroform which had been found.

Then she told the doctor about her marriage. She said

that her husband had always believed that every man should have two wives, one for companionship, the other "for use". He had married her when she was sixteen, intending that she should be a companion only. The marriage had been arranged by her parents. "My consent to my marriage was not asked, and I only saw my husband once before my wedding day." They had lived together happily enough without any sexual relations for six years, but then her longing to become a mother had led them to break the arrangement – just once. The child was born dead, and so the former platonic relationship was resumed.

When they had met the Rev. Dyson, the husband had seemed to view him as the ideal lover for his wife. He had tried to force them into one another's arms, encouraging them to kiss in front of him. He even told them they were affianced.

Later, when recovering from his illness, he had showed a desire to assert his conjugal rights, but she had rejected him. She regarded celibacy as a duty she owed to her womanhood – and to her "fiancée", the Rev. Dyson. Her husband had agreed with her views, but his animal passions were too strong for him. Having fended him off several times when his need was urgent, she had devised the idea of procuring chloroform, intending to sprinkle some of it on a handkerchief and wave it in front of him should he ever attempt to rape her.

She had never had cause to put her plan into effect – and had kept it secret from her husband. But the presence of the chloroform, hidden in her dressing-table drawer, had preyed on her mind. On New Year's Eve, while her husband was lying in bed, she had fetched the bottle of chloroform and given it to him, as a way of confessing everything. He had not been angry. He had simply looked at the bottle, then reached up and put in on the mantel-piece, close to the bed. She then reiterated how she had been awakened by cramp in her hand, only to find her husband lying dead. She had tried to pour brandy down his throat. . .

Dr Leach asked her how she had obtained the chloroform. She was reluctant to tell him. Very well, what had become of the bottle? She said that she was positive that it had remained on the mantelpiece throughout that night. But, at about eight o'clock in the morning, she had removed the bottle and hidden it in a drawer in her room. She left it there until the afternoon of January 6th, then took it with her when she left the lodgings because the rooms were to be sealed. She then told of emptying the bottle from the railway carriage and subsequently throwing it into the pond.

At the resumed inquest, Dr Stevenson stated that he had found a fatal quantity of chloroform in Bartlett's stomach, along with a small amount of alcohol. The inquest was further adjourned until the 11th, and by then Adelaide had been arrested for the murder of her husband. On February 18th, the jury returned a verdict of wilful murder against Adelaide and found that the Rev. Dyson had been an accessory before the fact, and he was also arrested. Both were taken before magistrates, who committed them for trial.

The case had aroused great national interest by the time the trial opened on April 12th, 1886, at the Old Bailey. Mr Justice Wills presided, with – as is customary in poisoning cases – the Attorney-General, Sir Charles Russell QC, prosecuting for the Crown. The defence, led by Sir Edward Clarke QC, applied for the prisoners to be tried separately. At that point the prosecutor rose and said that he did not propose to bring any evidence against the Rev. George Dyson, and the judge asked the jury to declare him "not guilty".

Sir Charles Russell told the court: "The jury will have no difficulty in arriving at the conclusion that the deceased died from chloroform which had found its way into his stomach. The question they will have to decide is: how did it get there? He may have taken it himself with suicidal intent or he may have swallowed it by accident. The third possibility is that it was administered to him by another person. The Crown says the person who administered the poison was Adelaide Bartlett."

Having described how the taking of chloroform orally would have caused such a burning sensation that it must have been accompanied by loud groans, or even screams, Sir Charles went on: "There was one way – and one way only – in which it could have been given. And that was by first inducing a state of stupor, then introducing it when the person was partly or wholly unconscious. Mr Doggett, the landlord, stated that when he entered the death-chamber, he noted a strong smell of ether. He sniffed at a tumbler on the mantelpiece, the contents of which were evidently brandy, with some drugs in it which smelt like ether."

Called as a prosecution witness, the Rev. Dyson said Bartlett had wished him to be Adelaide's guardian. He described how he had been persuaded to buy the chloroform, after having been told how Nurse Walker used to obtain it.

He said there was no great intimacy between himself and Adelaide. True, he had kissed her in her husband's presence, but no impropriety had taken place. Bartlett had once asked him if it was in accordance with the teachings of the Bible that a man might have two wives – one for companionship, the other for "service". He had told Bartlett that the Bible did not sanction such an arrangement. He and Bartlett had been like brothers – and Bartlett had left him in no doubt that he eventually wanted him to marry his wife, telling him that he had left Adelaide his entire fortune for that purpose. He had once said to him: "If anything happens to me, you two may come together." But, said Dyson, he had never promised Adelaide that he would marry her on her husband's death, and he had never considered himself engaged to her.

Nurse Walker, next into the witness-box, said that she had never at any time supplied Adelaide with chloroform. Dr Leach, who followed her, said that Mrs Bartlett had nursed her husband with great devotion, and he himself had found Bartlett to be extremely neurotic and unbalanced, so much so that he once suspected him of being insane. He described how Adelaide had told him about her peculiar marital arrangement, and how, on December 26th, Bartlett had told him an extraordinary tale. "When I asked him how he had slept, he replied: 'I could not sleep. I was nervous and restless. I saw my wife asleep in the easy chair, so I went and stood over her for two hours, holding up my hands and feeling the vital force being drawn up from her to me. I felt it through my fingertips. After that, I lay down and slept.' " (Bartlett had been a great believer in mesmerism.)

Dr Leach went on: "Prior to that, he had asked me if it was possible to be under someone else's influence from a distance, as both he and his wife had been mesmerised by a friend." The doctor concluded by saying that he had never heard of a case of poisoning by chloroform, and he had never given chloroform to a sleeping person. He thought it unlikely that chloroform could have been poured down Bartlett's throat, because he had had a large meal a short time previously, and would surely have vomited it up, yet he had not been sick.

Dr Stevenson, the Home Office analyst, said that he too knew of no case of murder by the administration of chloroform, but he did not think it would be difficult to pour it down the throat of an unconscious person – particularly if he was lying on his back and with his mouth open. In cross-examination, he admitted that it would be very difficult to do this without getting any chloroform into the air passages – and there had been none.

Rising to address the jury, Sir Edward Clarke told them: "You are asked to believe that a woman who had for years lived in friendship and affection with her husband, who had nursed and tended him night and day, who had called in doctors and tried to cheer him up, had suddenly been transformed into a murderess, committing a crime not only without excuse, but absolutely without any object, by the execution of a delicate operation difficult for the highest-trained doctors to perform. This is the first case in the world in which it has been suggested that a person was murdered by the administration of liquid chloroform. There is no other case of the kind – and yet it is now suggested to you that Adelaide Bartlett has committed an offence absolutely unknown in the history of medical jurisprudence.

"I think you will understand why chloroform has never been used – and probably never will be used – for the purpose of murder. It is because it is singularly variable in its effects. No one can define what a fatal dose is. We hear of persons swallowing from two to six ounces of liquid chloroform and yet life being retained. . .

"If Mrs Bartlett's account is to be accepted, the state of things was this – that the husband who had for so long not been unkind to her, but cold, was desiring again to assert his marital rights; that he, acting quite freely, had in effect given her to Dyson; had recognised the marriage which, after his death, might come to pass between these two; and had provided as far as he could for the contingency by making Dyson the executor of his will.

"Her statement is that he again desired to assert these rights, but she felt it would be wrong to her womanhood to allow their revival. She could not have been expected to tell Dyson that, so she made up the story of Nurse Walker having obtained the chloroform for her previously.

"When Dr Leach was first called in, there was something remarkable in Bartlett's condition. His symptoms told Dr Leach that he had been taking mercury. He denied it, but Leach had the impression that Bartlett had been to some quack who, for real or supposed syphilis, had dosed him with mercury.

"Now let us come to the night of the tragedy. On the last night of the year she was alone with her husband in that drawing-room. She was settling for the night in a chair at the foot of the bed. She had told him to what extremes she had been driven and given the bottle of chloroform into his hands.

"Soon after midnight she falls asleep. When she wakes up, probably an hour or two later, she finds her husband lying on his face. She gets up to turn him into a more comfortable position. She rubs his chest with brandy, but he is apparently cold and dead. She springs to his bedside. There is, close to the end of the mantelpiece, this wine-glass from which he had taken the fatal draught. Her woman's instinct is to give him brandy, in the hope of restoring him. She pours some brandy into the glass and tries to pour it down his throat. It is no use. She puts it back on the mantelpiece, where it was later found – this wine-glass which only contained brandy. . . We know the glass was there – and we know that this part of the mantelpiece was within Bartlett's reach.

"There was no scientific miracle worked by the grocer's wife under circumstances when it could not have been worked by the most experienced doctor. The rest of the story is known. 'What can he have died of?' she asks the doctor. The post mortem she does not shrink from. 'Spare no expense,' she cries. 'Fetch anyone so the mystery can be cleared.' "

Sir Edward sat down to a burst of applause from the packed courtroom. His had been a virtuoso performance.

In his closing speech Sir Charles Russell asked what had become of the bottle of chloroform. Why had it been removed before the doctor arrived? Mrs Bartlett had told Nurse Walker that her husband always used contraceptives – she did not want another child – and such things were found in the deceased man's pockets. This fact – and the symptoms of mercurial poisoning – might have a different explanation from that of the doctor. (This was an ambiguous – even baffling – reference to sexual practices which were taboo in the Victorian era.)

Mr Justice Wills, whose speeches always displayed his strong detestation of immoral practices, said that when he read, some weeks previously, that contraceptives had been found in Bartlett's possession, he'd had a strong suspicion that before the case was over they would throw some light on the matter. The pockets of a man's trousers were not the place in which he would keep these articles for domestic use, and this might well point to something else in Bartlett's habits. (The judge was implying that Bartlett had kept company with prostitutes).

He went on: "If there was one little grain of truth which is generally found in any romance to be inferred from these articles and in the habitual use of them between husband and wife, what becomes of the whole story of the use for which chloroform was to be employed?

"Chloroform was handed to her. Chloroform was in her possession. Chloroform killing the man – and the bottle of chloroform disappearing." He asked the jury to face these facts, in a clear invitation for them to convict Adelaide Bartlett.

The Old Bailey jury retired at 4.10 p.m, returning fifty minutes later with a verdict of "Not Guilty." They added this rider: "Although we think grave suspicion is attached to the prisoner, we do not think there is sufficient evidence to show how or by whom the chloroform was administered to the deceased." The verdict was greeted with applause, which the judge said was an "outrage."

Sir Edward Clarke wept silently. That evening, when he went to the Lyceum Theatre to see Henry Irving in *Faust*, the audience rose to give him a standing ovation. The audience might well have reflected on the Faust legend – a man selling his soul. . . Had Sir Edward sold his soul to enable a guilty woman to walk free?

After the trial Sir James Paget, of St. Bartholomew's Hospital, and surgeon to Queen Victoria, is said to have remarked: "Now she has been acquitted, she should tell us, in the interests of science, how she did it."

Adelaide Bartlett never did tell. After writing a graceful letter of gratitude to Sir Edward Clarke, she retreated into obscurity, returning to her native Orléans.

12
CHLOROFORM

Discovered in 1831 by the German chemist Baron von Liebig, this colourless, volatile liquid with its extremely low boiling point was first used as a solvent. It was excellent for removing stains from clothing, and its anaesthetic properties were quickly realised. In 1847 Sir James Simpson, Professor of Obstetrics at Glasgow University, published a paper on his use of chloroform as an anaesthetic for women in childbirth. It made the birth process a relatively painless affair and had few apparent side-effects.

This use of chloroform was bitterly denounced from the pulpits, the clergy holding that childbirth was intended by the Creator to be painful. However, the use of chloroform in this way became accepted after Queen Victoria used it during the delivery of her eighth child in 1853. If it was fit enough for a Queen, it was good enough for the public. Chloroform began to be widely used by doctors.

Used medically, the usual dosage was a concentration of one to two per cent of the vapour, given in controlled inhalations. It was sometimes given by mouth in minute doses to treat vomiting, but oral use was discouraged because liquid chloroform is an irritant to the skin – particularly the mouth and throat – and can produce severe blistering. The use of chloroform medically was discontinued when it was realised that it was liable to cause liver and kidney damage, an overdose causing fatty degeneration of these organs, leading to general blood-poisoning. It could often take four to five days for the victim to die.

Nevertheless, variations of chloroform began to appear in many remedies, like chlorodyne – a mixture of chloroform and morphine in tiny quantities – used to treat colds and stomach upsets. But it soon became apparent that some people became addicted to this mixture.

Readers of thrillers will be familiar with the use of pads soaked in chloroform pressed over victims' faces to make them unconscious. Chloroform has been used in kidnapping, robberies and rapes, but the use of chloroform to kill is rare, because it is so difficult to get anyone to swallow it. It burns the mouth and throat, with death resulting after hours of agony through heart failure and liver-damage. A fatal dosage is regarded as being 10 to 15ml. The characteristic smell of chloroform will be detected in the lungs at post mortem, with traces of the drug being found in all the body liquids.

Notable cases in which chloroform has featured include that of Ruth Snyder and Judd Gray, electrocuted in 1928 for the murder of Albert Snyder. Although a sash-cord weight was used to batter the unfortunate husband, chloroform and a picture wire finished him off.

Charles Jones and Albert Patrick used chloroform in the killing of Texas oil millionaire William Rice Marsh in 1900, and Dr Etienne Deschamps, a New Orleans dentist, used chloroform to drug patients so that he could sexually assault them. He went too far with a twelve-year-old girl and killed her, and was duly hanged in 1892. Chloroform also featured in the unsolved murder of model Dot King, fatally chloroformed in her New York apartment during a robbery in 1923. But the case of Adelaide Bartlett is for me the most intriguing of them all.

13
SADAMICHI HIRASAWA
The Polite Assassin
"Then the devil opened his mouth. . ." –
part of a memo from the Director of Tokyo CID.
*"Hirasawa is not the killer, I told the police he is not the
man." – Masako Murata, one of the survivors
of the mass poisoning.*

Imagine robbing a bank by offering all the staff doses of
poison which they readily swallow. . . This could only
have happened in Japan, where people are brought up
from birth to be submissive to authority, which they
equate with the Emperor himself. Just as they willingly
died in suicide attacks for him, so they complied when he
ordered them to obey the American Occupation Forces.
This attitude serves them well in their giant car factories,
but it was to lead to murder in the most sensational bank-
robbery in the country's history. The killer poisoned
sixteen people – twelve of whom died – just to steal the
equivalent of a few hundred pounds.

In 1948 Japan was still ravaged by the effects of the
war. Many city roads were still scarred with bomb-craters
and were little more than muddy tracks along which US
Army trucks ploughed their way.

The Teikoku Bank was just seventy yards from
Shiinamachi railway station in Tokyo, and was a simple
one-storey building of wood construction. The staff

worked at two rows of desks in the banking section behind the counter. In separate quarters attached to the bank lived the caretaker, with his wife and two children.

It was raining heavily on Monday, January 26th, 1948, with the temperature near freezing. Inside the bank the staff huddled around their heaters. Poor sanitation in the city had led to outbreaks of dysentery and typhoid, and when by two o'clock branch manager Ushiyama said he had to go home because of severe stomach pains, the staff nodded sympathetically. The under-manager, Yoshida, supervised the last hour of business, and at three o'clock the bank's doors were shut for the day. The staff sat at their desks transcribing the day's transactions into ledgers and adding up cash receipts.

At about 3.10 p.m. there was a sharp rapping at the bank's door. A woman clerk went to the door and opened it. She had no fear of robbery: robbing banks was a Western crime. A middle-aged man stood at the door, wearing a uniform covered by a white coat with an arm-band reading: Metropolitan Office, City Hall of Tokyo. He carried a small military-style medical bag. The girl, Miss Akuzawa, was to remember that he had two moles on his left cheek and a scar under his chin, and she thought him handsome. Oddly, though the street outside was knee-deep in mud, his rubber boots were very clean.

Politely, the man bowed and handed over his namecard. The Japanese are very scrupulous about having cards bearing their names, which they exchange with people they meet as a matter of courtesy. The namecard read: "Jiro Yamaguchi, M.D. Welfare Ministry." The man asked to see the manager as a matter of urgency and was invited in. He removed his boots outside the door, as is Japanese custom, and put on the proffered slippers.

The man approached the under-manager and told him that a public well in front of Mr Aida's house, just five minutes from the bank, had been responsible for a number of dysentery cases. In fact, one of Mr Aida's tenants had been stricken that very day and had been in the bank to make a deposit.

"How have you learned of this so quickly?" asked Mr Yoshida.

"The doctor who treated the stricken man made a direct report to the Occupation Forces," the caller explained. "I've been sent by Lieutenant Parker, who directs a disinfecting team with the Occupation. I have to inoculate everyone against dysentery, and I will also have to disinfect any items that might have been handled today. Receipts, money, accounts, books. Everything. No one will be allowed to leave until I do, which will be when Lieutenant Parker and his team arrive to check my work. They will be here soon."

The under-manager nodded. The doctor took from his bag a metal box containing two bottles, marked with English lettering. One read: "First Drug", the other "Second Drug."

What happened next was described as follows in a memorandum sent on January 27th, 1948, to all police stations by the Director of Tokyo CID:

> *This crime, which was committed at the closing hour of the bank and in the assumed name of the Occupation Forces, killing many lives at one time and attempting to rob much money of the establishment, is one of the rarest and boldest crimes ever seen in the history of all crimes . . .*
>
> *All the victims, wholly unsuspicious of the fiendish intention of the offender, whose perfect composure and plausible explanations as well as his armband of Tokyo Metropolitan office having satisfied them to lay full credit to his words, formed a circle around him, poor victims sixteen in all. Then the devil opened his mouth and said: "This medicine will damage the enamel of your teeth, and so I will show you how you must swallow it. There are two kinds of medicine. Take the second about a minute after you take the first. Be sure to drink it within a minute, or you will get a bad effect."*

After such explanations he poured into the victims'
cups some liquid medicine, then he took a cup in his
own hand and, saying "This is how to drink", gulped
its contents by dripping them drop by drop onto his
tongue, which he put out in the form of a shovel. So
the poor victims, without exception, gulped the fatal
water following the devil's example. The liquid in
question had a burning-taste . . . After about a minute
the tricky villain again showed them how to drink the
second medicine, and again the poor innocents
followed his example, not suspecting in the least that
they were actually killing themselves. The devil had
the audacity to advise them to rinse their mouths . . .

The under-manager had ordered all the bank staff,
including the caretaker and his family, to fetch their
cups. They drank the poison and ten died immediately,
their bodies being found around the water fountain,
blood and vomit trickling from their mouths. Two
more died in hospital. There were four survivors. One
girl, Miss Murata, crawled out of the bank on her
hands and knees and managed to gasp out to passers-
by: "The bank – it's awful! Help!"

The police were alerted, and inside the bank they
found a scene of unnatural calm. Money stood piled on
desks, but near the water fountain were the bodies of
those who had rushed there in a desperate attempt to
get water to alleviate the burning sensation in their
mouths. The dead and dying were rushed to hospital,
where some managed to gasp: "Dysentery – doctor –
medicine!" before passing away.

Chief Fujita of the Tokyo CID took immediate
charge of the case, but he arrived on the scene too late:
helpful neighbours had washed out the sixteen cups in
the bank. Traces of toxin in the victims' bodies were
too small to identify, although doctors believed the
poison to have been potassium cyanide or prussic acid.
An examination at the bank revealed that the killer had
taken 164,400 yen in cash and a cheque for 17,400 yen

– the equivalent of about £200. Inexplicably, he had left double this amount of money behind, lying in plain view.

The police memorandum, prepared just one day after the crime, gave this description of the wanted man, obtained from survivors: "Aged between 44 and 50, about 5ft 3in in height, rather thin with oval face, high nose, pale complexion. Two brown spots on the left cheek. A handsome man, well composed and looking like an intelligent man."

The memo went on to request all units to check if similar attempts had been made to rob banks, to find out where the killer's namecard had been printed, to check out all doctors and druggists, and to keep "secret surveillance over the daily habits and characteristics of the Metropolitan health officials and such others as are engaged in sanitary work . . ."

The killer had known just how much poison he needed to kill and how to administer it. In drinking from it himself, he had taken his liquid from that which floated at the top of the bottle, clear of the poison in suspension below, so he had some expertise. Yet police were subsequently to arrest a man who had no knowledge of poisons.

At that time the Tokyo police were under the supervision of American officials – the Allied Occupation Public Safety Division – who supervised their work to some extent and tried to stop them using brutal third-degree questioning tactics.

A printer was traced who had produced twenty cards for a "Jiro Yamaguchi, M.D." The description of the customer fitted that of the killer. Then a bank-manager came forward. Three months before the murders, a man had gone to the Ebara branch of the Yasuda bank and given the manager a card bearing the name: "Dr Shigeru Matsui. Japanese Welfare Ministry." He had persuaded eighteen members of staff to drink his "medicine," but the mixture had been weak and the staff merely felt ill. The man had mentioned "Lieutenant Parker," and had fled without attempting robbery. The manager had not thought the incident worth reporting to the police: it seemed more in the nature of a practical joke. But the manager had kept the card.

Then a second bank manager came forward. Just three weeks before the crime, his bank, the Mitsubishi Bank, had been visited by a man who handed over a card identifying him as "Jiro Yamaguchi, M.D." But the manager had become suspicious and declined the invitation to drink the medicine, and the man had run away.

Hampered at times by several men who falsely confessed to the crime, the police missed an early chance to catch the killer when the stolen cheque was cashed at a Tokyo bank the day following the killings, the murderer writing a false name and address as endorsement on the back. But at least the police had a specimen of his handwriting, and history was made when for the first time ever in Japan, an artist's impression was issued in an effort to catch the killer.

By this time the police were beginning to suspect that the killings had been carried out by a former member of the "731" germ-warfare unit of the Imperial Japanese Army.

This had been based in Manchuria during the war and had experimented on human beings – some of them Allied prisoners – with germs and poisons as part of research into chemical and biological warfare. Many of its members had kept their equipment after the war, taking it home with them. Now, however, the police were hampered by their American masters. The Americans shielded former members of the 731 unit from investigation, because they wanted the results of their experiments and were worried that the Soviets might discover the existence of this information. The commanding officer of 731, General Ishii, and his closest research assistants were taken to Maryland, USA, to work for the US Army Chemical Corps – even though it was known that they had experimented on US prisoners.

Checking on the two names the killer had used, police found there was no Dr Yamaguchi, but there *was* a Dr Shigeru Matsui, a man with an impeccable reputation who lived in Sendai, a few hours from Tokyo. He was interviewed at his home and said he had taken delivery of one hundred cards in March 1947, in preparation for attending a medical conference where he expected to hand out many. He had given ninety-six cards to people at the conference and elsewhere, and had four left. The card in the possession of the police was one of those ninety-six.

Although Dr Matsui kept no record of those to whom he had given cards, he did have their cards in return: ninety-six of them. So among the ninety-six cards might well be the real name of the killer. The police checked out each name laboriously, establishing that the man in question did not resemble the killer or had an alibi. This involved cross-questioning thousands of people given as alibi witnesses – altogether, more than 7,300 persons were interviewed in the investigation. Among those questioned was an artist who lived in a Tokyo suburb, Sadamichi Hirasawa.

Hirasawa was not at home when police called, his wife explaining that he had gone to visit his parents in Hokkaido because they were ill. He was questioned there by Tamigoro Igii, a bright Tokyo detective, who noted that Hirasawa's parents looked very well. The detective took Hirasawa to dinner – 180 days after the bank murders – and was surprised when Hirasawa supplied him with an alibi for January 26th. . . before he had been asked for one.

When asked about exchanging cards with Dr Matsui, he said he remembered the incident. They had met on a ferry going to Hokkaido. Cross-checked, Dr Matsui remembered meeting Hirasawa on the ferry. Hirasawa had said he was going to Tokyo to present a painting to the Crown Prince. Dr Matsui had been very impressed by that.

The detective noted that Hirasawa resembled the artist's likeness of the killer, even to the two moles on the left cheek.

When Igii asked Hirasawa for Dr Matsui's card, the artist said his pocket had been picked and he had lost the card, along with money. The detective phoned Tokyo, saying he felt Hirasawa was a definite suspect. He was told to stay on the case. Other detectives were sent to help, to keep watch on Hirasawa and question neighbours, some detectives posing as tradesmen. Letters were intercepted in order to compare the handwriting of Hirasawa with that on the stolen cheque.

Hirasawa had been desperately short of money before the bank murders, but now he was spending freely, having an extension built to his home . . . It was enough. Igii arrested him on August 24th, taking him back to Tokyo by train.

At the police station Hirasawa was found to be in possession of 40,000 yen, and he had given his wife 65,000 yen. Soon afterwards police traced a secret deposit Hirasawa had made in a Tokyo bank – 80,000 yen. When asked to account for this money, which came in total close to the amount stolen, Hirasawa said some had been a loan, some had come from selling paintings. But the men he named denied either having given him a loan or having bought paintings from him.

Eleven witnesses were asked to study him carefully and take their time: only one could pick him out as being the killer. While in custody Hirasawa tried to commit suicide, slashing his left wrist with a pen. In his own blood, he wrote on his cell wall: "I am innocent."

On September 3rd, after further questioning, Hirasawa admitted he had committed fraud on several occasions. On September 10th that secret bank deposit was traced, and by now his handwriting had been matched with that on the stolen cheque. Even so, at this point the evidence against him was circumstantial.

Then, on September 26th, came the confession without which Japanese police feel powerless to get a conviction. But how was that confession obtained? There were sixty-two interrogations over thirty-five days. Interrogations number 61 and 62 were virtually identical. Igii had questioned the suspect for the first forty-eight hours, and then the questioning had been taken over by Procurator Tagaki. The last two interrogations – 61 and 62 – had been conducted by the top man, Idei. According to the police, the fifty-eight-year-old artist wiped tears from his eyes and said: "I don't have adequate words to express the regret I have for committing such a horrible crime." The police celebrated by holding a large party.

Two months before his trial, Hirasawa retracted his confession, saying it had been coerced from him after days and nights deprived of sleep. On July 25th, 1950, he appeared in court, after twenty-three months in custody. He was convicted of the murder of twelve people and the attempted murder of four more, and sentenced to death by hanging. There had been no jury; Hirasawa had appeared before his judges in ceremonial robes, and when the death sentence was pronounced, he cried out: "A great wrong has been done!"

The case went to the Appeal Court, which ruled that he had been fairly convicted, and for the next three and a half years the appeal against execution was considered by the Supreme Court. During this time the Allied Occupation came to an end, and the case became purely a Japanese internal affair.

In 1951 Hirasawa's wife divorced him, and his daughters renounced him. In the spring of 1955 the Supreme Court ruled that Hirasawa's arrest, trial and conviction and death sentence had been correct, and they bound him over to the Justice Ministry for the execution to be carried out. But Hirasawa was not executed. He remained in custody until he died in 1987. According to *The Guinness Book of Records*, this was the longest ever wait by a prisoner on Death Row.

Why did the Japanese fail to execute Hirasawa? There are two theories. One is that every single Justice Minister had been too superstitious to sign the death warrant, because traditionally such acts bring bad luck. That seems unlikely, for many other prisoners were executed during the same period. The other notion is that the authorities knew that Hirasawa was innocent, or had serious doubts: thus, almost forty years later, Hirasawa still sat on Death Row, the authorities unable to release him because the prestige of their judicial system was at stake.

The case attracted much controversy and newspaper attention over the years, with many Japanese coming to believe that Hirasawa was innocent. In 1985 an American author, William Triplett, published a book on the investigation: *Flowering of the Bamboo*. He went to Tokyo and spoke to many surviving characters in the story, meeting representatives of the Society To Save Hirasawa. This had been founded in 1962, and the current secretary was Hirasawa's adopted son.

Before going to Japan, Triplett had examined papers in the National Archives in Washington relating to the case. His view was that Dr Matsui had been more involved than had ever been admitted. His medical skill would have made him far more knowledgeable about poisons than an artist, and he had served in Manchuria during the war . . . But Dr Matsui could not be questioned further: he died some thirty years ago.

The most convincing aspect of Triplett's attempt to prove that Hirasawa was innocent lies in his examination of Hirasawa's confession. That admission did not fit with the facts.

Hirasawa said he had walked from Ikebukuro station to the Teikoku Bank and this took him twenty-five minutes. It was part of the prosecution's case that he had left the company of his son-in-law shortly before two in the afternoon, and caught the 2.25 train to Ikebukuro station, arriving at 2.50 p.m, left the station and arrived at the bank by 3.15, introducing himself at the side door as "Dr Yamaguchi." The defence claimed that the artist, then aged fifty-six, could not have walked this distance in just twenty-five minutes. The crowds, the sleet and the atrocious mud would have made this impossible even for a young man. Triplett made the same journey with a group of Hirasawa supporters. It took him thirty-six minutes.

The trip itself displayed more inconsistencies. Why had Hirasawa gone on to Ikebukuro station, when the train stopped at Shiinamachi station, only seventy yards from the bank? He could have alighted and saved himself a long walk. In his confession Hirasawa said that he had seen an American Army jeep outside the house of Aida, supplying treatment for dysentery, and this had given him the idea for the story he told the bank manager. But it is impossible to see Aida's house from the station, and it is not on the direct route from station to bank. You have to make a seven-block detour to pass by this house. Why would Hirasawa have gone this way? And if he did, how could he have completed the journey in twenty-five minutes? And why would he have needed to witness the jeep scene to get the idea for the dysentery story? The real killer had already used the dysentery story twice as a ruse in his previous bank robbery attempts. Furthermore, the killer's clean boots suggested he had arrived in a vehicle.

Whoever the murderer was, he must have known the precise dosage to give. Too much, and the first few to take his potion would be dropping dead before he gave the rest their dose. Yet in his confession Hirasawa said he gave a one-gram dose of potassium cyanide to each person – in which case they would have died instantly. So did the police, coaching Hirasawa in his confession, supply him with the wrong information?

Other factors pointing to Hirasawa's innocence include a statement from Masako Murata, the girl who crawled from the bank. She told Triplett: "Hirasawa is not the killer. The killer had a round face. Very much like an egg.

I saw Hirasawa in the interrogation room and the first thing I noticed was how square his face was . . . I told the police he is not the man."

Triplett suggests that the killer was a member of the 731 unit experimenting with his toxin to see how powerful it was, and that the motive for the crime was not robbery, but was a political protest against the Occupation. The papers he uncovered in the National Archives in Washington, under the Freedom of Information Act, lend some weight to this.

The papers revealed that Chief Fujita of the Tokyo CID reported to the Americans that the technique employed by the bank robber-murderer was identical with that which Japanese Army chemical warfare personnel had been trained to use. The killer's equipment was similar to that used by the chemical warfare laboratory, and the use of the "First Drug" and "Second Drug" recalled the laboratory's jargon and suggested the killer had been trained there.

What about the money found in Hirasawa's possession, and for which he could not account? Triplett believes that Hirasawa had taken to painting pornography for wealthy patrons, but was so ashamed of this that he would sooner be convicted of murder than admit the truth.

On May 9th, 1985, officials from the Justice Ministry questioned Hirasawa in secret in connection with his appeal against execution. He declared his innocence, maintaining that he had been forced into confessing. The Justice Ministry never made their deliberations public.

Every day the white-haired prisoner would rise at 4 a.m. to recite his Buddhist prayers, and then return to bed to sleep until breakfast time. He refused to petition for a pardon, saying this would be "tantamount to admitting I am guilty. I am determined to prove my innocence. . . no matter how long I remain in this cell."

Romance blossomed for the artist, who had painted thousands of pictures while in prison, when Mrs Yakeo Ishita, 78, adviser to the Japan Music and Dancing

Federation, visited him in gaol and fell in love. In the Japanese equivalent of *Woman's Own*, she declared that "no man with such clear innocent eyes could have committed such a crime." Mrs Ishita expressed the hope that Hirasawa would be freed to marry her and live graciously in her large, eight-roomed house on the slopes of Mount Fuji. It was not to be . . .

In February 1987 Hirasawa, now seriously ill with pneumonia, spent his ninety-fifth birthday in his prison on the outskirts of Tokyo. He told a reporter that if ever he were free he would sell his paintings to finance a campaign for election to public office: "My purpose in running will be to save those convicted on false charges."

Though his case remains baffling, one thing is certain: if Hirasawa *did* poison those sixteen people merely to steal a few hundred pounds, he joins the ranks of the great eccentrics of crime.

14
CYANIDE

Cyanide is a vegetable poison which can be distilled from laurel leaves, as well as from the stones of peach, apricot, plum and cherry. It is a useful poison, employed in industry for case-hardening steel. Although it is the stuff of spy thrillers – the cyanide capsule to bite on when arrested – death is not so instantaneous as those stories would have you believe. A fatal dose of about four grains will kill the victim in about five minutes. A fatal dose of hydrocyanic acid (sometimes known as prussic acid or Scheele's acid and a derivative of cyanide) is considerably less than one grain and will kill a little quicker – within a few seconds. The smell of bitter almonds, also mentioned extensively in thrillers, is not all that pronounced. Many Nazi war criminals, including Heinrich Himmler and Hermann Goering, cheated the hangman by biting on capsules of potassium cyanide. American gas chambers use cyanide gas to execute condemned criminals.

The basic property of this poison is that it blocks the natural function and ability of the blood to take up oxygen, thus causing death through asphyxiation. The Romans, Arabs and Indians made extensive use of this poison. It is believed that Livia used it to murder the Emperor Augustus, applying it in the form of laurel water, which had been distilled to drive off the water and leave the poison behind. She dusted it on some figs. . .

There is a painting – 'The Death of Chatterton' – showing the poet lying gracefully on a couch after having taken poison. Although he had taken arsenic – which would have caused terrible stomach pains – his face is peaceful. Had he taken cyanide, the scene would not have been so pleasant. As the poison starves the body of oxygen, the result is the same as suffocation – or even hanging.

The victim would find his heart beating faster in an effort to suck in more blood and get it around the system quicker, and there would be a pounding in his head from an increased pulse. His limbs would become numb and his chest would heave rapidly as he fought for breath. A roaring in the head would give way to blackness – unconsciousness would take place before death itself.

After death all muscles would relax, including the involuntary muscles, so the bowels might be voided and the bladder emptied. The smell of faeces and urine might be the first noticeable thing. The body itself would be cyanosed – that is, all exposed parts would show a deep purple colour, almost like the sheen on a damson. The tongue would be swollen and extended. The eyes would be open and staring, showing broken blood vessels. There would be irregular red blotches on the body.

Notable killers who have used cyanide include John Tawell, tried in 1854 for murdering his mistress, Sarah Hart. It was proved that Tawell went to a chemist in Bishopsgate Street in London and casually bought two grams of Scheele's acid. This he added to a glass of beer he offered Sarah at her Slough home on January 1st, 1845. She died, but not before mumbling to a neighbour what had happened. The Slough police used the new-fangled telegraph to warn London police that Tawell was on the train to Paddington – a police "first" – and he was arrested on arrival. He was duly hanged.

Roland B. Molineux, a New York factory manager, sent his enemies bottles of Bromo Selzer through the post in 1898, laced with mercury cyanide. Twice tried, he entered an asylum in 1913 and died there four years later.

In 1907, Richard Brinkley made the acquaintance of an

old lady in Fulham, London, and after getting her to alter her will in his favour, killed her with cyanide. When relatives contested the will, Brinkley attempted to dispose of one of the will's witnesses with a cyanide-laced bottle of stout. Two others inadvertently drank from the bottle and died. Tried at Guildford, Brinkley was hanged.

Adolph Hofrichter was an Austrian army officer who, in December 1912, sent several fellow-officers boxes of capsules of a "strength-preserving remedy." Only one officer took a capsule – and promptly died. Apparently, Hofrichter wanted to remove those newly-promoted officers who stood in the way of his own promotion. He was sentenced to twenty years.

Dr Pierre Bougrat, heavily in debt, had a patient visit his Marseilles surgery on March 14th, 1925, carrying a bag full of his firm's wages, some 20,000 francs. Succumbing to temptation, the doctor poisoned his patient with cyanide, hiding the body in a cupboard, which he pasted over with wallpaper. When police eventually found the decomposing body, Bougrat stood trial for murder and was sentenced to life on Devil's Island. He became one of the few to escape, in 1927, getting to Venezuela where he was allowed to stay because of his skill as a doctor. He died in 1962, aged seventy-five.

There have also been many modern cases, too numerous to mention. Unlike arsenic, cyanide has never gone out of fashion.

15
EDMOND DE LA POMMERAIS
A Gambling Man

*"Look more closely into the death of Madame de Pawr.
It was murder. Her physician was also her lover and her
beneficiary" – Anonymous letter received
by Chief Inspector Claude, head of Sûreté.*

It was in 1863 that France's leading toxicologist, Dr Ambroise Tardieu, was confronted with an apparently insoluble problem. He was convinced that he was faced with a case of poisoning by digitalis, but no test existed to detect this poison . . .

Doctors called in to treat a sick widow in Paris in November 1863 were baffled by her condition. The heartbeat of the young Madame de Pawr was so erratic that any likely cause defied logical explanation. Her heart was racing one minute, then slowing the next. . .

The case was exacerbated by the fact that the patient insisted on being treated by her own physician, Dr Edmond de la Pommerais. This twenty-eight-year-old homeopathic practitioner was her lover. He had also tended her late husband prior to his untimely death . . .

Born in Orléans, Pommerais had arrived in Paris in 1859, then aged twenty-four, using his perfect manners and good looks to charm his way into the company of aristocrats. He convinced his new friends of his right to the title of "Count", when in fact it was self-granted.

Although a quack who treated his patients with homeopathic remedies, many of which were self-made vegetable alkaloid poisons, Pommerais soon established a thriving practice. One of his patients was an artist named de Pawr, who died leaving behind a pretty young widow with three children. Pommerais quickly took her to bed and became her lover.

Then she became unwell, telling friends that she was suffering from a "light case of cholera". After a short illness, characterised by stomach pains and copious vomiting, she died on November 17th, 1863. Pommerais issued a death certificate giving cholera as the cause of death, and his mistress was duly buried. But she was not forgotten.

Chief Inspector Claude, head of the Sûreté, soon received an anonymous letter suggesting that Pommerais had a financial interest in the widow's death. Taking personal charge of the inquiry, Claude discovered that the dead woman had taken out a large insurance policy shortly before her death, naming Pommerais as the beneficiary. In fact, the doctor was already in the process of claiming the money, 500,000 francs, from the insurance company.

De la Pommerais, known to be a big spender and gambler, had actually dumped the widow before her death, because he was in desperate need of money. Instead, he married a wealthy daughter of the rich Dubiczy family. His new mother-in-law, however, was sufficiently wary of Pommerais to make sure her daughter did not have control of her inheritance, but two months after the wedding the mother-in-law was taken ill after dinner with Pommerais, and died soon afterwards. Pommerais certified her death as being caused by Asiatic cholera, and no one questioned his diagnosis. After all, he had been the woman's doctor. . .

Now able to get his hands on his wife's money, Pommerais had used to it pay his pressing debts. And in

March 1863 he had got back in touch with Madame de Pawr, becoming her lover again, only for her to die eight months later.

Claude talked to the dead woman's sister, Mme Ritter (who was almost certainly the author of that anonymous letter), and he was told by her of a scheme that Pommerais had devised to make her financially secure and end her money worries. She was to take out a large insurance policy, then feign an incurable illness as a means of persuading the insurance company to change her policy for an annuity payable on her now shortened life expectancy. It would save the insurance company money. Pommerais would furnish the medical proof of her terminal medical condition. . .

Completely under his influence, the woman had taken out the policy, then made a will in Pommerais' favour. Fortunately, she had not had time to put the rest of the plan into operation – and had thus saved her life. There was no doubt in Claude's mind that Pommerais was insuring women only to murder them for financial gain.

He had the body of Madame de Pawr exhumed and an autopsy carried out. Dr Ambroise Tardieu, Professor of Forensic Medicine at Paris University, examined the various organs. He found no trace of cholera – the "official" cause of death. Next he did all the tests for the usual poisons, like arsenic and antimony, but found no trace of them. Yet he was certain the woman had been poisoned. Had Pommerais used his medical knowledge to choose a poison which he knew could not be detected?

The police had called at Pommerais' surgery and had taken away various bottles of liquids and powders, all of which had to be tested by the laborious Stas method, which could not detect some vegetable poisons.

Tardieu did not have a sample of the dead woman's vomit, which would have made things easier, so he made a compound of the liquids he had extracted from the various body organs, and then injected this into a dog.

The dog vomited, then its heartbeat raced and slowed

– exactly like the symptoms exhibited by Madame de Pawr – and within a few hours the dog was dead. Tardieu examined the collection of bottles taken from Pommerais, and noticed one labelled digitalis. It was empty – yet the doctor's records indicated that he had bought three grains recently. Then the police supplied Tardieu with dried vomit scraped from the floor-boards of the sickroom. He was able to make extracts from this which, when injected into frogs, duplicated exactly the effects of digitalis and proved that to be the murder substance.

The body of Pommerais' mother-in-law was exhumed, but she had been buried too long for any trace of digitalis to be found, although that was believed to be the poison which killed her, since no sign of cholera was found.

At the trial of Pommerais, the defence challenged the medical evidence, saying it had not been proved beyond doubt that digitalis had been the murder poison, and citing the fact that alkaloid poisons develop naturally in the corpses of people who die from natural causes.

But the jury were convinced by the mass of circumstantial evidence, and Pommerais' guilty behaviour – he had not insured Madame de Pawr in his own name but had persuaded her to take out the policy, though he provided her with the premium. To prevent the insurance money going to her children after her death, he had taken her to a lawyer to sign a document agreeing that she owed him 500,000 francs – promising to look after her children if anything happened to her. Getting his victim to sign that document was proof of motive. It was enough to convict de la Pommerais, who was executed in June 1864.

Tardieu's method of testing for digitalis with the aid of a frog is still in the modern textbooks on toxicology. He had made forensic history.

16
DIGITALIS

Digitalis is an extract from the foxglove, *Digitalis purpurea*, which has been used for centuries as a heart stimulant in folk medicine. It was a Dr Withering who first "discovered" digitalis in England in 1775, having extracted it from the leaves of the purple foxglove. The dried leaves can be boiled and the resulting liquid distilled to draw off a compound which contains several drugs, the most important of which is digitoxin. This has the effect of making the heart contract much more forcibly than usual, thus increasing the blood pressure and circulation. It is of great medical help in cases of heart failure, since it regulates the rhythm of the heart when used in minute doses, but in a normal healthy person, an overdose will cause the heart to beat irregularly and bring on cardiac arrest.

A toxic dose is about 2g. The symptoms experienced, usually within three hours of taking the drug, are headaches, mental confusion, affected vision, delirium and nausea. Overdoses taken orally are not usually fatal, as the victim will tend to vomit the poison.

17
HAWLEY HARVEY CRIPPEN
The Henpecked Husband

*"Do you think an advertisement would be any good?" –
Dr. Crippen questioning a detective, following his wife's
disappearance. "I am not sorry. The anxiety was too
much." – Crippen's words when arrested on board ship.*

Dr Hawley Harvey Crippen was an American, born in
Michigan in 1862. He obtained a somewhat dubious
medical degree from the Cleveland Homeopathic
Hospital, and the highest position he ever achieved in his
profession was as assistant to an optician. He married at
twenty-five, but his first wife died early of tuberculosis,
leaving an infant son.

As a thirty-year-old widower, the slight, weedy-looking
Crippen – he stood five feet four inches, had a straggling
moustache and weak, bulging eyes hidden behind small
"granny" spectacles – met a young New Yorker in 1892
who had ambitions to be on the stage. Crippen immediately fell in love with seventeen-year-old Kunigunde
Mackamotzki – she was of Polish origin, and for obvious
reasons changed her name to Cora Turner – and paid for
singing lessons for the new woman in his life. Crippen
knew what Cora was: she was living with a man as his
mistress when Crippen met her. She had no moral
scruples, and probably viewed Crippen as her meal-ticket
for life.

If opposites attract, then the marriage should have been a success. Crippen was quiet and timid; Cora was noisy, vulgar and drank too much. Although she never got a stage part, she did bed a number of young actors. The couple travelled, settling first in Brooklyn, then St. Louis, Salt Lake City, Toronto and Philadelphia.

It was in 1900, the eighth year of their marriage, that they came to England, where Crippen, now aged thirty-eight, became the English representative of an American firm which manufactured patent medicines. He could not practise as a physician because his medical diploma was unorthodox.

The couple moved to 39, Hilldrop Crescent, off Camden Road, in the Holloway district of London, where Cora took in lodgers to make ends meet. Her henpecked husband did most of the housework. At this stage Crippen was still deeply in love with his wife, vainly spending a fortune on her "artistic" career.

Cora Crippen was a dominant woman, and Crippen a mild-mannered man. . . until he took a mistress who put fire into his veins. Ethel le Neve (real name Neave) was also a dominant woman but much younger – in her early twenties when Crippen first met her, and a quiet and shy girl at that stage. She came to work as a typist in the office which Crippen managed, and he soon began visiting her in her shabby bedsitter. To Crippen, now going through the male menopause, she must have seemed the very opposite of his fat, blowsy, coarse wife with her nagging tongue. When the firm which employed him went bankrupt, Crippen bought up some of the stock and set up in business for himself, with Ethel as his book-keeper and typist.

Meanwhile, his wife was trying her luck on the London music halls, under the name Belle Elmore, but she tended to get booed off the stage during her rare appearances. Crippen tried to appease her by buying her expensive gifts of jewellery, but during her drunken parties at Hilldrop Crescent, surrounded by her bohemian friends, she screamed abuse and taunts at her husband.

The strange thing was, Crippen bought Ethel exactly the same items of jewellery as he bought Cora, as if to even things up.

Mrs Crippen soon discovered the existence of Ethel, who had been a visitor to Hilldrop Crescent, and loudly declared her intention of leaving her husband, and punishing the "common" typist who had stolen her husband's affections. Crippen realised that not only had he spent a great deal of money on jewellery to keep both women happy, but his savings of about £600 were in a bank account, and more than half of this was in his wife's name . . .

Crippen and Ethel were far better suited; she was a quiet, retiring soul, though capable of hard bargaining. She refused to have sex with Crippen until they were legally married, and kept pressing him to divorce Belle. When Crippen discovered his wife in bed with one of the lodgers, Ethel took this as sufficient proof that his marriage was over and surrendered her virginity to him in a hotel room on December 6th, 1906, some years after they had first met. The situation did not improve for the couple. For a time Crippen became a dentist, with Ethel as his assistant, but sex was still an illicit act performed in cheap hotels. As with all such "eternal triangle" situations, there was only one solution: Cora had to go.

On January 1st, 1910, the fifty-two-year-old Crippen ordered five grains of hyoscine hydrobromide, which came in the form of small soluble crystals, from a chemical wholesalers, using his firm's name and headed notepaper for the transaction, and in the early morning of February 1st he poisoned his wife. There had been a typical noisy party the night before, and Mrs Crippen was last seen alive at about 1 a.m. That night Ethel slept at Hilldrop Crescent. After dismembering his wife and burying her in the cellar, on February 2nd Crippen pawned some of her jewellery for £80, under his own name and without attempting to disguise what he was doing, and told anxious friends who enquired about her that his wife had gone back to America.

On March 20th he wrote to a Mr and Mrs Martinetti to tell them that "Belle", as they called her, was ill. On the 24th he sent them a telegram reading: "Belle died yesterday at six o'clock. Please phone Annie. Shall be away a week." In fact he had gone to Dieppe for a sort of "honeymoon" with Ethel, who had given up her job and begun to live openly with Crippen since March 12th, wearing Mrs Crippen's jewellery and furs. It is probable that Crippen took the opportunity during the sea trip to Dieppe to drop pieces of his wife overboard.

Cora's friends made enquiries of the various shipping lines, and in New York. Nobody of her name had sailed on any line, nor was anything known of her whereabouts in New York. A Miss Hawthorne, who knew Cora well, had seen Ethel wearing her jewellery and feared the worst. On June 30th another friend, a man called Nash, went to Scotland Yard to report his suspicions, and Chief Inspector Walter Dew of Scotland Yard's famed "Murder Squad" visited Crippen on July 8th at his office to ask: "Where is your wife?" Crippen said that she had left him to go and live with a man in Chicago. He even named him, a handsome young actor and singer called Bruce Miller. He claimed he had made up the story about his wife's death to try to conceal the scandal and his shame. Asked why his secretary had been seen wearing his wife's jewellery, Crippen said that his wife had left England in such a hurry that she had forgotten to take all her jewellery. The house was searched, but nothing was found to indicate foul play.

As he was leaving, the detective said: "Of course, I shall have to find Mrs Crippen to clear this matter up."

Crippen replied pleasantly: "Yes, I will do anything I can. Do you think an advertisement would be any good?" Dew agreed that Crippen should advertise for his missing wife, even making suggestions as to the wording. Crippen appears to have been a far better actor than his wife had ever been. . .

He might have got away with it if he hadn't panicked and fled the day after that interview with Dew, first sailing to Antwerp, then leaving that port on July 20th on board the *SS Montrose* for Canada, as "Mr Robinson and son" – Ethel was dressed as a boy, with her hair cropped. Meanwhile Dew, alerted by Crippen's flight, had returned to Hilldrop Crescent on June 11th with a team of officers, and on June 15th, under the cellar floor, he found, covered in quicklime, what he described as "a mass of flesh."

Dew later reported: "The coal cellar had a brick floor . . . I found that the poker went in somewhat easily between the crevices in the bricks, and I managed to get one or two up and then several others came up pretty easily. I then produced a spade from the garden and dug the clay that was immediately underneath the bricks. After digging down to a depth of about four spadefuls, I came across what appeared to be human remains. . ."

Crippen had not only dismembered his wife's body; he had mutilated it, even dissecting her sex organs as if wanting ritually to destroy her both as a human being and as a woman.

The *Daily Mail* carried the story of the wanted "cellar murderer," and Captain Kendall of the *SS Montrose* recognised Crippen from the newspaper photograph. He radioed London to report that he suspected he was carrying Crippen aboard as a passenger and Dew took a faster ship. Disguised as a pilot, he arrested Crippen on July 31st, 1910, as his ship reached landfall, just inside the St Lawrence River on the way to Quebec. Taken into custody, Crippen said: "I am not sorry. The anxiety was too much."

He thus became the first murderer to be arrested by means of Marconi's transatlantic wireless telegraphy. Ethel had been wearing some of Crippen's clothes, and as the captain later stated: "Master Robinson squeezed his 'father's' hand immoderately, and . . . his trousers were very tight around the hips, and were split down the back and fastened with large safety pins." Ethel had a large bottom . . .

It fell to the pathologist Bernard Spilsbury to conduct the autopsy on what were presumed to be the remains of Mrs Crippen; the head, skeleton and limbs were never found, and all he had to work with was a pile of flesh and internal organs. Essentially, the case revolved around the question of identification: the prosecution had to prove to the satisfaction of a jury that the remains were those of Cora Crippen. First it was established that the remains contained traces of hyoscine. This was done by Dr. William Willcox, the foremost toxicologist of his day, who showed that hyoscine had been the agent involved in the Crippen case by dropping an extract from the internal organs into a cat's eyes and seeing the pupils widen dramatically. Two-fifths of a grain showed up in the analysis, and the estimate for the entire body was half a grain. A fatal dose can be as little as a quarter-grain, although much larger quantities have been recorded where the patient recovered. It all depends on the individual's metabolism.

The next important clue was a piece of flesh from the area of the abdomen which bore an operation scar – as had Mrs Crippen in life. Defence experts at the Old Bailey trial, which began on October 18th, claimed it was a piece of flesh from the thigh, and the "scar" was just a fold in the skin. Spilsbury showed that it came from the abdomen, pointing out that part of the rectus muscle of the abdominal wall was still attached to the specimen.

The trial, with the Lord Chief Justice, Lord Alverstone, presiding, was concerned mainly with technical medical matters, although the jury wanted to know why an innocent man would have fled to foreign shores with his mistress in disguise. Sir Richard Muir, prosecuting, put this to Crippen, but received no satisfactory answer. Instead, Crippen told him: "I might have thought, well, if there is all this suspicion and I am likely to have to stay in gaol for months and months and months, perhaps until this woman is found, I had better be out of it."

Crippen remained loyal to Ethel to the end, defending

her and emphasising that she had no knowledge of what he had done.

There was other damning evidence, particularly the fact that the remains had been wrapped in Crippen's own pyjama jacket. The jury took less than half an hour to find him guilty, and he was hanged on November 23rd, 1910, at Pentonville Prison.

Ethel le Neve was tried separately and was acquitted. She had told the police one interesting thing: when they boarded the steamer to Dieppe, Crippen had been carrying a hatbox, but it had vanished by the time they landed. Had it contained Cora's head?

Ethel later emigrated to Australia, where she died in 1967 at the age of eighty-four. It was reported in the British Press in 1981 that Sir Hugh Rhys Rankin, former vice-president of the World Buddhist Federation, had met Ethel le Neve in Australia in 1930. He said she had told him that Crippen killed his wife because she had a venereal disease.

Although not involved in this trial, Sir Edward Marshall Hall, the great advocate and defender, speculated publicly that had he been retained as defence counsel, he would have won an acquittal by arguing that Crippen had obtained the hyoscine to dull his wife's excessive sexual demands and keep her quiet during his nights with Ethel, but had accidentally given her an overdose, afterwards panicking and disposing of her body.

Alternatively, it could have been pointed out that as "Belle Elmore", Mrs Crippen drank to excess because she was a failed artiste, and when drunk abused her husband with an even more vicious tongue than when sober. So Crippen was secretly trying to cure her alcoholism without her knowledge with hyoscine . . .

Both of these theories are unlikely. Cora was simply in the way.

18
HYOSCINE

Hyoscine is one of the drugs extracted from the plant henbane, *Hyocyamus niger*, which is closely related to deadly nightshade, from which we get atropine and is also found in Jimson Weed, *Datura stramonium*. Another name for it is scopolamine, the drug often featured in thrillers as a "truth-serum" to extract information from unwilling agents. It is chemically related to atropine, also found in henbane, often used in ophthalmic work because it widens the pupils of the eyes.

Hyoscine depresses the central nervous system, and for that reason is often used in travel sickness preparations and to treat anxiety. But that is in very tiny doses of hundredths of a grain. In larger doses it slows down the reflexes and impairs judgement, which is why it was used as a truth drug. A man with impaired judgement and suffering from hallucinations is more likely to "spill the beans" than a sober person. But then, alcohol in excess has much the same effect. Ointments made with henbane were popular with witches for this same reason. It can be absorbed through the skin, like atropine, and is rapidly absorbed through the mucous membranes, but does not cause the initial giddy excitement associated with that drug. Death from a fatal dose results from respiratory failure.

In the last century, hyoscine was often prescribed to

treat alcoholism and nymphomania. Strangely, it was never taken up by the drug culture of the Sixties as a hallucogenic drug.

Hawley Harvey Crippen is the only poisoner known to have chosen this particular drug to kill.

19
KENNETH BARLOW
A Non-Confessor

"Anybody gets a load of this – and it's the quickest way out" –
Kenneth Barlow discussing insulin with a fellow nurse.
"It is supposed that he (Barlow) was an ogre planning to
murder a woman he had not yet married" –
Mr Bernard Gillis QC, defence counsel.

Kenneth Barlow served most of his life sentence in Wakefield top-security prison in Yorkshire. He was not a typical convict. He worked in the office of the Tutor Organiser. This was the officer responsible for directing the educational activities of prisoners attending evening classes or taking correspondence courses.

The job had its perks. Barlow was a red-band or trusty – and that red band around his arm denoted that he had the freedom to walk unescorted around the prison, to deliver messages or pick up exam papers.

He was not only self-effacing; he was also remote and solitary, taciturn and reserved, hiding the most important part of himself away. There was an air of indefinable superiority. Obviously intelligent, he was essentially an observer, casting a cool sardonic eye over the goings-on around him. Never a part of the prison fraternity, he made no friends, and he was very controlled, never exhibiting emotion. He was a calm, calculating watcher, with precisely the qualities one might expect a poisoner to possess.

In 1957 Barlow was a male nurse at a large Yorkshire hospital. His first wife had died eighteen months before, at the age of thirty-three. Now his thirty-year-old second wife, Elizabeth, was pregnant. What the state of the marriage was we shall never know. What went on behind the walls of their home in Bradford was known only to themselves, but one thing is certain: the pregnancy was not acceptable to one or other of the partners.

Late on the night of May 3rd, 1957, Barlow phoned for an ambulance, saying that he had found his wife dead in the bath. She had left their bedroom to take a bath, he later explained, leaving him dozing on the bed. Suddenly he had woken, realising that she had not returned to bed and that her bath was taking far too long.

He had gone into the bathroom and seen his wife lying with her face under the surface of the water. He pulled out the bath plug and, he told the doctor who examined his wife's body, he attempted artificial respiration – as one would expect from a trained nurse. Yet his pyjamas were dry . . .

The doctor noted that the pupils of the eyes of the dead woman were oddly dilated. He could find no bruises on the body; no injuries. An apparently healthy young woman had died: there would have to be a post mortem.

The police questioned Barlow while the autopsy was being carried out, taking a statement from him. Tests indicated that the woman had indeed drowned in her bath, and as there were no signs of violence on her body, and no trace of poisoning was detected, she was duly buried.

Yet Detective Chief Superintendent Philip Cheshire, head of Bradford CID, was not satisfied. Instinct told him that something was wrong. Perhaps Barlow had been too calm, had not exhibited the expected degree of grief. Whatever the reason, Barlow was questioned again, with the police probing his background – until Barlow cracked.

Barlow conceded that he had given his wife several injections of ergometrine – at her request – to induce a miscarriage. But he insisted that he had never intended to bring about her death. Thus, when Elizabeth Barlow was exhumed for a second post mortem, special attention to the skin was paid by the pathologist, who found tiny puncture marks made by a hypodermic needle in the buttocks.

Had Barlow injected ergometrine, or had the substance been something else? The police questioned Barlow's colleagues and found one who had an interesting tale to tell. He said that Barlow had once told him that insulin – the drug vital for diabetics – was the perfect instrument of murder, as it was designed to dissolve in the bloodstream, to replace a natural substance that the pancreas failed to produce in diabetics, a substance one would expect to find in the body, and hence it left no incriminating trace behind.

Barlow worked at St. Luke's Hospital, Huddersfield, where part of his duties was to inject diabetic patients with insulin, and a quick stock-check revealed that three ampoules of ergometrine were missing, but it was impossible to say if any insulin had gone. No strict check of insulin stocks was kept: it was not a dangerous drug, unless given in overdose to a person *not* suffering from diabetes.

Had Barlow injected ergometrine, as he admitted, or had he injected insulin? Perhaps the most important witnesses at his subsequent trial for murder were one thousand mice. They had been injected with extracts taken from Mrs Barlow's organs and had reacted with convulsions, coma and ultimate death. These tests were consistent with Elizabeth Barlow having received a massive dose of insulin.

Barlow was tried at Leeds Assizes before Mr Justice Diplock in December 1957. Sir Harry Hilton-Foster, the Solicitor-General, prosecuted, and Barlow was defended by Mr Bernard Gillis QC.

Harry Stork, a male nurse at Northfield Sanatorium, Driffield, who had worked with Barlow two years previously, described a conversation in which Barlow had mentioned insulin as being the perfect murder drug. The accused had said the same thing to another colleague, Miss Waterhouse, a nurse at East Riding General Hospital, where even a patient, Mr Arthur Evans, had been told by Barlow of the homicidal potential of insulin.

This witness claimed that Barlow had added: "Anybody gets a load of this – and it's the quickest way out." It seemed that Barlow had made the careless mistake committed by many murderers. He had talked too much.

Dr David Price, pathologist to West Riding County Council, said that at a post mortem examination he had found four injection marks on Mrs Barlow's buttocks. Some of these were old, but one seemed to have been made shortly before she died. Describing his experiment with the mice, he said that ergometrine could not have caused Mrs Barlow's death.

Police Sergeant Naylor of the Bradford Police had arrived quickly on the scene in response to Barlow's emergency call. He testified that there was no condensation on the painted walls of the bathroom, nor was there any moisture on the floor. He confirmed that Barlow's pyjamas were dry.

Barlow told the court that his wife of less than a year had worked that morning and had come home very tired. She had gone to bed early, at about half-past six that evening, but was later sick in the bedroom. At ten o'clock she said she would have a bath as she was feeling better. He was unable to explain why a healthy young woman could not have prevented herself from drowning in the bath.

The defence claimed that there was insufficient proof that the body had contained insulin – despite those thousand mice who had perished to prove Barlow a killer. No motive for murder had been established, and if Barlow had intended to kill with insulin, he would not have been so foolish as to talk about its homicidal possibilities.

The defence called its own expert witness, Dr Hobson, of St. Luke's Hospital, Muswell Hill. He testified that at moments of great emotional excitement, such as fear or anger, the body poured adrenaline into the bloodstream, which in turn would increase the level of sugar in the blood, which in turn would lead to an increase of insulin being secreted by the pancreas.

"If this woman knew she was slipping down and drowning in the bath, and she could not get out, she would be terrified, and I think that would produce all the symptoms the chemists have described," Dr Hobson said.

Prosecution medical experts refuted this. Fifteen thousand units of insulin had been found in Mrs Barlow's body, far more than ever could have been produced naturally.

In his closing speech, defence counsel stressed that there was no evidence that the Barlows had not been a happy couple, and made a telling point: "This chatter of the various nurses regarding things about insulin that Barlow is alleged to have said dates from as long ago as 1954. It is supposed that in 1954, *before he even knew the dead woman*, he was planning murder; that he was an ogre planning to murder a woman he had not yet married!"

The evidence was sufficient to convince the jury, however, and after one-and-a-half hours' deliberation they found Kenneth Barlow guilty. He had injected his wife with a massive dose of insulin, then dumped her unconscious body in the bath to drown, and the judge remarked that it was "a cold, cruel and carefully premeditated murder," before sentencing Barlow to life imprisonment. Had he been tried a few weeks earlier, before the new Homicide Act was passed, he might well have hanged.

In gaol, he became Britain's second-longest serving prisoner, being released only after twenty-six years. Only child-killer John Straffen has served a longer sentence – thirty-five years and still inside.

Most murderers serve between nine and ten years before being released on licence. Some released during Barlow's long stretch had committed murders far more horrific than that for which he was convicted.

Why was Barlow's release delayed so long? He had pleaded not guilty at his trial, and was to maintain his innocence throughout his ensuing twenty-six years in gaol.

In failing to confess his guilt, the parole board felt, he was not demonstrating remorse and rehabilitation and he was therefore unsuitable for release.

So if he were *truly* innocent, he would have to lie in order to gain release.

In the last couple of years, nearly two dozen people have been officially found to have been victims of a miscarriage of justice and have been freed with great fanfares of publicity. All of them were serving life imprisonment, and many had completed up to seventeen years – casualties of the procedure which insists that innocent or not, you must at least *pretend* to be guilty if you want parole . . .

If Barlow was guilty, why did he persevere with the lie which denied him release? I can only offer an opinion based on psychological insights gained by studying more than three hundred convicted murderers. There is a type of personality which cannot admit to error, to guilt, and which puts up a mental wall behind which to hide from the ugly truth. This type of criminal can actually convince himself of his innocence, for to admit guilt, even to himself, would destroy his psyche.

Perhaps Barlow was of this type. Perhaps, even, he was not guilty.

Following his release, on January 3rd, 1984, at the age of sixty-five, he said: "I feel very bitter. I have been in prison for twenty-six years for a crime I didn't do, but IRA bombers get out after nine years. Where's the justice in that?"

Kenneth Barlow will probably continue to protest his innocence until the day he dies, considered guilty by those of us who are unable to believe that one thousand mice can be wrong.

20
INSULIN

Insulin is a typical example of a life-saving drug which is not regarded as a poison, yet can be used to kill – like chloroform and morphine. The pancreas in normal healthy people secretes a hormone called insulin, a substance which deals with sugar in the blood, converting it into energy and storing it in receptor cells. It controls the level of glucose in the blood, much like a kind of thermostat. Most people produce twenty to forty units of insulin a day. People suffering from diabetes have a faulty pancreas which produces little or no insulin, and their blood sugar levels soar to the point where they go into a hypoglaemic coma. Until Drs Banting and Best made their famous discovery in 1921 of how to process insulin from natural sources, patients simply deteriorated and died.

For a long time, doctors had to rely on human corpses for their supplies of insulin, but now it can be extracted from cattle and pig sources. Insulin is a great life-saver, yet if given in overdose, it causes a coma which can lead to death, since it gives rise to low blood sugar levels.

Kenneth Barlow was the first person known to have used insulin to kill.

21
BODKIN ADAMS
A Doctor's Ordeal

"Easing the passing of a dying person is not all that wicked" –
Dr Bodkin Adams's alleged remark to Detective
Superintendent Herbert Hannam of Scotland Yard.
"He was as guilty as hell. He deserved to hang twenty
times over" – Detective Chief Superintendent
Charlie Hewitt.

Just twenty-six years after his notorious trial for murder,
Dr John Bodkin Adams died in Eastbourne District
General Hospital on July 4th, 1983, aged eighty-four,
having outlived most of the other leading figures in his
case – including his Nemesis, Detective Superintendent
Herbert Hannam of Scotland Yard.

The Bodkin Adams case was perhaps the last of the
classic trials, belonging more in essence to the pre-war,
rather than the post-war era. It aroused enormous
interest, with reporters from all over the world flocking to
a genteel seaside town. Many of these were from the
USA, where they could hardly be said to be short of
sensational murders of their own.

In retrospect, the public's fascination with this case is
difficult to understand. A middle-aged doctor in Eastbourne, a place where the elderly and wealthy went to
spend their declining years, was accused of poisoning one

of his female patients with drug overdoses in order to gain, among other things, a Rolls-Royce car and some silver cutlery. He was also charged with the murder of another elderly female patient, but the Crown did not proceed with this. It is a peculiarity of English law that a person can only be charged with one murder at a time. And in a case where a person is accused of more than one murder, it is for the prosecution to choose the murder most likely to secure a conviction.

In this case the victim – rich widow Edith Alice Morrell – had died six years previously and had been cremated at her own request. It is always difficult to prosecute without a body, and in this instance the evidence looked very flimsy, since there could be no autopsy, with proof of poison in the corpse. Yet such were the rumours surrounding the case – particularly that the doctor was suspected of the deaths of dozens of his former patients – that the physician was to stand in the famous No.1 Court at the Old Bailey in peril of his life.

Perhaps it was simply the fact that he was a doctor which aroused the interest. Britain, after all, has a long tradition of killer-doctors. Buck Ruxton, Hawley Crippen, Neill Cream, William Palmer – the list is long, because doctors are in a privileged position when it comes to murder. They can prescribe the poison and sign the death certificate . . .

The Bodkin Adams case illustrates several weaknesses in law, undermining the belief that we have a near-perfect legal system. (The recent rash of admitted miscarriages of justice has firmly put the nail in the coffin of that particular myth). Men have been found guilty of murder on evidence which is vague in the extreme, and but for medical records – which were supposed to have been destroyed – Bodkin Adams might well have hanged.

A confirmed bachelor, the Irish-born Dr Adams became a physician in Eastbourne in the 1920s, aged twenty-three, buying his way into a lucrative private practice patronised by hundreds of elderly female patients. He began his first rounds on a motorcycle, but within a few years was driving a Rolls-Royce complete with chauffeur. In 1930 he bought a detached villa, 6 Trinity Trees. His mother lived there with him, together with servants. Later he became engaged to a butcher's daughter, but the romance came to nothing.

Business flourished, to the extent that he had to bring in three other doctors to cope with a practice of more than a thousand patients. He was the leading physician in the town, not brilliant, but a good, competent general practitioner with a nice bedside manner and a soft Irish brogue.

Not unnaturally, several of his wealthy patients left him small legacies as a token of their gratitude. Usually these were small bequests – perhaps a silver salver – but in one case he received £3,000, a considerable sum at the time. Since many of his patients were old and in pain, he regularly prescribed sleeping-pills and even morphia or heroin. Many of his patients lived in Eastbourne's numerous nursing homes, cared for in comfort until death. Perhaps he was *too* successful, arousing envy. He tended his patients throughout the German bombing of Eastbourne in the war, was a leading contributor to local charities, and between 1944 and 1955 he received fourteen bequests totalling £21,600 from patients who had averaged eighty years of age at the time of death. He did not need this money – he was a wealthy man in his own right – and although it was perfectly proper to receive such bequests, it was perhaps foolish of him to accept them. Jealous tongues in Eastbourne were wagging about how Dr Adams was murdering wealthy patients to get his hands on their fortunes. It was gossip loud enough to reach the ears of the Coroner and the Chief Constable.

During 1956 Eastbourne Police began investigating the death of one of his patients. What set events in motion was the demise of Jack Hullett, and then that of his widow four months later. Jack Hullett was an extremely wealthy man who retired in 1938, buying a house in Eastbourne.

Bodkin Adams was doctor to both Mr and Mrs Hullett. A frequent visitor to the house was a young widow, "Bobbie" Tomlinson. With a mixture of sedatives and psychology, Dr Adams had helped her overcome her grief at the loss of her husband. When Jack Hullett's wife, Theodora, died in 1951, he was sixty-one and did not mourn for long. He soon married "Bobbie" Tomlinson and the couple were very happy together.

At seventy, Jack Hullett was found to be suffering from cancer of the bowel. After an operation, he insisted on returning home to be nursed. Dr Adams was unhappy about this, and only agreed to it because his patient had servants and promised to engage a night nurse. As he was recuperating, Jack Hullett said to Dr Adams: "When I'm well again I'm going to buy you a car. That's the least you deserve." But after three months the patient's condition deteriorated and he died as a result of cerebral haemorrhage.

The widow was distraught with grief, often threatening suicide. The doctor tried to give her spiritual help – he was a devout Christian who had started a Bible class in the town. Then he resorted to giving her sedatives, and she became dependent on drugs. When she was in a better frame of mind she reminded the doctor about her husband's promise to buy him a car, and wrote him a cheque for £1,000. Unwisely, the doctor accepted this and asked the bank to clear it speedily. That was on July 17th. On July 23rd the widow died. She had become depressed and had lapsed into a coma. Dr Adams' partner, Dr Harris, was called in to attend to her, and Dr Adams joined him later, the two striving to save her life.

Because of the patient's threat of suicide, both doctors asked a local pathologist to carry out a post mortem. The results were negative. Dr Adams then wrote to the Coroner, setting out the facts of the case. The patient was aged fifty. She had lost the will to live following the death of her husband, and had become generally ill. She had been treated with sedatives – sodium barbiturate – to help her sleep, but she had refused to see a psychiatrist. When she died the doctors had searched her room for evidence of empty pill bottles, etc., but none had been found – "and nothing to suggest poison." Dr Adams concluded by stating that because the pathologist had been unable to determine the cause of death, he did not feel able to issue a death certificate in the circumstances.

It was not the letter of a guilty man. If it had been, he would not have ruled out suicide by drugs, and might well have "planted" an empty container. However, the Coroner – after consulting the Chief Constable – ordered a second post mortem, which was also inconclusive.

Dr Adams attended the inquest on Mrs Hullett to give evidence, and after the Coroner's verdict of suicide, he told reporters: "I hope the verdict will clear up the ugly rumours and innuendos that have been going round the town. My conscience is clear."

But Eastbourne's Chief Constable chose that moment to announce that his officers were investigating reports that "several wealthy women have died in mysterious circumstances." Asked by reporters if there was anything suspicious about the death of Mrs Hullett, he said that there was "a possibility of foul play." A month later, he called in Scotland Yard. The *Daily Sketch* carried a headline: "WAS THE £1,000 WOMAN MURDERED?" The disclosure that the dead woman had written Dr Adams a cheque for that amount presumably came from police sources: it was to be trial by newspaper, with the police leaking details to the Press.

The sober *Daily Telegraph* reported: "Detective Superintendent Hannam will go to Eastbourne tomorrow to examine the records of 400 women who have died in the area in the past ten years." And a French newspaper headlined the case: "THE BLUEBEARD OF EASTBOURNE?"

Enter Detective Superintendent Herbert Hannam of the Yard, known to his colleagues as "The Count" because of his stylish attire. He was an unconventional detective, adept at exerting psychological pressure on a suspect. Publicity-conscious, he enjoyed having his name in the newspapers, and with his team of detectives he began questioning dozens of Dr Adams's patients. Impromptu Press conferences in the pub opposite the police station became a feature of the investigation, Hannam quietly smoking his cigar. He also encouraged gossips to make scurrilous remarks about Dr Adams, for he was convinced that the good doctor was guilty.

His next step was to have the body of Gertrude Hullett exhumed. Dr Francis Camps carried out the autopsy, but found nothing amiss. Undaunted, Hannam applied for exhumation orders for two more of Dr Adams's patients, but only one of these was in a state to be examined, both having been buried for several years. The autopsy revealed death was due to cerebral thrombosis – just as Dr Adams had stated on the death certificate.

Still undeterred, Hannam bided his time. The suspense mounted, the world's Press becoming restless. The effects of three months of this pressure on Dr Adams can only be imagined. Hannam questioned him for long periods, searching his home. Then, on November 23rd, 1956, Hannam pounced, charging Dr Adams with thirteen offences under the forgery, cremation and larceny Acts. By law, a doctor making out a cremation form has to state whether he is a beneficiary under the will of the dead person. The doctor had written "No." On December 18th Hannam charged Dr Adams with the murder of Mrs Hullett, and the doctor was remanded to Brixton Prison as prisoner No. 7889 to await his trial.

Meanwhile, Hannam had the bodies of Julia Bradnum and Clara Miller exhumed and examined. Professor Camps carried out the post mortems but again found nothing untoward. The cause of death was in accordance with the doctor's death certificate, but the Press were not told that.

In his fascinating autobiography, *Forty Years of Murder* (Harrap, 1978), Professor Keith Simpson devoted a chapter to this case. Appropriately entitled "The Innocence of

Dr Bodkin Adams," this records that Simpson was retained by the Medical Defence Union to "watch" the exhumations. He reports: "Only one of the bodies was in a good enough condition for Camps and me to agree on the cause of death, which was cerebral thrombosis – precisely what the doctor had certified."

In January 1957 Hannam applied to Eastbourne magistrates for permission to examine the doctor's bank accounts, and the following day Dr Adams was charged with the murder of eighty-two-year-old Edith Morrell, who had died on November 13th, 1950. During an interview the doctor was alleged to have said to Hannam: "Murder – can you prove murder? She was dying in any event."

The committal proceedings at the magistrates' court on January 14th, 1957, attracted much publicity, with the prosecution outlining a "system" of murder, detailing the deaths of Mr and Mrs Hullett, and Mrs Morrell. Mr Melford Stevenson told the magistrates: "The same pattern repeats itself. A rich patient. Heavy drugging over a period of months, ending up with a fatal dose. A patient obviously under the influence of Dr Adams. A patient from whose will Dr Adams benefited."

Yet – as her solicitor was to testify – Mrs Morrell had been annoyed because Dr Adams took a holiday, and had cut him out of her will. She had intended to leave him her Rolls-Royce. So it was being claimed that Dr Adams killed Mrs Morrell for a car which she hadn't left him.

Nevertheless, the magistrates decided that there was a case to answer, and Dr Adams was committed for trial at the Old Bailey.

Mr Justice Devlin (subsequently Lord Devlin) was to preside, and in accordance with tradition in poisoning cases, the Attorney-General, Sir Reginald Manningham-Buller (known to *Private Eye* readers as Bullying-Manner) was to prosecute. The defence barrister, Mr Geoffrey Lawrence QC, was an unknown factor, having had little experience of criminal trials. In the event, he was to prove to be a brilliant advocate, devastating in cross-examination.

The trial itself was indeed a classic, lasting seventeen days – a murder hearing record not exceeded until the A.6 trial of James Hanratty five years later. It was also notable for the fact that the accused man spoke only six words: "I am not guilty, my Lord."

Opening for the prosecution, the Attorney-General said that charges of murdering one of his patients, knowing that he was to benefit under her will, would be proved against Dr Adams by four nurses who had attended the dying woman. He would also call an expert medical witness who would state that, in his opinion, "Mrs Morrell could not possibly have survived the administration of drugs prescribed in her last five days." And although Dr Adams was only charged with the murder of Mrs Morrell, facts about the deaths of Mr and Mrs Hullett would be brought in to prove "system."

Mr Lawrence began with a spirited attempt to have the trial held in camera, arguing that publicity accorded the magistrates' hearing had prejudiced a fair trial. His legal submission was unsuccessful, but this defect in legal procedure was to be corrected ten years later with the passing of the Criminal Justice Act (1967) forbidding the reporting of evidence at a committal, unless the defence waives its right to this prohibition.

Hannam testified that when he had questioned Dr Adams about the death of Mrs Morrell, the doctor had replied: "Easing the passing of a dying patient is not all that wicked. She wanted to die. That cannot be murder."

The detective said he had "accidentally" bumped into Dr Adams during his inquiries in Eastbourne, and a conversation had ensued in which he reminded the doctor that he had said on the cremation certificate that he was not a beneficiary under Mrs Morrell's will. Adams had replied: "Oh, that was not done wickedly. God knows it was not." Mr Lawrence attacked in cross-examination. That meeting had not been "accidental." Hannam had waylaid Dr Adams at the rear of his house as the latter was putting his car away in the garage. He had known at the time that Dr Adams was *not* a beneficiary under the will.

Mr Lawrence went on: "You were drawing his attention to the cremation certificate at that time, as if he were not only a beneficiary under that will, but *knew* he was a beneficiary and had told lies about it?"

"Yes."

"And all the time you knew that he was *not* a beneficiary under the will!"

When Hannam had gone with Inspector Pugh of Eastbourne Police to search Dr Adams's house for dangerous drugs, only Inspector Pugh's name was on the warrant. Hannam was technically a trespasser, with no authority to enter the house. In his testimony Hannam said that Dr Adams, who had been weeping, wanted to ring his solicitor. "He asked me if he might do so, and I gave him permission," Hannam said.

Mr Lawrence commented caustically: "*You*, a trespasser in his house, giving him permission to ring his own solicitor? How very kind of you!"

The Crown had claimed that during a period of eleven months, Mrs Morrell had been given 1,629 grains of barbiturates, 1,928 grains of Sedormid, 164 grains of morphia and 139 grains of heroin. This was based on the prescriptions issued, but Mr Lawrence realised that such doses would have killed a horse, let along a woman, long before Mrs Morrell died. The only logical explanation was that Mrs Morrell had never received these drugs. Having established in cross-examination that in her will Mrs Morrell had expressed the wish to be cremated and that her death certificate (and all the others) had been countersigned by another doctor, Mr Lawrence dealt with the Crown's claim about those prescriptions: a director of a chemist's shop agreed that of the seventeen prescriptions alleged by the Crown to have been for Mrs Morrell, in fact only twelve items had been for her.

The Crown's case that an eighty-one-year-old woman had been turned into a drug-crazed addict by Dr Adams began to crumble.

81a George Street, Edinburgh, where the Chantrelles lived

Eugene Marie Chantrelle and his young wife Elizabeth, whom he poisoned with opium

THE EDINBURGH COURANT, SATURDAY, JUNE 1, 1878.

TRIAL OF M. CHANTRELLE FOR ALLEGED WIFE-POISONING.

VERDICT OF GUILTY, AND SENTENCE OF DEATH.

This trial was resumed, before Lord Justice Moncreiff, and a jury, at half morning, and after occupying

EXECUTION OF CHANTRELLE.

Yesterday morning, a few minutes past eight o'clock, Eugéne Marie Chantrelle suffered the extreme penalty of the law in the Calton Prison, Edinburgh. His crime was that of the murder of his wife by the administering of poison, her death taking place on 2d January

Seducer of Innocents:
see page 178

Ten of the poisoned victims lined-up by Tokyo police at the Teikoku bank

Victims of the cyanide laced drinks lie in the bank hallway. Note the cups on the floor

The Polite Assassin: see page 107

Bodies of the caretaker and his family as found by the police

Sadamichi Hirasawa at his trial in 1949

After drinking the "second drug" this bank employee had tried to reach the water tap

Dr. George Henry Lamson.
He had to be carried, almost unconscious to the gallows

The Saint who Strayed: see page 32

Now came the evidence of the four nurses – potentially the Crown's most damaging witnesses. The first of these nurses to take the stand was Helen Stronach, a stocky no-nonsense sort of woman. She explained that her regular procedure was to give Mrs Morrell a quarter-grain of morphia at 9 p.m., as prescribed. But at 11 p.m. one night, Dr Adams arrived and, while Mrs Morrell was still asleep, he gave her an injection of an "unknown substance".

Her evidence was to the effect that an unconscious woman was being pumped full of drugs. That allegation, if substantiated, might well have proved fatal for the defence . . . and fatal for the Doctor too!

Nothing showed on the bland face of Mr Lawrence as he rose to cross-examine. He was about to spring a legal trap of his own. He began in a deceptively languid manner, prefacing his questions with: "I wonder whether you can help me?"

Nurse Stronach agreed with him that she, like nurses in general, noted down, at the time, each injection they gave.

Quite right and proper, remarked Mr Lawrence. He went on: "All experienced nurses do it?"

Nurse Stronach replied primly that they should do.

"That is what you did?" Mr Lawrence asked blandly.

"Indeed we did," she replied, clearly under the impression that her professional competence was being questioned. "Every time we gave an injection we wrote it down, what it was, and the time, and we signed our names."

"And whatever you wrote in that book," Mr Lawrence suggested, "that would be accurate, because it would have been done right at that very moment?"

"It would."

Mr Lawrence led her one further step down the path towards his carefully prepared trap. "Everything that happened of significance in the patient's illness would have to go down in the book? Everything that was of any importance?"

Nurse Stronach nodded firmly. "We reported everything. A proper report is written day and night."

"As distinct from your memory of six years later, these reports, of course, would be absolutely accurate?"

Suddenly there was a stir on the prosecution bench, whispering, heads close together. Wiser in the ways of courtroom tactics than Nurse Stronach, they sensed the approaching danger, although for the moment they couldn't define it.

Mr Lawrence pressed on, bland as ever. "So that if only we had those reports now we could see the truth of exactly what happened night by night, and day by day, when you were there?" There was regret in his voice and a certain sadness. It was as though he were saying, "What a shame we haven't the books in front of us, because then everything would be so simple and straightforward."

The no-nonsense Nurse Stronach shrugged such regrets aside, firmly: "But you have my word for it."

His face relaxed. It was just the answer he wanted, for he had more than her word. He had the books! He produced one of them suddenly, like a magician pulling a rabbit out of a hat, and asked Nurse Stronach to identify it.

This was one of the most dramatic moments the Old Bailey had ever known. An audible buzz swept through the court like a rustling wind. The denizens of the Press benches leant forward to hear her answer. The judge was suddenly sitting a little straighter. The Attorney-General, clearly dismayed, rose to his feet but stayed silent. And the briefest of smiles flitted across the face of Bodkin Adams.

Mr Lawrence continued as though totally unaware of the furore he'd caused. "Is this the night report for June 4th, 1950?" he asked the nurse. "Is it in your handwriting? And is it signed by you?"

Nurse Stronach, all confidence washed away, replied in a mute voice, "It is."

Mr Lawrence pressed on. "There is no doubt about it? This is the very book and nightly record kept by the nurses who attended Mrs Morrell and contains your own record?"

Nurse Stronach's voice dropped to a whisper. "It is."

The judge intervened. If the book was to be used in evidence, he reasoned, the Attorney-General had a right to see it. Mr Lawrence's reply was so quiet that it barely reached the Press benches. But he seemed to be saying that it was essential the books should be identified first.

Fresh alarm was being sown in the ranks of the prosecution. Again there was sudden whispering with heads close together. *Books?* Did he say *books?*

And then came Lawrence's bombshell: "At this stage, my Lord, I desire to say that we have the whole of the nurses' reports on this case from June 1949, to November 13th, 1950, when Mrs Morrell died."

Mr Lawrence, seemingly the calmest man in the arena, read out entries, eventually telling Nurse Stronach: "We have now been through the whole of your records for that time, and have not found a single instance where you gave that quarter-grain of morphia you mentioned. You recorded only one or two visits by the doctor – and then we find you knew exactly what injection was given." (It was paraldehyde).

The nurse looked stunned. Her credibility had been destroyed. She had nothing left to say. And the Attorney-General, aware now of the existence of the report books, realised that he had to steer the prosecution's next witness, the tall, slim and quietly-spoken Sister Mason-Ellis, away from any evidence which might conflict with them.

In cross-examination, Mr Lawrence took Mrs Mason-Ellis through her nursing reports:

"May 11th: Very difficult and depressed. Said she wished she were dead and that she knew a doctor who would put her to sleep forever.

"May 30th: Brighter. Cytamen injection given by the doctor.

"June 18th: Had an outburst. Called me a slum woman and a brute.

"November 12th (the day prior to Mrs Morrell's death): Awake but quiet. Half a glass of milk and brandy taken."

Mr Lawrence asked Sister Mason-Ellis, "Would you agree it's quite obvious, from that report, that she was not in a coma?"

"Well, not according to my report," came the reply. Another prosecution witness had bitten the dust.

Nurse Randall was to have been the Crown's star witness, having attended Mrs Morrell in the last few hours of her life. In his opening speech the Attorney-General had promised that she would tell of having been forced to give 5 cc injections to a woman in a coma – and he had held up a 5 cc syringe to show how large it was.

Once again Mr Lawrence read from the nurse's own report: "August 2nd 1950: Patient irritable and muddled. Very worried about tablets in drawer beside her bed. When she thought I was not in the room, watched her hold bottle and unscrew cap. Would not let me have them. Found tablets loose in bed." And on the night of her death: "Patient weak and restless. Paraldehyde given intravenously by the doctor. 11.30 p.m., very restless, no sleep. 12.30 a.m., restless and talkative. 12.45 a.m., appears asleep. 2 a.m., passed away quietly."

"Just point out to me," said Mr Lawrence, "an entry of yours for the last three nights that indicates this woman was in a coma. Can you do it?"

"No, sir."

"Your memory isn't very trustworthy?"

"It appears not to be," the nurse agreed sourly. Then she added: "I think 5 cc of paraldehyde is a very large dose."

Mr Lawrence was back on his feet like a jack-in-the-box. "Do you know that the British Pharmacopoeia's full dose is 8 cc?"

The fourth nurse, Sister Bartlett, was dealt with in short order, after attempting to repeat the evidence she had given at the magistrates' court about the patient having been in a coma. Mr Lawrence quietly read out her own words from the record books: "Patient awake, restless, talkative."

The nurses' testimony had been demolished. Only the Crown's expert witness remained.

Throughout those seventeen days the subject of the trial appeared to be almost a forgotten figure, a silent, chubby and bespectacled presence sitting grimly in the dock. Now came his most bitter hour: a colleague was ready to condemn him. Dr Arthur Douthwaite, a Harley Street specialist and a senior physician at Guy's Hospital, was a recognised authority on medicines.

Some of his thunder had been stolen, however, since the injections which Morrell "could not possibly have survived" had not, in fact, been given. The report books had revealed a discrepancy between prescription and dosage. The Crown had stated that Gertrude Morrell had received 41 grains of morphia and 39 grains of morphia in her last five days. Yet the reports had revealed an actual dosage of 30 grains of morphia and 22 grains of heroin.

Tall and distinguished, an impressive figure in the witness box, Dr Douthwaite was asked by the prosecutor if there was any justification for injecting morphia and heroin immediately after a stroke.

"No justification whatsoever," he said firmly.

"It it right or wrong to do so?"

"Wrong. In all circumstances wrong."

The Attorney-General put the clinching question. "What conclusion do you draw from the dosage administered in the last days?"

"The only conclusion I can come to is that the intention on November 8th was to terminate her life." (Mrs Morrell died on November 13th).

Mr Lawrence rose to cross-examine. Obviously, the expert had been at fault in the evidence he gave to the magistrates' court about the lady having been in a coma? Yes. And she hadn't, in fact, received the dosage the Crown had originally claimed? No. Had the expert made any inquiries about the treatment Mrs Morrell had received for her stroke *before* coming under the care of Dr Adams?

"I was told the information was not available."

"It would be most *important* to know before condemning the doctor as you did?"

"It would be interesting to know," the witness countered.

Once again Mr Lawrence produced another "lost" document: Gertrude Morrell's medical records from the Cheshire Hospital. She had spent ten days there, and on each of those days she had received a morphia injection. Was the witness condemning the hospital doctors too?

"If that was the treatment for the stroke, yes."

Hour after hour Mr Lawrence pounded away at the witness, at his certainty about a patient he had never seen, his willingness to condemn the treatment she had received from four separate doctors who had seen her – and moreover, examined her. Dr Douthwaite wilted, eventually having to admit that sometimes old ladies were given morphia for pain relief. He also confessed: "I don't know what was in the doctor's mind."

"But you did *before*, when you accused him of murderous intent?" Mr Lawrence retorted.

Dr Douthwaite did not reply. He had been routed, and not only as a witness but also professionally. It was said that he would have been elected President of the Royal College of Physicians the following year, but for his involvement in the Bodkin Adams case. He was later to say that his ordeal in the witness box had been "the most exhausting test of my body and mind I have ever endured."

In his autobiography, Professor Simpson remarks: "I suggested that we should inspect the order book for hard drugs in a private London clinic used by Dr Douthwaite – and this showed that he had considerable recourse to both morphia and heroin for his own patients. I prepared charts to demonstrate this fact. Happily, we never had to confront him with them . . . Amounts of morphia and heroin actually administered to Edith Alice Morrell were considerably less than amounts commonly given by Dr Douthwaite himself in his private clinic, in particular for elderly patients of precisely the kind treated by Bodkin Adams. And this could be proved from my charts."

In his closing speech, Mr Lawrence said he had not wished to put the doctor in the witness box "for the entertainment of the spectators in this court . . . He would have had to search his memory for events of six years previously . . . by the mercy of heaven there has been provided for you, members of the jury, one witness which is but eloquent and unchallengeable – that's the witness in these notebooks, made by the nurses day by day, month after month, when their memory was as fresh as paint."

Manningham-Buller chose to view the survival of those notebooks as sinister. Dr Adams kept those notebooks to protect himself. "Who kept them? From 1950 to 1957? Who had an interest in keeping them? There was only one person: Dr Adams . . ."

In his summing-up, Mr Justice Devlin told the jury: "The question of whether a doctor is entitled to shorten life to save pain cannot be left to doctors to decide. It must be a question of *law*."

The jury might come to the conclusion that "the doctor was a fraudulent rogue, but all fraudulent rogues are not murderers," he continued. "Mr Lawrence said that the suggestion that the doctor had anticipated her (Mrs Morrell's) death by a few days or weeks for the sake of a chest of silver worth £275 was ludicrous. Ludicrous is a strong word. But, members of the jury, *it is a strong point*. I listened carefully to the Attorney-General's speech to hear what the answer was. I did not hear the answer." He concluded: "I do not think I ought to hesitate to tell you that the case for the defence seems to me to be a manifestly strong one. But the final verdict is with you . . ."

After retiring for only forty-four minutes, the jury returned with a verdict of not guilty. The judge looked hard at the prosecution bench. "Mr Attorney-General," he said, "there is another indictment?" The Attorney-General stood up, flustered, to reply: "The further indictment – that he murdered Mrs Hullett – it would be even more difficult to secure a fair trial. In view of the length of the trial and the publicity and the ordeal which the doctor had undergone, the Crown does not intend to proceed with the indictment."

Within half an hour, friends gathered at Dr Adams's home to celebrate.

After a short holiday, he returned to his practice. He successfully sued various newspapers for libel, but he was soon to be tried at Lewes Assizes for failing to keep proper records of dangerous drugs and for National Health prescription offences, and he was fined £2,400. A few months later his name was ordered to be struck off the Medical Register. Four years passed before it was restored.

His friends did not desert him. Councillor Charles Aldous, who had Dr Adams as his guest at his mayoral lunch, was later to say: "Dr Adams suffered a terrible injustice. He was a very gentle, caring man, a great comfort and friend to his patients. He served them devotedly, helping them with family, social and legal problems, as well as treating them." A former Medical Officer of Health for Eastbourne described him as "a good doctor," and his patients remained loyal.

Others, however, were biding their time. They waited for more than twenty-five years for the doctor to die. Then they published allegations which would have been criminal libel while he was alive.

Attacks on the dead doctor stemmed from the reminiscences of a former policeman – police sometimes tending to regard their quarry as guilty even after acquittal. So it was with retired Detective Chief Superintendent Charlie Hewitt, who as a detective sergeant had worked on the Bodkin Adams case for over a year. In *Where There's a Will. . .*(Capstan Press), by crime reporters Rodney

Hallworth and Mark Williams, the seventy-one-year-old ex-detective was quoted as saying that the prosecution had picked the wrong murder – "it was madness to go for one without a body, when we had so many better cases – and what was more important, bodies."

Appearing to ignore all those fruitless exhumations, he went on to claim that during a two-day period when detectives had to go to London to confer with the Director of Public Prosecutions, Bodkin Adams murdered the only witness who could have nailed him – Mrs Elizabeth Sharp, a nursing-home matron. She was ready to talk, declared the ex-detective. So why didn't they exhume *her* body? A study of the death register for the relevant period contains no mention of any Elizabeth Sharp ...

Hewitt said the doctor had been a beneficiary in 132 wills and had forged signatures on his patients' cheques. Why wasn't Adams prosecuted for that? Because, I suspect, there was no evidence. Retired policemen may retain all the suspicion they like, but under the English legal system a man has to be proved guilty in a court of law, not by the Press, which had a field day with Hewitt's allegations.

"He was as guilty as hell . . . He deserved to hang twenty times over," the ex-detective concluded. A more balanced view of the Bodkin Adams case is provided by Lord Devlin's book, *Easing the Passing*.

The ordeal of Bodkin Adams illustrates how close an innocent man could come to the gallows. If those report books had not been kept, the jury would have been largely reliant on four nurses' accusations. However strongly the defence protested, that jury would have found it difficult to believe that four nurses would unite to hang a blameless man.

22
MORPHINE

Morphine is the principal drug which can be separated from the complex mixture of drugs – called alkaloids – found in opium, which is the resin extracted from the white poppy, *Papaver somniferum*. A solution of opium in alcohol is called laudanum, to which the poet Coleridge, among others, was addicted. Opium has been used for centuries as a narcotic, usually smoked in pipes.

Morphine, like insulin, was developed for its medical properties, principally as a powerful pain-killer. It was discovered in 1806 by the German chemist Friedrich Sertürner, who found that morphine reacts with acids to form salts, principally morphine hydrochloride – commonly called morphia. As it is soluble in water it is easy to administer, and it became even handier when a French doctor invented the hypodermic syringe in 1853. Morphine is much more powerful than opium, and proved its benefit during the First World War, when given to wounded soldiers to ease their suffering.

However, it is also a powerful depressant of the central nervous system (which is why it kills pain), and is poisonous and addictive. Patients treated for a painful illness quickly develop a tolerance for the drug and require ever-increasing amounts to maintain relief. Consequently it is difficult to establish a normal therapeutic dose.

A fatal dose for the average adult without tolerance is about five grains, which is enough to cause the respiratory system to fail within a few hours. The victim will go into a deep narcosis, with heavy sweating and reduced respiration, and a marked drop in temperature. Convulsions may occur prior to death. The give-away symptoms of morphine poisoning are pin-point contraction of the pupils of the eyes and the smell of opium on the breath or in the stomach during an autopsy.

The highly addictive narcotic heroin, can be extracted from morphine. It was introduced by Dresser in 1874 as a product to wean addicts away from morphine, and is in fact converted back to morphine by the body.

Morphine has been employed by murderers practically ever since its introduction, and if its use as a killing-agent seems confined to the medical profession, that is because only medical personnel normally have access to the drug. Would Barlow, discussed in a previous chapter, have murdered his wife if he had not had easy access to insulin?

The first recorded murder by morphine occurred in 1823, when Edmé Castaing, a young Paris doctor, murdered two of his patients to benefit under their wills. A more celebrated case is that of Carlyle W. Harris, a twenty-three-year-old medical student in New York whose grandfather was a distinguished professor of medicine in the same city. Carlyle attended lectures on pathology and toxicology given by Dr George L. Peabody, and was especially attentive when, on three successive afternoons in January 1891, the doctor talked about the problems of morphine overdose, and how it was impossible to detect this.

Harris had listened intently because he had a problem. His girl friend, Helen Nielson Potts, aged nineteen and a student at the Comstock School for Young Ladies in New York City, was pregnant by him. In fact, Harris had secretly married the girl on February 8th, 1890. Her wealthy parents were sure to disown her and cut her off without a penny, and would expose Harris to shame – and the necessity to earn a living to support a wife and child. He shuddered at the thought.

From the dispensary at his college – the New York College of Physicians and Surgeons – Harris stole enough morphine to ensure her death. But he was careful to establish a non-criminal source for any trace of opiates which might be found in her system. He wrote Helen a prescription for capsules containing one-sixth of a grain of morphine and four grains of quinine, which was a conventional remedy for stomach chills at that time. A chemist readily dispensed the prescription: after all, one-sixth of a grain of morphine would not harm an infant. And even if the girl took all six capsules provided at once, that would amount to only one grain, well below a dangerous dose.

Harris had to sign the prescription, giving his full name and address, and listing his status as "student." He took the six capsules and opened one of them, removing the contents and replacing them with five grains of morphine. Then he gave them to Helen, telling her to take one a day. There was an element of Russian roulette in this, since he would not know when she took the fatal capsule, but he probably wanted to appear as much surprised and shocked by her death as anyone else.

On January 31st, 1891, Helen was found unconscious, breathing with difficulty. Attempts to waken her resulted in her mumbling about her weird and pleasant dreams. A doctor was called and attempted to treat the girl, but she died at 11 a.m. that same day. Although the doctor noticed her contracted pupils, she was buried after a coroner ruled her death accidental. Following newspaper revelations about Harris's sexual behaviour, Helen's family hired a pathologist, Dr Rudolf Witthaus, to carry out a post mortem, following exhumation. He discovered, first, that the girl had been pregnant. Then he was able to prove – despite Dr Peabody's lecture – that the girl's body contained about five grains of morphine. Once her mystery husband had been identified as Carlyle Harris, he was duly arrested and brought to trial in January 1892. Although the evidence was for the most part circumstantial, Harris was convicted. He died in the electric chair at Sing Sing Prison on May 8th, 1893.

The case had attracted enormous newspaper publicity – it was *The New York World* which had published details of the secret marriage of Harris and his victim – and reading about it with disapproval was Dr Robert Buchanan, a New York physician. He believed he could have done the job far more effectively than Harris, and his work would not have been detected.

Buchanan had established a successful practice in New York, but had tired of his wife, preferring to visit brothels for his sexual pleasure. He fell for an obese madam called Anna Sutherland, in 1890 divorcing his wife and marrying the former prostitute three weeks later. He probably believed rumours that Anna had made a fortune from running brothels over the years. After the marriage Anna made a will leaving everything to Buchanan. He had installed her as receptionist at his practice, but as his patients did not take kindly to a fat ex-whore with a foul mouth, business began to dwindle. Anna had to die. Her death would enrich Buchanan – via her will – and improve his business.

Having studied reports of the Harris trial, Buchanan was scornful of the pin-point contraction of the pupils clue. Any clever doctor ought to be able to get around that, he told his saloon bar cronies. In 1892 he announced that he was travelling to Edinburgh in the April, to further his medical studies. A few days before he was due to sail, Anna Sutherland fell ill, dying on April 23rd ostensibly of brain haemorrhage. Two days later Buchanan sailed for Europe, $50,000 to the good.

In his absence friends voiced suspicions about Anna's death, and the authorities were persuaded to order an exhumation and autopsy. It was the same pathologist, Dr Witthaus, who found evidence of poisoning by morphine. He was puzzled by the absence of those pin-point pupils, until he found traces of belladonna in both eyes. This drug, used by opticians to enlarge the pupils, had been Buchanan's method of preventing that morphine-poisoning symptom from occurring. When Buchanan was tried in March 1893, the prosecution staged a dramatic demonstration for the jury, having a cat killed with morphine, then showing how belladonna dropped into its eyes caused the pupils to widen, thus masking the true cause of death. Found guilty of murder, Buchanan went to the chair in July 1895.

An interesting English case of morphine poisoning came in 1926, when Hillary Rougier, an elderly retired farmer from Jersey, went to live with William Lerwill and his wife at their house in Lower Knaphill in Surrey. He died a month later, after some respiratory problems, and the cause of death was diagnosed as cerebral haemorrhage. Instead of leaving the fortune everyone knew he was worth, he left just £50. In 1928 suspicious relatives forced the exhumation of Rougier, and at the post mortem Bernard Spilsbury found traces of morphine. Detectives discovered that Rougier's fortune had been spent in the form of cheques made out to Lerwill over a two-year period. The largest cheque was for almost £2,000. Questioned by the police, Lerwill said that Rougier had been a paying guest – hence the cheques. Although a coroner's jury concluded that Rougier's death had been caused by morphine poisoning, not self-administered, no charges were brought against Lerwill because of a lack of evidence. He even successfully sued two newspapers for libel, and then left England to live in Canada.

Returning to England in 1933, Lerwill travelled around leaving a trail of worthless cheques in his wake. While staying at the Devonshire village of Combe Martin, and possibly in a fit of guilty conscience, he committed suicide by swallowing cyanide, thus adding a moral element to his story.

Also in England – Nottingham this time – came the case of Nurse Dorothea Waddingham. The title of "nurse" was self-granted, and she opened a nursing home in Nottingham in 1935, together with her handyman-lover, Ronald Sullivan. She had taken two patients into her care, a mother and daughter named Baguley, eighty-nine and fifty respectively. Although Waddingham had initially agreed to care for them for thirty shillings a week each, she soon realised that they needed a high degree of care "worth five guineas a week," as she put it.

After getting them to change their wills in her favour, by threats of evicting them, Nurse Waddingham murdered them with morphine overdoses. On May 12th, 1935, the mother died, followed four months later by the daughter. When Waddingham produced a forged letter, supposedly from Ada Baguley, requesting to be cremated and adding "I do not wish my relatives to be informed of my death," suspicious officials had the body examined, and traces of morphine were found. When old Mrs Baguley was exhumed, morphine was found in her remains also.

Waddingham and Sullivan appeared at Nottingham Assizes in February 1936. Sullivan was discharged because of lack of evidence. Waddingham was tried alone and made the mistake of going into the witness box, condemning herself out of her own mouth. Although the jury which found her guilty added a strong recommendation to mercy, she was hanged on April 16th, 1936.

Again in England, in 1947, Dr Robert Clements called a doctor to his Southport home to tend to his ailing, fourth wife. She was found to be in a coma, and died the following day. Although the examining doctor issued a death certificate confirming death from leukaemia, and this diagnosis was confirmed by another doctor who carried out the post mortem, other physicians noticed the pin-point contraction of the pupils and notified the Coroner of their suspicions.

Police soon learned that Dr. Clements had prescribed large doses of morphine for a patient who had never received them. Where had the missing doses gone? The funeral of Mrs Clements was halted, pending a second post mortem. Meanwhile, Dr Clements committed suicide with a morphine overdose. And the doctor who performed that first post mortem and made the wrong diagnosis also committed suicide – but he took cyanide: much more painful, but quicker. Inquiries revealed that Dr Clements had signed the death certificates for his previous three wives, each time gaining financially from their demise. Owing to the lapse of time – and the death of the suspect – it was decided not to make any further inquiries.

Any one of the above instances might have provided the last chapter, but I chose to examine in detail the case of Dr Bodkin Adams because it illustrates the ambiguous nature of such drugs as morphine, which are both life-savers and life-takers. Doctors have long been known to ease the suffering of terminally-ill patients with overdoses of narcotics, thereby practising euthanasia. But the physician who does this treads a very thin and dangerous line between mercy and murder, as Dr Bodkin Adams discovered.

23
HIPPOLYTE DE BOCARMÉ
The Busted Count
"I hope the blade is sharp" – De Bocarmé's comment when confronted by the guillotine

One of the great names in the history of toxicology – it would be no exaggeration to say that he founded the science – was a young Spaniard, Mathieu Joseph Bonaventure Orfila. Born on the island of Minorca in 1787, he proved to be an infant prodigy. Although the island lacked a school, Orfila read every book he could get his hands on, being particularly fond of the history of ancient Greece and Rome. Most of his learning came from itinerant priests – many of whom had fled from the terrors of the Revolution in France – and by the time Orfila was fourteen he was fluent in five languages, including Latin and Greek, and had written a book on philosophy entirely in Latin.

For such a boy, with his voracious appetite for knowledge, the island quickly became a prison, confining his intellect. He did once go to sea, travelling to Alexandria, but was so sea-sick from violent storms that returning home came as a relief. It was there that he met a German professor named Cook, who instilled in the boy a love for chemistry and a desire to learn more about it. At the age of sixteen Orfila enrolled as a student at the chemistry class in Valencia.

He found his new school petty and parochial, its teachings out of date. He began buying books by the masters in the field, men like Lavoisier and Vauquelin, reading them at such length that he barely averaged two hours' sleep a night. As a result, his exam results were astounding and he was given a scholarship to the University of Barcelona.

So swift was his rise there, so great his advancement in knowledge, that the authorities decided to create a chair in chemistry for him at Barcelona, first sending him to Paris to complete his studies. He was never to return. At that time Paris was regarded as the leading centre of medical learning, with Germany a close second. Had Orfila been sent to Germany the whole course of science might have been delayed, waiting for another Orfila to appear . . .

He arrived in Paris without much money, and had to live as a typical penniless student of the time, but ambition drove him on, making him oblivious to hunger. On the day he received his medical degree, he had only six francs to his name, but he had made friends in Paris who recognised his genius. They saw to it that he did not starve, providing him with a large room in which he could give lectures. These were so successful that soon he had sixty students, each paying forty francs for the privilege of being taught by a master. Soon he was able to set up his own laboratory, and add botany to his courses.

The event which changed his life – and history – came about by accident. One day in April 1813 he was lecturing to a large class about the effects of arsenious acid, explaining that when it was mixed with various liquids, like wine or coffee, there would always be a white chalk-like precipitate left at the bottom of the cup or vessel. To prove his point he took his cup of coffee from the chair beside him and mixed it with the acid. To his surprise, instead of a white chalk-like precipitate, he got a murky one. He tried again, but once more got the same result. Puzzled – and not a little embarrassed – he explained to his students that there must be some impurity in the acid which caused this effect.

After his students had left, Orfila took samples of broth, wine, coffee, milk and other substances and mixed them with various poisons. Then he performed the standard text-book chemical tests in an effort to detect these poisons, one after another. In more than half the samples, he failed to detect the poisons. He studied all the volumes on chemistry he could find. Not one of the eminent authors realised that there existed no tests to detect many poisons! Orfila was stunned. He was to write later: "The central fact that had struck me had never been perceived by anyone else. My first words were these: 'Toxicology does not yet exist!' "

So Orfila rose to the challenge. He first went to a publisher and asked if a book on poison detection in two volumes would be profitable. Assured that it would, he left with a contract and set about writing the work which would make him famous through Europe: *Traité de toxicologie générale*. Published in 1813, when Orfila was only twenty-six, this became a best-seller and marked the end for many types of poisoner.

Orfila himself was to become a scientist-detective, involved in many cases of suspected poisoning.

In England, in 1836, James Marsh devised his Marsh test for arsenic, and Hugo Reinsch produced his refinement of the Marsh Test in 1842. But Orfila had not lagged behind. In 1840 he helped convict Marie Lafarge of the arsenical poisoning of her husband. But although most of the metallic poisons could now be detected, there were many vegetable poisons, like aconitine, belladonna, strychnine and opium, for which no tests had been devised. And even such poisons as mercury, phosphorus and chloroform were undetectable. As late as 1847, Orfila admitted sadly that it was possible that the vegetable poisons would remain forever unidentifiable. But even as he spoke, one of his pupils was ensuring that such tests would be devised.

Jean Servais Stas was a young Belgian, who had studied under Orfila and shared his passion for knowledge. In 1850 he was called in to help the police with a mysterious affair of poisoning, and was to make history. He was to devise a test for nicotine poisoning, a test which is still in use to this day.

The police were embarrassed. That 1850 case was one of apparent murder, it involved the local aristocracy, and proof was lacking. All they had were suspicious circumstances. Gustave Fougnies had a sister called Lydie who was married to Count Hippolyte de Bocarmé. Lydie was the daughter of a successful apothecary, and Bocarmé had married the girl for her money, only to discover that she was not as wealthy as he had thought. He and his new wife were soon deeply in debt, trying to maintain a count's life-style on a peasant's income. They lived in the Château Bitremont, near the village of Bury, in Belgium.

Their hopes lay in Lydie's brother, Gustave. He was wealthy and unmarried, and on his death his property would go to his sister. It was promising that he had been in poor health for years, and the recent amputation of a leg seemed likely to hasten his end. His legacy would save the Bocarmés from ruin.

Then came a shock: Gustave announced that he was in love. He had bought a château, fallen for its previous owner, and persuaded her to marry him. Although they had to pretend delight, the Bocarmés were dismayed. Gustave had to be killed before the marriage could take place.

On November 20th, 1850, they invited Gustave to lunch. The children were sent to the nursery to eat, while the countess herself served the meal. It was late afternoon when the servants in the kitchen heard a loud thud and rushed in to find Gustave Fougnies lying unconscious on the floor. The countess was hysterical, saying: "Gustave has fallen ill – I think he is dead!" She said she thought that her brother had had a stroke. The count was masterful, taking charge of the situation and sending a servant to fetch vinegar, which he poured down Gustave's throat through a funnel, apparently in the belief that this might revive him. When this failed, he ordered a servant to strip the clothing from Gustave, and wash his body all over with vinegar. The countess took the clothing and hurried to the laundry with it, putting it into boiling water. Then both the count and countess were seen on their hands and knees scrubbing the dining-room floor and scraping it clean with an knife.

The death had to be reported, and when the examining magistrate arrived he found the body of Gustave lying naked on a bed in a servant's room, his cheeks red and bleeding, and his mouth and throat scarred with burns. A post mortem was carried out, and the doctors reported that death had not been caused by a stroke, but by the dead man drinking something caustic, like acid. Vinegar, of course, would not cause such burns. . .

The magistrate was suspicious. Accounts of the count and countess scrubbing the floor suggested something fishy. He had the Bocarmés placed under arrest, and the stomach contents of the dead man sent to the military school in Brussels.

Jean Servais Stas was the professor of chemistry at the École Royale Militaire in Brussels, and it fell to him to examine those stomach contents. He noted the presence of vinegar in the stomach, and when told about the washing of the corpse in vinegar he suspected that this had been done to mask some other smell. But what?

The stomach contents had been preserved in alcohol, so Stas set about mixing them with water and filtering and distilling the result: body substances are soluble in water or alcohol, but not in both. So any body substances which passed through the filter with alcohol would be caught by water, and vice versa. The result should be a fairly pure solution of the poison used.

Stas repeatedly distilled the resulting liquid, at first getting a smell like mouse urine – which suggested coniine, the derivative of hemlock – before arriving at a much stronger smell: that of tobacco. Nicotine – that had been the poison!

The problem now was to separate the poison from the liquid distillate. Stas got an idea of how to do this. He mixed the liquid with ether, which is lighter than water. After a time the ether separated out on top of the water, taking with it the brownish colouring which smelled of tobacco. Stas poured off the excess ether, leaving the remainder in a dish to evaporate. When it had done so, it left behind a dark brownish oily liquid which burned the tongue and smelled of tobacco. Now Stas used the standard tests to prove that the substance was nicotine, mixing it with tannic acid, mercuric iodine of potassium, and so on. Each test proved positive. When Stas had removed all the nicotine from the stomach contents, he had sufficient to fill a small flask – enough to kill several men. He reported his results to the police.

Further investigation showed just how ingenious the murder had been. Bocarmé had a laboratory at his château, as he was interested in the scientific side of agriculture. He had heard of the deadly toxicity of pure nicotine and knew that as a vegetable poison it was undetectable. So he had grown tobacco in a patch in the garden, distilling the resulting leaves over and over again to obtain a colourless liquid, explaining to his half-witted gardener that he was making eau-de-Cologne. The police questioned the coachman, who told them that his master had been to Ghent to confer with a professor of chemistry. The police traced this professor, who said that Bocarmé, giving a false name, had asked him about the process of obtaining nicotine from tobacco leaves. The professor had innocently told him.

Behind secret panelling in the château, police found laboratory apparatus and some left-over nicotine in a flask. And buried in the garden they discovered the remains of animals on which Bocarmé had tested his deadly concoction.

As the police reconstructed the crime, they reasoned that Gustave had been seized from behind and thrown to the floor, being held down by the much stronger

Bocarmé. Then the murdered man's sister had poured the nicotine down this throat, until he lost consciousness. Even so, much of the liquid had splashed onto the floor – hence all that scrubbing, which did not prevent Stas from subsequently finding traces of nicotine on the floorboards.

Then the count had made his mistake, pouring vinegar down the victim's throat to hide the smell of nicotine. It was an error which was to cost him his life. When nicotine and vinegar (which is acetic acid) combine, they form a corrosive liquid. Stas carried out experiments with two dogs, poisoning them both with nicotine, but only pouring vinegar into the mouth of one. Only this dog developed mouth burns.

At their trial the defendants blamed each other. The countess pleaded that her husband had forced her to take part in his murder plot, and she was acquitted. But Bocarmé went to the guillotine on July 19th, 1851, in Mons, saying he hoped the blade was sharp. At least his death had not been in vain: no one else could ever again hope to get away with nicotine poisoning.

24
NICOTINE

The word nicotine makes one think of cigarettes, smoking, nicotine-stained fingers – and possibly lung cancer.

Every schoolboy is brought up to believe that tobacco was brought to Europe from the Americas by the dashing Sir Walter Raleigh – who also brought us potatoes, among other things. However, while Raleigh may have brought tobacco to England, the tobacco plant, *Nicotiana tabacum*, was first introduced into Europe in 1561, having been brought from the New World by the adventurous Spanish, who had observed Red Indians smoking it. The new import was first landed at Lisbon. The French Ambassador there, one Jean Nicot, took an interest in the plant, introducing it to France, where it flourished. Nicot was primarily interested in the plant's medical properties, and it is from his name that the word "nicotine" derives.

Nicotine is an alkaloid, and is a compound found naturally in certain plants and fungi. It belongs to the same group of classic vegetable poisons as morphine, strychnine and aconitine. When extracted from the tobacco plant it is an oily drug, and in its purest form it is a very rapid poison – as swift as prussic acid. It is particularly dangerous because it is soluble in water and can easily penetrate the skin, quite apart from being addictive.

The initial effect of nicotine is that of a stimulant, but

taken in overdose it causes nausea and eventual cardiac irregularity, ultimately paralysing the respiratory system and leading to death from asphyxiation. The lethal dose is around 40 to 60 mg (or less than one grain) and it was once included in horticultural sprays as an insecticide, but had to be withdrawn because of its toxicity. Farm workers would accidentally get it on their skin and drop dead minutes later. The amount of nicotine in one cigarette, if distilled to a pure form, would kill the average adult. However, the smoker gets very little nicotine, most of it going up in smoke in the burning process.

25
EUGÈNE MARIE CHANTRELLE
Seducer of Innocents
*"Mama, if you do not want me to be murdered outright,
you must see that all I can do is leave him at once" –
Elizabeth Chantrelle's letter to her mother.
"Send in three bottles of champagne and a whore" –
Chantrelle's request to the prison governor on the eve
of his execution.*

There is a sub-section of Criminology called "Victimology"
which asserts that certain people – predominantly women
– are predisposed to become victims, and in effect go
around looking for someone to kill them. A recent novel
by Martin Amis, *London Fields,* deals with a woman of this
type.

But while some women are undoubtedly careless and
enter into the most extraordinary and dangerous liaisons,
carelessness alone is not enough for them to be regarded
as participants in their own murders. Sometimes, despite
all precautions, the woman seems destined to become the
prey of the rogue male.

Such was the case with Elizabeth Cullen Dyer. She
knew she was in danger, and even warned her parents,
but they dismissed her fears. She had complained too
often. . .

The daughter of a respectable middle-class Victorian
family, Elizabeth had been a pupil at a private academy

for young ladies in Newington, and was now ready to spread her wings. The academy had concentrated on manners, a little culture, and a thin veneer of sophistication. But Elizabeth was still a child.

Her father was a commercial traveller for several London firms and was consequently away a good deal. At this time, 1867, the Dyer family lived in a flat in Buccleuch Place, in a fashionable area of Edinburgh.

While at the academy Elizabeth, a pretty if dewy-eyed girl with a head filled with romantic effusions, had developed a "crush" on one of her teachers, Eugène Marie Chantrelle, who taught French, Latin and Greek. Not only was he a Frenchman, but he was also tall and handsome, with a high forehead, wavy brown hair, and imposing whiskers. He was the very picture of a Victorian hero, as a photograph taken in 1867 testifies. But he was more than twice Elizabeth's age, and he preyed on susceptible women wherever and whenever he met them. He found a fifteen-year-old's love letters quite enticing.

Born in Nantes in 1834, Chantrelle received a good education, as befitted the son of a wealthy Breton ship-owner, and attended Nantes Medical School, later continuing his studies in Strasbourg and Paris, followed by a year in Edinburgh. But he never qualified as a doctor, never obtained his degree in medicine, although he called himself a "medical man," wrote prescriptions for friends and acquaintances and generally gave the impression of having, in his own words, "studied medicine in the highest degree."

His early history is vague, because he gave conflicting accounts at various times. He once said he left France in December 1851, following Louis Napoleon's coup, presenting himself as a romantic political refugee. Sometimes he displayed a scar on his arm, claiming it had been a sabre wound from when he fought on the barricades; he admitted to strong Communist opinions. He had also travelled widely in the United States, without putting down any roots.

But on another occasion he said he had studied medicine at Strasbourg from 1850 to 1855, which contradicted the "soldier at the barricades" story. Whatever the truth, by the early 1860s he was in England, teaching French at Newcastle, then at Leicester and other places. In the mid-1860s he moved to Edinburgh where, after first attempting to continue his medical training, he earned his living as a teacher.

Edinburgh produced many fine doctors and perhaps the competition was too fierce for Chantrelle. But as a teacher he was a success, having text-books published and finding his air of culture sympathetically received by head-mistresses. It was as a teacher that he first met Elizabeth Dyer in 1867, when she was his pupil and he the successful scholar who had found his niche in the world: a cultured Frenchman with an aura of glamour.

But behind the façade of sophistication lay a deeply buried secret: Chantrelle was a man with unbridled sexual passions who could not keep his hands off young girls. This compulsive lust had led him into trouble more than once. We know of Chantrelle's affairs because of his obituary in *The Scotsman:* "While acting as a tutor in various families of the highest respectability in England, Chantrelle committed what, so far as is known, was the first outrage which brought him into the hands of the police – an outrage of a very gross nature which would, it is believed, have been followed with penal servitude, had it not been for the high testimony to his character borne by the family with whom he had resided, and which, as it was, brought about a sentence of nine months' imprisonment . . . In 1866, soon after this term of confinement was over, he came to Edinburgh, where he was guilty of an act which was nothing less than a shocking repetition of his former offence. For this heartless crime no steps were taken against him."

Chantrelle's offence was to seduce minors – just as he was to seduce Elizabeth Dyer. There is in existence a letter from one of his victims, a governess, Lucy Holmes, whom he seduced in his lodgings one New Year's Day. She wrote: ". . . What happened in your house on the 1st of January, and how you shielded my fears by assuring me that nothing would result from what you had done, which I in my simplicity believed, but now I find that you have been deceiving me all the time, if not yourself as well. Think for a moment what you would feel were your only sister to be treated as you have treated me. . ." It was a vain appeal to a conscience which Chantrelle did not possess.

It was perceptive of Lucy Holmes to suggest that Chantrelle might also be deceiving himself. He was, of course, in that he adopted the role of "ladies' man" with aplomb, little thinking that just as he stole his victims' innocence, so he depleted his own.

Chantrelle stalked Elizabeth as a cat hunts a mouse – although there is evidence that the fifteen-year-old was more than willing to play her role in the melodrama she made of their passion. She had been his pupil for two years when she fell under the spell of the thirty-four-year-old Frenchman. The courtship leading to the seduction was full of intrigue, with passionate letters exchanged.

Lizzie wrote: "Oh Eugène, you would not know how I love you. I could never bear anyone to kiss and pet me. If it was broken off I should die . . . I could not live without your love . . . I feel my love increasing . . . I want you to ask them to let me come to school for French as we will be out together walking. How different it will be when we are married . . . "

The courtship was dominated by drama. Sudden fits of jealousy, bitter partings, followed by sweet reconciliations and vows of devotion. In October 1867 Elizabeth wrote: "My Darling Eugène, as it would make me very unhappy should our arrangement be continued, I therefore release you from all your engagements to me." This was ten months before her marriage to him.

Chantrelle replied swearing his eternal love, but saying: "My house is always open to you whenever you choose to come, but I will NEVER enter yours again . . ."

Elizabeth became pregnant, writing: "My Darling Eugène, I scarcely know how I managed to pass last night. I try to think you are right and know better than me, but still I expected you would come . . . But what is the use of speaking about it when it is not to be? The only thing I can do is to go away as it is evident I cannot stay and have a baby at home . . . It is quite true what Mama says that when you give yourself to a man he loses all respect for you. But I do not say so of you, Eugène . . . I do not complain, the thing is done and I am ruined for life. The only thing for me to do is to go to the street and shorten my life . . . " This was a schoolgirl's notion of high drama.

Chantrelle replied: "Why do you want to die, you foolish little puss; there are many happy days in store for you yet . . . "

Then came a hurried and secret marriage on May 10th, 1868, in Chantrelle's rooms in George Street. It was a strange wedding. The couple simply exchanged notes and vows pledging themselves to one another, but it was sufficient under Scots law to make them legally man and wife.

Relations between Elizabeth and her mother were strained since the daughter had become a "scarlet woman," but by August the mother had relented enough to attend a public marriage for her seven-months pregnant daughter. The strict Presbyterian parents had prevailed upon Elizabeth to marry her licentious teacher, even though she herself was by now disenchanted. She wrote the day after her marriage: "I know I shall not be happy. He is not a kind man, and I can't trust him." The mother was later to state: "I visited my daughter occasionally throughout the period of her married life, and she and the children called on me sometimes, but not as frequently as I visited them." The Dyer family had been disgraced by their daughter's flouting of conventional morality, and they never let her forget it. They were determined never to allow her to disgrace them again.

The marriage was stormy from the start, full of rows

and emotionally-charged scenes. Chantrelle felt he had been tricked into a marriage he never wanted, and in his mid-thirties he now had to provide for a wife of seventeen and a child. More were to follow. The polished Frenchman had become a harried husband.

The entire ten years or so of the marriage were spent living in George Street, a central address if not fashionable. The accommodation was a double-flat occupying the top two floors of 81A, and consisted of a kitchen, dining room, parlour, and classroom (Chantrelle gave lessons at home to earn money) on the lower floor, with two bedrooms in the attic. The family was to comprise three children and a live-in maid, who slept in the annexe to the kitchen, and conditions were cramped.

By 1877 Chantrelle was no longer sharing a bedroom with Elizabeth, but was sleeping in the front room – called the nursery – with his two boys, Eugène and Louis. Possibly this physical separation was a form of birth-control. Possibly it was a symptom of strained marital relations. Chantrelle was not by nature a family man.

Supplementing his school salary with a lot of private tuition, he had a full work-load. He needed the money and was always in desperate financial straits. Prior to his marriage he had shared his apartment with a family, his lodgers paying him £250 per annum. However, Elizabeth objected to sharing her home and Chantrelle was obliged to make them leave. He missed that extra income and blamed Elizabeth bitterly for its loss. He seemed to be working all hours and yet he was always short of money, constantly worried about bills. He needed to get his hands on some cash and it was now, at a peak of desperation, that he took out insurance on his wife's life . . .

The strain had begun to tell on Chantrelle. He began to drink heavily, and by the mid 1870s he was getting through a bottle of whisky a day.

This was not his only vice. He was also a regular patron of a brothel in Clyde Street, a narrow lane to the north of George Street. In 1876 Elizabeth contacted a private detective with a view to his keeping an eye on her husband's movements. The detective told Elizabeth not to bother: he himself had seen Chantrelle in the brothel. The madam of the brothel was a Barbara Kay, who was to say that Chantrelle often came to her establishment with a pair of loaded pistols, which he would sometimes discharge for fun. Only a well-paying customer could have got away with that.

Chantrelle's language, too, had degenerated. He used obscene terms, often calling Elizabeth a bitch and a whore. He struck her too, and sometimes threatened to kill her, boasting that he knew more about poisons than any professor and could outsmart them. The violence had begun early in the marriage. On holiday in Portobello in 1871, Chantrelle displayed his brutal nature, as Elizabeth was quick to report to her mother by letter.

"I might have been sleeping for an hour or more when I was awakened by several severe blows. I got one on the side of my head which knocked me stupid. When I came to myself I found I could not move my face, and this morning I find my jaw out of its place, my mouth inside skinned and festering and my face all swollen. The servants who sleep in the next room heard it all. . . They heard him say he would make *mincemeat* of me . . . well, Mama, if you do not want me to be murdered outright you must see that all I can do is leave him at once . . . I am sorry to trouble you but if he murders me you might have been sorry not to have heard from me . . . " In further letters she complained about Chantrelle's "fearful threats" and his threat to murder her and the children.

None of these letters bothered Mrs Dyer. She was well-aware that Elizabeth tended to dramatise everything, and she was a girl who cried wolf too often; after a time her warnings and complaints were ignored. Besides, in those days the husband was regarded as lord and master of the household, and if he chose to beat his wife, he had the right . . .

Elizabeth ran away from Chantrelle several times,

taking refuge with her mother, but she soon returned to the battleground of her marriage. She could not live without conflict. Servants saw Chantrelle strike her and threaten her with loaded pistols, and in 1876 Elizabeth and her servant were so alarmed by his behaviour that they went out in the middle of the night to fetch a policeman. Sergeant Robert Brass was later to testify: "On Sunday, 30th April 1876, when I was in Hanover Street, Madame Chantrelle and a servant came up to me about 4.30 in the morning. Madame told me that her husband had come in and broken into the servant's bedroom, and threatened herself. He threatened to use violence to her."

The sergeant testified that when he arrested Chantrelle, the man took up a knife, and as he took him to the Police Office he said: "I will do for the bitch yet." Chantrelle was subsequently bound over to keep the peace.

Elizabeth was extremely jealous of her husband, constantly accusing him of making eyes at other women. Chantrelle was jealous too. On one occasion he wrote to Elizabeth's twin brother, John, virtually accusing him of incest: "Sir, I find that on the 21st ulto, you were in my house for a considerable time and remained with my wife alone . . . " This was the letter of a man on the verge of insanity.

In September 1877 he applied for the position of insurance agent with the Star Accidental Assurance Company in Edinburgh, being appointed on the basis of his written application and with no references taken up. He got one or two former acquaintances to take out policies, and he questioned his manager about what constituted an accident. Chantrelle himself had been injured in the hand when one of his sons accidentally fired his loaded pistol. That was indeed an accident, but would a drowning suffice? Death from poisoned food, even if the doctors could not identify the poison? And so on. The manager explained that there would have to be "an outward and visible sign – an ascertained cause of death." Then Chantrelle went to another insurance company where he took out three policies. One, for the servant Mary Byrne, was in the sum of £100 in the event of death. The second was in favour of Elizabeth and was for one thousand pounds against accidental death, at a cost of thirty shillings. The third, in his own favour, was in the same terms as his wife's. He conducted this transaction in the middle of October, when he was heavily in debt.

Mrs Dyer was later to say: "About six weeks before her death she (Elizabeth) told me that Mr Chantrelle wished to insure her life . . . My daughter said she did not care to have it done . . . On the Thursday before her death she reverted to the subject . . . she said to me . . . 'my husband is insured now and, Mama, you will see that my life will go soon after this insurance.' I said 'You are talking nonsense . . . ' She replied: 'I cannot help thinking of it; something within me tells me it will be so . . . ' "

On New Year's Eve Elizabeth was in good spirits, according to the servant. She had played with the children, and had eaten some of the cake and shortbread her mother had sent. The baby was put to bed at six-thirty, and when Chantrelle came in a little later he brought champagne. After supper the other two children were put to bed, and Elizabeth went out to post two New Year cards. At midnight Mary Byrne joined her master and mistress in the parlour to listen to the bands in the Castle welcome in the New Year. Then they all went to bed.

It was a different story the following morning. Elizabeth had very little to eat: a cup of tea and a slice of toast, and she complained of a headache. At eleven, she gave Mary Byrne the rest of the day off as a holiday, although she had to be back for ten. She returned at about nine-thirty to discover that her mistress was ill in bed, "very heavy-looking and did not look so well." Elizabeth said she would like a little milk, but the shops were shut by this time. Mary noticed a tumbler of lemonade by the bedside, three parts full. Elizabeth mumbled some complaint about the lemonade, brewed by her husband . . . Mary peeled an orange for her mistress, giving it to her in quarters, and then left her to go to her own bed.

She got up the following morning at a quarter to seven to find the parlour a mess, with an empty whisky bottle and an ashtray full of cigarette stubs. She had gone to the kitchen to make tea for her mistress when she heard a strange sound. She described it as being "a moaning like a cat's." She went up to Elizabeth's room, finding the door open and the gas light out – both unusual occurrences. Elizabeth was lying near the edge of the bed, on her back but bent over to one side. Her head had slipped off the pillow, and there was no sign of the baby. The servant noted that her mistress seemed "awfully pale-looking" and saw green-brown vomit stains on the bedding. She shook Elizabeth to get some response, but received no answer, just a continual moaning. Going through to the other room to alert Chantrelle, the servant was surprised to find all three children in bed with him. It was later to be alleged that he had deliberately removed the baby from its mother so that it should not be gassed too.

Chantrelle got out of bed immediately and went to his wife's bedside, kneeling beside her and holding her hand. He asked if his wife had spoken at all. No, said Mary Byrne, asking if a doctor should be called. Chantrelle told her to check on the baby in the other room. It was as if he wanted her out of the way. She went to see to the baby – finding him fast asleep – and on her return found Chantrelle near the window, having opened the bottom sash. He asked Mary Byrne if she could not smell gas. The servant could smell it faintly, but not to the extent of what she termed a "suffocation smell."

Chantrelle asked Mary to check the gas bracket on the wall, while he set off to fetch a doctor. He left a message with Dr James Carmichael of Northumberland Street – by no means the nearest doctor, but a fellow-Mason. Dr Carmichael arrived at the Chantrelle home at about twenty-past eight. He could smell gas, and ordered the patient to be removed to another bedroom, assuming it to be a simple case of gas-poisoning. However, he sent a note to Dr Henry Littlejohn, the Police-Surgeon, and Medical Officer of Health to the City of Edinburgh. He also sent Mary to fetch a bottle of brandy, which he used as an enema. Although his efforts were in vain, the doctor was puzzled to note that the brandy in the bottle was beginning to disappear – "though neither Madame Chantrelle nor myself took any." It was a mystery soon solved when Carmichael's assistant arrived at ten-fifteen to find Chantrelle drunk. He was sitting by his wife's bedside, holding her hand, but looking far from concerned.

Dr Littlejohn arrived at about the same time and was at once suspicious. He had been involved with the Chantrelle family before and was aware of the death threats. He thought the patient's condition was so grave that she ought to have her mother at her bedside. Chantrelle pretended not to know the address of his mother-in-law, not wishing to have Mrs Dyer in his house. Littlejohn brusquely ignored him and sent the young son to fetch his grandma. He also urged that Elizabeth should be removed to the Royal Infirmary. Chantrelle made no objection to this, and Littlejohn left, after sending word to the gas company to inspect the fittings at Chantrelle's house. At this point he considered gas-poisoning "the only possible explanation" for Elizabeth's conditions.

Mrs Dyer arrived together with her family doctor, who came as a friend rather than as a physician. He claimed later that he immediately concluded that the patient's symptoms indicated narcotic rather than gas poisoning. However, he did not tell anyone else of his suspicions, and Elizabeth was admitted to hospital at a quarter to two as someone suffering from gas poisoning. There she was examined by Dr Douglas MacLagan, Professor of Medical Jurisprudence at the University. He reported that he found her "lying totally insensible, with the muscles relaxed and the pupils of the eyes contracted. She was incapable of being roused; the respiration was interrupted and the heart's action was scarcely discernible. The pulse of the wrist was not to be felt . . . "

He had to use his stethoscope to detect a faint heart-beat, but more significantly, when he put his nose to the patient's mouth, he could detect no smell of gas. Rapidly coming to the conclusion that this was a case of narcotic poisoning – he suspected opium or morphia – he applied artificial respiration and another brandy enema.

Chantrelle arrived at the infirmary at this point, to be told that narcotic poisoning was suspected. He repeated his story about an escape of gas, and turning to Mrs Dyer in fury, declared that Lizzie was being murdered by the doctors. He said he could not bear to stay and watch such cruel treatment – he had a low opinion of medical men, he said – and stormed out of the hospital to return home. He gave the maid money to buy food for the children, finished off the brandy and sat for an hour brooding. If the gas poisoning was discounted, then the insurance company would refuse to accept Elizabeth's death as being accidental, and he would lose the thousand pounds he so desperately needed. He returned to the hospital at just after four. Elizabeth was dead. No trace of carbon monoxide was found in her body.

Meanwhile the doctors had been considering what poison had killed their patient. Opium was considered the most likely, but it was difficult to detect in the system with a post mortem examination, since it was rapidly absorbed into the bloodstream. The most likely clue lay in the vomit on the pillow in the Chantrelle home, and this was taken away for analysis. It had lain in the house all day, and Chantrelle had plenty of opportunity to get rid of this evidence had he wanted, just as Mrs Dyer had ample opportunity to tamper with it, as Chantrelle was to suggest. The question of the gas escape had to be investigated, since there had certainly been one.

Two gasfitters found a pipe torn loose in Elizabeth's bedroom, behind the shutter to the window, the broken piece lying on the floor. It would have taken only a couple of seconds to wrench that pipe off its bracket.

The criminal investigation officer, William Frew, was now certain in his mind that murder had been committed, that Chantrelle was the culprit, and that the method had been poison. Chantrelle had tried to fix the blame on a gas escape, by sending the servant out of the room so that he could wrench the pipe free. Mary Byrne had seen him coming away from the window when she returned to the room.

The post mortem examination found no trace of coal-gas poisoning, but an analysis of the vomit on the pillow revealed traces of opium. Chantrelle was arrested on the afternoon of January 5th, immediately after the funeral of Elizabeth, during which he had been very emotional.

Examined by magistrates, he claimed that Elizabeth had been unfaithful to him, having had two affairs. "She took a great deal of persuasion, and at length confessed to repeated adulterous intercourse," he said. He admitted his own affairs, and patronage of the local brothel, but in Victorian times there was one law for men, and another for women . . . Chantrelle also claimed that on the night prior to her death, he had made love to his wife – but medical evidence showed that he had not, and Elizabeth had been menstruating at the time.

The trial of Chantrelle for his wife's murder began on May 7th, 1878, at the High Court of Justiciary in Edinburgh. He still wore mourning dress, just as his wife had been buried in her wedding-gown. It was the "done thing." He answered "Not guilty" to the charge in a firm and clear voice.

The prosecution began by dismissing any possibility of suicide. The devotion of the mother to her children ruled that out. Nor could accidental gas-poisoning be accepted. That left murder. Opium had been found in vomit on the victim's pillow, and when he was arrested Chantrelle had in his possession a solid block of opium – 60 grams – which he had bought on November 25th, 1877, just a month prior to the murder . . . The Lord Advocate in his summing-up of the Crown case said that this amount of opium was "twenty or thirty doses, each sufficient, if administered, to prove fatal to human life." But Chantrelle had bought opium previously which had not been found. And if not accounted for, this was the opium found in his wife's vomit.

The defence countered by producing a bottle of fluid opium, Chantrelle's lawyer, Mr Traynor, saying: "It is just as obvious as two and two make four, if a man would open his eyes and look at the fact, that that was what had become of the drachm of opium unaccounted for. It had been reduced to a fluid, and that was where it had gone to . . ."

Mrs Dyer said that her daughter had told her that Chantrelle had threatened to shoot her if she left him. Elizabeth had once sent her a note saying: "Come and see me at once if you want to see me alive. E has a revolver." And he would blow up his mother-in-law's house if Elizabeth went to live there. Mrs Dyer admitted that she had never consulted a professional man to see about her daughter's rights "to have the children if she was separated from her husband when he was ill-treating her." It was obvious that she preferred her daughter to suffer in silence rather than create a fresh scandal.

The eldest son, Eugène Chantrelle, admitted having seen his father strike his mother and call her bad names, but added: "He was kind to Mamma too. It was a long time before Mamma died that the hard words and the swearing took place. Papa was kind to Mamma lately . . ."

Chantrelle's counsel excused his conduct – his heavy drinking and admitted immorality – by reminding the jury that his client was a Frenchman and could hardly be expected to behave as morally as a Scot.

The prosecution pointed out that Chantrelle had threatened to poison his wife in a way that could not be detected, and she had died. He had been the last person to see her alive, and on his own account had given her lemonade and a piece of orange. As to the motive and what interest Chantrelle could have in his wife's death, "the prisoner was interested to the extent of one thousand pounds sterling in the woman's death being accidental . . . "

The manager of the insurance company had testified that it was very rare for "policies to be taken out in the name of females." In fact, of eight hundred policies issued in this the first year of operation, Chantrelle's "was the first and only application of this kind." What was more sinister was that Chantrelle had asked his own insurance company what constituted accidental death "and then took out policies from another office where he asked no questions of the kind."

Defence counsel protested that the taking out of insurance had been nothing more than a sensible precaution, in view of Chantrelle's own accident with a pistol. As for the threats Chantrelle had made against his wife, her own mother had testified that she had felt no real apprehension.

It was a strange case. The defence claimed that death had been due to gas poisoning, but had the prosecution based its case solely on that, Chantrelle would have been convicted, for only he could have broken the pipe. Instead, the prosecution insisted on death from opium poisoning. Mr Traynor insisted on death from gassing, obviously hoping to so befuddle the minds of the jury that they would return a verdict of Not Proven.

Found guilty, however, and sentenced to death, Chantrelle rose: he wished to make a statement. In a hysterical voice he told the court: "I am willing to admit that the dark stains on the sheet and on the nightgown . . . contained sufficient evidence that opium was there. I go further: I say opium was there . . . I am further satisfied, gentlemen, that I did not put it there; that it did not proceed from Madame Chantrelle's stomach; that it was rubbed in by some person for a purpose I do not know – an enemy . . . "

This was an obvious allusion to his mother-in-law, and

the judge cut him short, telling him to proceed no further.

In the condemned cell Chantrelle said through gritted teeth to a warder: "Would that I could but place a fuse in the centre of this earth, that I could blow it to pieces, and with it, the whole of humanity. I hate them." Similar resentment can be found in many other murder cases. Henry Lee Lucas, reputed to have killed 360 people, explained his actions by saying: "I was bitter at the world." Carl Panzram wanted to destroy all mankind. This hatred is the suicidal cry of the man who feels he has been cheated of recognition; it is a sense of thwarted self-esteem.

On the night before his execution Chantrelle was asked by the prison governor if there was anything he would like to have. He retorted: "Send in three bottles of champagne and a whore." The request was denied.

When dawn broke, Chantrelle breakfasted on coffee and eggs and a glass of brandy, followed by a cigar. He still maintained his innocence, and when given a last chance by the chief warder to confess, he declined to do so.

Hanged on May 31st, 1878, he had not destroyed the world, neither did the world destroy him. He destroyed himself.

26
OPIUM

From the innocent opium poppy comes a sticky resin which is a compound of many drugs, morphine and heroin among them. The poppy grows in many places. Much publicity has been given to the "golden triangle" of Laos, Burma and Thailand, but the poppy also flourishes in Afghanistan and elsewhere, notably Columbia and other South American countries. Pound for pound, it is the most valuable cash crop of modern times. Yet it was not always so. In Victorian days you could go into a chemist's and buy opium and laudanum, and the price was cheap. Only when a substance is banned – as alcohol was in America during Prohibition – does the price shoot up and the criminal element move in.

It has been argued that drug addiction is a "victimless crime" and should be decriminalised: if the addict wants to ruin and cut short his life, why not let him? Why not supply him with cheap drugs – as they do in Amsterdam – so that he does not steal to feed his habit?

Meanwhile, the product of the poppy is killing American youth in that country's big cities. But whatever the philosophic argument, one thing is beyond dispute: there certainly was a victim in the Chantrelle case.

27
LOUISA MAY MERRIFIELD
A Careless Chatterer
"I've had a slice of real luck! Where I'm living the old lady
has died and left me her bungalow worth £3,000" –
Mrs Merrifield speaking to a friend, three weeks before
the death of the 'old lady'.

The case of Louisa May Merrifield reminds me of an observation made by literature's most celebrated opium addict, Thomas De Quincey. In his essay "On Murder Considered as One of the Fine Arts," he noted: "If once a man indulges himself in murder, very soon he comes to think little of robbing; and from robbing he comes next to drinking and sabbath-breaking, and from that to incivility and procrastination."

He was writing tongue-in-cheek – the essay having been inspired by the Wainewright poisoning case – but in turning conventional morality upside down, he was making a valid point. Murderers often arrive at the ultimate crime from a beginning in petty thievery.

Mrs Merrifield had served a prison sentence for ration book frauds. Married three times, she had also had twenty domestic jobs in three years. She was unable to hold down either a marriage or a job, and was also to fail in the trade of murder . . .

One of five daughters born to a miner in Wigan, Louisa broke away from the family devotion to Methodism and instead joined the Salvation Army. At twenty-five she married an ironworker named Ellison, bearing him four children. But she was never a domesticated person, much preferring the snug in the local pub. In 1945 the local authority considered her not to be a fit mother and placed her children in care.

They were returned to her after a couple of years, but were removed again in 1949, being placed in foster-care. It was in 1949 that Louisa's husband died, and within three months she had married her lodger: Richard Weston, aged seventy-eight, a former under-manager at a colliery. As Louisa was forty-two, it seems that she married for security rather than love.

Within ten weeks her aged husband died. Undaunted, the following year she married sixty-seven-year-old Alfred Merrifield, but if she had been looking for financial security, she was to be disappointed. He had no money, and the couple had to go into domestic service.

On March 12th, 1953, they secured a position with a Mrs Sarah Ann Ricketts, who had advertised in a newspaper for a live-in companion. Mrs Ricketts was a woman of seventy-nine with a bad temper and a hand-some bungalow in Blackpool. She had been married twice, both husbands committing suicide by gassing themselves.

On April 13th, 1953, a delivery man from a local wine-store called at the bungalow with a bottle of rum for Mrs Merrifield. Mrs Ricketts answered the door, grumbling: "I don't know what they are doing with my money!" She told the deliveryman that she was getting fed up with the Merrifields and they would have to go. She complained that she was not getting enough to eat.

She died the next day, which was providential for the Merrifields. Their employer had been almost eighty and her death might have been expected and accepted, but for the fact that Mrs Merrifield had been making some indiscreet remarks. On March 25th, she had told a friend: "I've had a slice of real luck! Where I'm living the old lady has died and left me her bungalow worth £3,000."

She told another person about her lucky bequest, and when asked when the old lady had died, replied: "She's not dead yet, but she soon will be." On the day the rum was delivered – the day before the death – Louisa started talking to a complete stranger at a bus-stop, and said: "I've been to Wigan to see my son, and when I got back I found my husband in bed with the old lady. If it goes on again, I'll poison the old bitch and my husband as well. She's leaving the bungalow between me and my husband, but he's so greedy he wants it all on his own."

Three days before the death, Louisa told a Mrs Brewer: "We're landed! I went to live with an old lady, and she died and left me a bungalow." When Mrs Brewer read about the death of Mrs Ricketts taking place a week later, she telephoned the police.

The doctor had refused to issue a death certificate on April 14th, for on April 9th Louisa had called him to the bungalow to certify that Mrs Ricketts was fit enough to make a new will. Because the doctor was not satisfied as to the cause of death, there had to be an inquest with a preliminary post mortem examination. This revealed phosphorus in Mrs Ricketts' stomach.

Meanwhile Mrs Merrifield, conscious of police suspicions, produced the will leaving her the bungalow jointly with her husband, and had the local Salvation Army band play "Abide With Me" outside the bungalow in tribute to the memory of the dead woman.

The police, who had been told that death was due to phosphorus poisoning, began searching the bungalow while the couple were still in residence. Looking for any receptacle which might have contained the poison, detectives even used a mine-detector in their two-week fruitless hunt. While this continued, Louisa gave interviews to reporters, saying she had an enemy in Blackpool who was trying to ruin her, and adding, "I shall remain here and face it out."

But not for long. On April 30th she was arrested and

charged with murder. Her husband was not allowed to visit his wife, but when she appeared before the magistrates he was told that he might now see her. Taken to her cell, he was arrested there and was also charged with the murder of Mrs Ricketts.

Mrs Merrifield seemed confident of being acquitted, telling staff at the prison where she was held that she would not be coming back. The trial at Manchester Assizes was before Mr Justice Glyn-Jones. The Attorney-General, Sir Lionel Heald QC, led the prosecution, and Mr Jack Nahum, QC, appeared for the defence. The prosecution contended that Mrs Ricketts had died of phosphorus poisoning, and since it was unlikely to have entered the body either by accident or due to suicide, it must have been deliberately administered. For three of the trial's eleven days Mrs Merrifield was in the witness box, and she appeared to enjoy being the centre of attention. But then, she was an inveterate gossip . . .

She was forty-six at the time, plump and unattractive. She seemed impatient listening to the various witnesses testifying, but when her turn came she told a fellow-prisoner: "Today is my day; I'm going to get my own back." Her counsel had warned her that coarseness and argumentative talk would not help her cause in the eyes of the jury, but she didn't listen. She imagined that she could button-hole and transfix the jury just as she had people she met at bus-stops.

The mystery of the will was never resolved at the trial. It was undisputably in Mrs Ricketts' handwriting; the signature was genuine, but she had only known the Merrifields for six weeks and was on the verge of sacking them. Yet she left her bungalow to a drunken and unsatisfactory servant.

Mrs Merrifield was in her element in the witness box, cocky and defiant, and the account she gave of Mrs Ricketts' sickness agreed completely with the symptoms of phosphorus poisoning.

"I was up and down with her five or six times that

night," she said. "And then I heard her go to the bath-room again. She was under the tap. I asked her if she was sick and she said 'No.' I got her into bed again. She went to the toilet and cried bitterly and said: 'You don't know how ill I am.' I got her into bed. She seemed to go a bit quieter. Next thing I heard her up again and she was in the hall, on the floor. I picked her up. I got her into bed. She said she thanked both my husband and me for what we had done for her. Those were her last words. She had apparently lost her speech by that time. Her teeth came out and I pushed them back and found she had five pink cough lozenges in her mouth at once. I just gave her a sip out of the egg cup which was prepared for her by herself the night before."

Mrs Merrifield was to spend a total of nine and a half hours in the witness box, describing Mrs Ricketts' death and then being cross-examined. She loved every minute of it.

The prosecutor did his best to discover how the poison had been administered. He asked Mrs Merrifield: "She had a raging thirst, didn't she?"

"Well, she just wanted a drink and gave the motion a woman would do who had lost her speech – or a man."

"She was thirsty?"

"Yes, sir."

"Where do you say the brandy came from?"

"It was already mixed on the table."

"Mixed with water?"

"I don't know."

"Why do you say mixed?"

Mrs Merrifield paused, thinking. Then she said: "Mrs Ricketts always prepared the table herself before she went to bed."

Dr G.B. Manning, the pathologist who had conducted the post mortem examination, said that after experiment-ing with various mixtures he had found that rum masked the characteristic phosphorus smell of garlic, but brandy, while it hid the taste, did not entirely disguise the smell.

The Attorney-General had hammered away at Mrs Merrifield for hours, exposing her to the jury as a cheat and liar who could offer no explanation for her sinister remarks prior to the death of Mrs Ricketts. Her case had been damaged badly.

Mr Nahum, for the defence, produced an expert witness of his own: Professor Webster, director of the Home Office Forensic Laboratory at Birmingham, and Professor of Forensic Medicine and Toxicology at the University in that city.

He had not attended the post mortem, but based his opinion on the medical findings. In his view Mrs Ricketts had not died from phosphorus poisoning, but from a disease of the liver called necrosis. (Basically, this meant cirrhosis of the liver.) He said: "The sequence of colour and swelling of the liver as described by Dr Manning is totally wrong. It is quite wrong to say that this lady died of phosphorus poisoning before the liver began to swell."

In other words, although phosphorus was undoubtedly found in the dead woman, it had not caused her death. By coincidence, phosphorus had been introduced into the stomach of a woman who had already been dying.

It had been proved that Mrs Merrifield had purchased a tin of Rodine, a popular rat-poison of the time. A Blackpool chemist's assistant had testified that she had sold her a shilling tin. It could be bought openly over the counter, and a shilling tin contained ten grains of phosphorus: enough to kill ten people.

Only 0.141 grains of phosphorus had been found in Mrs Ricketts. The judge happened also to be a qualified pharmacist, and he questioned Professor Webster himself, asking him how he thought phosphorus had got into Mrs Ricketts' body.

"I think it entered by the mouth," said the professor.

"Would you suggest any form, as far as you know, in which it could have entered the body save in the form of Rodine rat-poison?" asked the judge.

"I think it is the most likely way in which it entered the

body," the professor replied.

The defence was that Mrs Ricketts had died of necrosis of the liver, before the phosphorus had any chance to do her any damage. It was a defence of *coincidence*.

In effect, the defence was arguing that if you poison someone who is already dying and is beyond all help before the poison is administered, then this cannot be murder.

The jury deliberated for six hours, wondering why Mrs Merrifield had bought that tin of Rodine, and what had happened to it subsequently. Why had Mrs Merrifield been so anxious to have Mrs Ricketts cremated? And what about the new will leaving everything to comparative strangers? No, it just would not do . . .

The jury found Mrs Merrifield guilty of murder but were unable to agree in the case of Mr Merrifield, who was discharged and went back to the bungalow to live there alone. He was sitting in that bungalow when his wife was hanged at Strangeways Prison on September 18th, 1953, and he lived on to enjoy his half-share in the property, later making a living appearing in Blackpool side-shows. He died in 1962, aged eighty.

With her streak of vanity and her love of publicity, his wife had talked cheerfully of her employer's death before it happened. She had also talked her way into the hangman's noose.

28
PHOSPHORUS

Once used for making matches, phosphorus is a volatile, dangerous material. As a waxy yellow solid, it bursts into flame when exposed to air, and during chemical factory processes it is kept under water. As little as one grain can prove fatal, the symptoms being liver damage, haemorrhage, intense thirst, delirium, convulsions, and finally coma leading to death. There is a characteristic smell which can be detected in the intestines at a post mortem; and the vomit and excreta of a phosphorus-poisoned victim will glow in the dark . . .

Chemical factory workers in the last century, exposed continuously to phosphorus, used to develop chronic phosphorus poisoning, typical symptoms being necrosis of the upper and lower jaw, the bones failing to develop normal growth and teeth falling out, a condition stoically known in the trade as "phossy jaw."

Phosphorus was a common ingredient of rat-poison, until its use was banned – probably due to the case of Mrs Louisa Merrifield. The first person known to have used phosphorus to kill was Dr J. Milton Bowers, a 42-year-old San Francisco physician who married three times in fifteen years, each wife dying suddenly. It was the death of his third wife which attracted the attention of the police.

Bowers had seemed distraught at the death of 29-year-old Cecelia, his wife of three years. She had been ill for a couple of months, dying of an abscess of the liver. It was an anonymous letter to the insurance company which alerted investigators. The body was exhumed and phosphorus was found in the remains.

Tried in March 1886, Bowers was also strongly suspected of performing abortions as a sideline, and the jury lost no time in finding him guilty of first-degree murder. Then, while he was in jail waiting for his appeal to be heard, there was a dramatic development in the case.

Henry Benhayon, brother of the murdered Mrs Bowers, who had testified against Dr Bowers at his trial, was found dead in a rooming-house. On the bedside table was a bottle of potassium cyanide, and three suicide notes, one of which was addressed to the coroner in the Bowers case. In this note, Benhayon confessed to having poisoned his sister.

Suspecting a conspiracy, police arrested John Dimmig, who was known to have visited Bowers in prison and to have bought potassium cyanide. Charged with Benhayon's murder, he was tried in December 1887, but the jury failed to agree on a verdict. At his second trial a year later, he was acquitted. Meanwhile, Dr Bowers had been writing fruitless petitions from his cell demanding a new trial, but in August 1889, after almost four years in prison, he was released. He resumed his practice, married a fourth time, and died in 1904, aged sixty-one. His case remains one of the great mysteries of San Francisco.

In England, in the late 1950s, the case of the "Widow of Windy Nook" attracted much Press attention. Mary Elizabeth Wilson, sixty-six, lived at Windy Nook in Felling-on-Tyne. A lover of romantic fiction and fed up with her husband of many years, she took the local chimney-sweep as her lover, but both sweep and husband died within five months of one another, apparently of natural causes, and Mrs Wilson was left a widow with prospects. In 1957, when she met Oliver James Leonard, a retired estate agent living in lodgings, she asked his landlady: "Has the bugger any money?" The couple were married in the September, and two weeks later Leonard died – of "natural causes," according to the death certificate. But the widow's question about his finances was not forgotten. She next married another elderly man, Ernest Wilson, who wanted a housekeeper. Two weeks after the marriage he too was dead. Just being around this woman was fatal . . .

Greed and meanness went together in Mary Wilson, and they were her undoing. She asked the undertaker for the cheapest possible funeral, and this, together with her indiscreet remarks, set tongues wagging. When the gossip reached the ears of the police, the corpses of Mrs Wilson's former husbands were exhumed and were found to be glowing with phosphorus, like neon-tubes in the cemetery. Tried for murder, the prosecution alleging that she had fed her husbands phosphorus in tea or cough mixture, she was convicted and sentenced to death. A reprieve followed on account of her age, and she died in prison at seventy. Her four murders netted her just £200.

There can be little doubt that phosphorus was used to kill many times over in undetected cases. It was easy to obtain as rat-poison, and it is inconceivable that the would-be poisoner would have ignored such a convenient agent. In 1958, American research into homicide suggested that one in ten murders goes unsuspected. The true figure, I believe, must be much higher, especially in poisoning cases where doctors fail to recognise the symptoms and put down cardiac failure as an easy diagnosis. When a study was carried out, comparing death certificate diagnosis with post mortem results, it was found that the cause of death given on those certificates was incorrect in nearly fifty per cent of the cases. Doctors, like anyone else, can make mistakes. As a result, killers escape justice . . . though as we've seen, that careless chatterer, Louisa Merrifield, was not so fortunate.

29
THOMAS NEILL CREAM
The Poisonous Prankster
"I am Jack the . . . " – Neill Cream's last words,
interrupted by the hangman

There seems to be a curious element of the practical joker in some poisoners – Ethel Major and her poisoned sweets being one example. Another came in 1923, when in February of that year Sir William Forwood, Commissioner of the Metropolitan Police, received a box of chocolates through the post with a note reading: "A good lunch and a hearty appetite." After eating one of the poisoned sweets, and giving one to his secretary, Sir William began to feel extremely ill. Later, a public-schoolboy was arrested and charged with attempted murder.

There is undoubtedly a learned treatise to be written about such instances. John Franklin Bardin wrote three surrealistic crime novels during 1946-48, one of which was called *The Deadly Percheron*. In this his psychiatrist-hero reflects: "In the last analysis the psychology of the murderer and the practical joker differed only in degree. Both were sadists, both enjoyed the pleasures of the grotesque and of inflicting pain on others. Murder might be termed the ultimate practical joke; similarly, a practical joke might be termed the social form of murder." The case of John George Haigh – the "Acid-Bath Murderer" – who was noted at school for his nasty practical jokes, demonstrates how prescient Bardin was.

If ever a man poisoned people as a form of practical joke, it was Dr Neill Cream. He did not do it for gain, and he got nothing out of it except perhaps the pleasure of *imagining* his victims' death, for he didn't see them perish. If I were writing a book with the title *Murder as a Practical Joke*, I would start with Dr Cream . . .

It was G.K. Chesterton who observed: "Society is at the mercy of a murderer without a motive." He might have had Dr Cream in mind. Once a killer begins operating at random, with no discernible motive and nothing to connect him with the victims, then he becomes extremely difficult to catch. With the Yorkshire Ripper we at least had the motive, but it still took five years to catch Peter Sutcliffe. Dr Cream could not have been caught by sheer logic, normal police routines, or by a thinking-machine like Sherlock Holmes. In fact, he was caught by a chain of coincidences.

The bizarre series of events which shocked London began on the evening of October 13th, 1891, when a man standing outside a pub near Waterloo Station saw a young girl on the opposite side of the Waterloo Road suddenly collapse against a wall, sliding down to fall on her face. The man went to her aid, lifting her to her feet and helping her to walk home. She was in considerable pain, but managed to tell the man that her name was Ellen Donworth, she was nineteen, and she thought her pains were due to a "tall gentleman" who had twice given her a drink out of a bottle "with white stuff in it."

Back at her lodgings, when a doctor had been called and a policeman arrived to question her, the girl, by now having terrible convulsions, managed to describe the "gentleman" as being tall and dark with cross-eyes. The policeman noted that she was obviously a prostitute, one of the poor drabs who eked out a living on the streets of London. She was taken to hospital but died on her way there, her death being recorded as being due to strychnine poisoning. Detective Inspector Harvey had the task of investigating her murder, but his enquiries got nowhere.

The coroner at the girl's inquest received a letter from someone signing himself "A. O'Brien, detective," and offering to solve the mystery for the sum of £300,000. Another letter, sent to Fred Smith of the W.H. Smith book chain in the Strand, accused him of being the murderer of Ellen Donworth. Signing himself "H. Bayne," the writer of the letter said he was willing to meet Mr Smith to talk the matter over, and if Mr Smith wanted a meeting, he should place a paper on his office window. The police advised Mr Smith to display the paper, and kept watch on his office, but "Mr Bayne" never turned up. Both letters were dismissed as being the work of cranks. Scotland Yard gets thousands of such letters every year.

A couple of days later a London magistrate received a letter from "Bayne" stating that he was in possession of enough evidence to hang Smith, and would make it hot for the police if they failed to take action against him.

A week after the murder of Ellen Donworth and before the inquest on her had been concluded, the occupants of a house in Lambeth Road, in that same London district, were woken at three in the morning by the screams of a woman in great pain. Hurrying to the room of Matilda Clover, a twenty-seven-year old prostitute, they found her in convulsions on her bed. A servant in the house, Lucy Rose, tended to the sick woman. In between spasms of pain, Matilda Clover was able to tell her that she had entertained a gentleman named "Fred" in her room earlier that evening, and he had poisoned her with some "long pills." (She meant capsules, which were a novelty in England at that time). The servant had caught a glimpse of the mysterious "Fred" in the dimly-lit hall, but all she could remember was that he had been tall, wearing a cape overcoat with a high silk topper. After hours of agony Matilda Clover died, and a doctor issued a death certificate stating the cause of death as delirium tremens due to acute alcoholism. The case was buried and forgotten. The victim had been a "nobody" . . .

In late November a reputable physician, Dr Broadbent of Portman Square, received a letter signed "M. Malone" accusing him of having murdered Matilda Clover with strychnine and demanding £2,500 to keep his mouth shut. If the doctor wanted to do a deal, he was to put a personal advertisement in the *Daily Chronicle*. The doctor went straight to the police, who advised him to place the ad. so they could lay a trap for "Mr Malone." Two detectives lay in hiding in the doctor's home, but "Malone" did not appear and never followed up his letter.

Later, police were to learn that Countess Russell, living at the Savoy Hotel, had received an anonymous letter in December accusing her husband, Lord Russell, of having murdered Matilda Clover. Naturally, she had dismissed the letter as the work of a crank . . . In April the following year, guests at the Metropole Hotel were startled to receive a printed circular headed: "ELLEN DONWORTH'S DEATH." It went on: "To The Guests Of The Metropole Hotel. Ladies and Gentlemen, I hereby notify you that the person who poisoned Ellen Donworth on the 13th last October is in the employ of the Metropole Hotel and that your lives are in danger as long as you remain in this Hotel. Yours Respectfully, W.H. Murray. London. April 1892."

Matters came to a head later that month. In the early hours of April 11th, Constable Cumley, walking his beat, was passing along Stamford Street, in Lambeth, when he saw a man being let out of a house by a young girl. He recognised the girl as being a local prostitute, Emma Shrivell, aged about eighteen. Even in such an unsavoury area it was an unusual sight, since it was two in the morning and the man was obviously a gentleman, wearing a top hat. By the light of a street gas-lamp the observant constable noted the sudden reflected glint of spectacles.

Less than an hour later the constable was back at the house. The occupants had been woken by the sound of two girls shrieking in pain, and they found Emma Shrivell, and her friend, Alice Marsh, both writhing in agony. They managed to tell the landlady, in between spasms of pain, that they had entertained a man called "Fred" who said he was a doctor. Before he left them, he gave them each "three long, thin pills" which he hinted were good for female complaints. Perhaps imagining they were to enjoy some narcotic delight, after he had gone, both girls took the pills – and promptly went into the terrible convulsions of strychnine poisoning. The constable took both girls to hospital in a cab, but Alice Marsh died on the way, and Shrivell expired five hours later.

Inspector Harvey now knew that there was a connection between these murders and that of Ellen Donworth. Furthermore, one of his sergeants had mentioned that Matilda Clover had exhibited the same symptoms before her death, so Harvey had her body exhumed. The post mortem revealed strychnine poisoning.

Detective Chief Inspector John Tunbridge of Scotland Yard was placed in charge of the investigation, which the Press was now blazoning as the "Lambeth Poisoning Mystery." All he knew was that he was seeking a madman who wore a topper and needed spectacles. At best, he could have his officers question prostitutes in the hope that one of them might know of a gentleman who handed out capsules.

It wasn't such a bad idea. A prostitute called Lou Harvey wrote to a London magistrate telling him that she had met such a man, who gave her some pills "to improve her complexion." She had not taken them, but had thrown them away. Several days later, when she met the man by accident, he seemed startled to see her and hurried away. Another girl, Violet Beverley, said that she had met the same man and he had offered her "an American drink" which she had declined.

Now pure chance came into operation – proving that there must be a Providence somewhere. John Haynes was an engineer with a friend in the Special Branch at Scotland Yard, Detective Sergeant McIntyre; or to be more precise, Haynes was an informer on suspect political groups. He lodged with a photographer named W. Armstead, at a house in Westminster Bridge Road.

A frequent client of the photographer was a Dr Neill, who had a passion for being photographed. He spoke with an American accent, and explained that although he was a qualified doctor with a British degree, he did not practise. Instead, he was a representative in England for an American drugs company. Frankly, he explained, he was more interested in having a good time.

The photographer introduced his new client to his lodger, and soon Dr Neill and John Haynes became friends, going out together in the evening, visiting music-halls or drinking clubs. In about the middle of May, Haynes noticed that they were being followed by a man acting furtively. He asked Dr Neill if he knew of any reason why he should be followed.

Dr Neill had a ready – and fascinating – story. He said that a fellow-lodger at his boarding-house, a young medical student named Harper, lived off an allowance from his rich father, but was a dissipated Don Juan-type who had been involved in the "Lambeth poisoning affair." As Dr Neill explained it, both Alice Marsh and Emma Shrivell had been blackmailing Harper, who in desperation had attempted to buy strychnine from Dr Neill. He, Neill, had therefore written anonymous letters to both girls, telling them that their lives were in danger. Obviously the girls had ignored his warnings . . .

In the course of further conversation, Dr Neill said that Harper had disappeared shortly before the inquest on the girls, but had also claimed to have poisoned girls named Clover, Donworth, and Lou Harvey. When Haynes asked him why he had not gone to the police with this information, Neill retorted that he was not a fool. There was money to be made out of Harper's rich old father, by a little blackmail.

Haynes did not take this account seriously, nor had he any suspicions about the affable Dr Neill. But one day Detective Sergeant McIntyre visited Haynes at the photographer's studio. While the two men were talking, Dr Neill came in, and Haynes introduced him to McIntyre, neglecting to mention that he was a policeman.

McIntyre and Dr Neill became friends, often enjoying an hour or two at the pub. But then one day Neill complained that he was being shadowed by police officers. McIntyre, now on his guard, listened to the complaint politely.

Afterwards, he went to see Detective Inspector Harvey and discovered that Neill was indeed being watched. Detective Sergeant Ward had spotted Neill in Westminster Bridge Road and had immediately remembered Constable Cumley's description of the man seen leaving the house in Stamford Street. The sergeant, never losing sight of the suspect, sent for Cumley, who arrived in civilian clothing and confirmed that Neill resembled the man he had seen. The constable was given the job of discreetly dogging Neill's footsteps.

Following McIntyre's visit, Harvey arranged a meeting with Neill in a public house, where he explained that Neill's difficulties arose from the fact that he was a stranger in the area, and that naturally placed him under suspicion in some minds. If he could just confirm his identity and the nature of his business, then no doubt he would cease to be spied upon.

Neill accordingly fetched his sample case, and some letters to show that he was acting as an agent for an American company. Harvey said he was satisfied and left, leaving Neill drinking with McIntyre. Neill complained that surely no one could suspect him of being implicated in the Lambeth poisonings. Harvey had never mentioned the poisonings, but McIntyre did not point that out. Instead, he cultivated Neill's friendship more assiduously.

Meanwhile, Scotland Yard officers were taking a closer look at this Dr Neill, Inspector Jarvis being sent to the United States and Canada to check on the suspect's background. Other detectives concentrated on talking to all Neill's friends, and to any woman with whom he had any contacts. They were soon talking to the girl who had refused an American drink from Neill.

At the end of May, Neill complained to McIntyre that he had been pestered by a detective named Murray who questioned him about the medical student, Harper. (There was no detective named Murray involved in the investigation. The story was concocted by Neill to draw attention to himself). The doctor now produced a letter which had gone through the mail, addressed to Marsh and Shrivell, warning both girls to beware of Harper – or he would serve them as he had Matilda Clover and Lou Harvey. McIntyre had never heard of Lou Harvey at this point.

The medical student, Harper, was soon traced. He was able to establish that Neill's stories against him were a complete fabrication. He revealed that his father, Dr Harper, had received a letter from someone signing himself "W.H. Murray" and demanding £1,500 as the price of his silence about the fact that Dr Harper's son was the Lambeth Poisoner. Negotiations were to take place through the advertisement columns of a daily newspaper. Det. Chief Insp. Tunbridge took possession of this letter and placed the ad. in the paper, but it led to nothing.

By now the police had several letters of this type in their hands, at least two from W.H. Murray. The letter from "M. Malone" sent to Dr Broadbent was particularly significant. It accused the doctor of having murdered Matilda Clover with strychnine, at a time when only the killer could have known that she had died of this poison.

McIntyre was instructed to try to get samples of Dr Neill's handwriting. He went to see him and listened sympathetically as once again Neill complained about the "impertinent detective Murray." McIntyre indicated some notepaper on the table and suggested: "Just write down the facts about the way you have been bothered. I shall see that it gets into the right hands and puts a stop to any further persecution of your good self." Neill eagerly obliged, penning a few lines in his neat handwriting. When McIntyre suggested that he also record his movements while in England – to prove that he could not have been in Lambeth, for example – Dr Neill thought that an excellent idea, and said he would compose this list the following day.

At Scotland Yard, McIntyre, Tunbridge and Harvey compared Neill's handwriting with that on the various anonymous letters. It matched some of them, but the clincher came when the watermarks on the note Neill wrote for McIntyre, and the letter received by Dr Harper, were found to be identical: "Fairfield Superfine Quality." This was a paper manufactured only in the United States and not available in England.

Neill was not arrested, although the net was closing around him. Detectives traced Lou Harper to Brighton and questioned her. What she told them showed how Neill chose his victims, and his method of administering strychnine in the guise of innocent capsules. A chemist was traced who had sold strychnine to the doctor.

The following day McIntyre visited Neill in his lodgings, at 103 Lambeth Palace Road, ready to collect the statement about his movements. He found him still in bed, dictating the statement to his landlady's daughter. McIntyre glanced at the document and saw that there was no reference to anything on the day Shrivell and Marsh had died. He pointed this out, and Neill said: "That can easily be rectified. I will look up the dates once I get up. I think I was in Berkhamsted that day."

Detectives went to Berkhamsted and found a girl, a respectable dressmaker, who had been engaged to Neill for some months. She had even written some of those anonymous letters at his request: the ones signed "W.H. Murray." The doctor's landlady's daughter was questioned about Neill and said he had talked a lot about the Lambeth poisonings, mentioning Lord Russell as one culprit. Tunbridge decided it was time he had a talk with Neill.

He called at the doctor's lodgings, ostensibly to answer his complaints about police persecution. They chatted amiably. Then the detective asked Neill if he was still an agent for a drugs company. Neill fetched him his sample bag. The detective looked at some strychnine capsules and remarked how dangerous they might be if they fell into the hands of the general public. Neill said primly: "It is not intended to sell them to the public direct, but only to druggists and doctors."

Tunbridge wanted more time, but events forced his hand when McIntyre announced that Neill was getting restless and was talking of going away, perhaps back to America. Tunbridge went straight to Neill's rooms on June 3rd and told him he was under arrest for the blackmailing of Dr Harper. He was careful to make no mention of murder. Neill shrugged. "Fire away," he said cheerfully. "You have got the wrong man."

Tunbridge immediately began a search of Neill's rooms, finding an envelope on which Neill had scribbled the initials of the murdered girls, and the dates of their deaths. In one of Neill's pockets was found a piece of paper in Marsh's handwriting, with her address. Also in the doctor's rooms police found seven bottles of strychnine, but the oddest discovery of all was a birth certificate in the name of Thomas Neill Cream, born in Glasgow on May 27th, 1850.

Now everything fell into place. Inspector Jarvis had returned from the USA and Canada with the results of his inquiries. Dr. Neill was in reality Thomas Neill Cream, who had been taken to Canada at an early age by his parents, who had emigrated there in 1854-5. Cream had graduated in medicine at McGill University in 1876, but had never been a success at it.

At the age of twenty-four he had insured his possessions, and had then arranged to have a little fire. Two years later he had attempted to pull the same trick again, but found the insurance company no longer so gullible. At this time he met a Miss Flora Eliza Brooks in

Montreal, becoming engaged to her. The girl's father had forced Cream at pistol-point to marry her after discovering that Cream had been drugging his daughter. Cream had left Canada immediately after the wedding, having arranged to go to England to complete his medical training. He arrived in London in October 1876.

He had taken a post-graduate course at St Thomas's Hospital in London and gained a British medical degree. As his wife had died in the meantime, he returned to Canada in March 1878, setting up a practice in London, Ontario. A short time afterwards a chambermaid named Kate Gardener was found dead in the room next to his premises, a bottle of chloroform by her side. The police suspected murder and questioned Cream, who attempted to implicate a local merchant who retorted that Cream had attempted to blackmail him. There was insufficient evidence to bring any charges, but Cream found his practice and reputation ruined, and moved to Chicago.

He was arrested in that city in 1880, on suspicion of causing the death of a woman named Faulkner during an illegal abortion, but was released for lack of evidence. Four months later a girl named Stack died after taking medicine prescribed by Cream, and he sent blackmailing letters to the chemist who had made up the prescription. Meanwhile, Cream had been arrested for sending scurrilous postcards to another man, but had been released on bail.

The police kept an eye on him, however, because of another more serious matter. Cream had been having an affair with Julia Stott, the young wife of an elderly station-agent who suffered from epilepsy, and lived some miles from Chicago, at Garden Prairie, Illinois. Mrs Stott had originally visited Cream in the hope that he could cure her husband. After a few months, with Mrs Stott making frequent visits to Cream's surgery for fresh "medicine," Cream made an unsuccessful attempt to insure Mr. Stott's life.

Then he gave Mrs Stott a new prescription which she

had made up by a nearby chemist. She took the medicine back to Cream, who added a white powder to it. When Mrs Stott gave this medicine to her husband, he died within twenty minutes. That same night, before news of the death was known, Cream told an acquaintance that Stott had been poisoned.

The cause of Stott's death had been attributed to an epileptic seizure. Cream was outraged at this misdiagnosis and fired off an angry letter to the coroner telling him that the chemist had blundered in making up his prescription, and had inadvertently poisoned his patient. When the coroner ignored this letter, Cream went to the District Attorney, who was happy to listen and had the body exhumed. When strychnine was found in the remains, the police went looking for Cream.

He had skipped bail on the postcard charges, but was traced to Canada where he was arrested. With Mrs Stott he faced trial for murder. Mrs Stott, who had turned State's evidence, was acquitted, but on November 1st, 1881, Cream was found guilty and sentenced to life imprisonment, serving ten years in Joliet Prison.

While he was in prison a relative died, in 1887, leaving him $16,000. People now agitated for Cream's release, saying he had been punished enough, and the Governor of Illinois commuted his sentence. When he was released he made a brief trip to Canada to collect his inheritance, before returning to England, landing at Liverpool on October 1st, 1891. He had arrived in London on October 5th. On October 9th he met Matilda Clover. On October 13th he murdered Ellen Donworth. He didn't kill Matilda until October 20th.

The police now knew the explanation for the long gap between the October and April murders. In January 1892 Cream had sailed to Canada, where he had those Metropole Hotel circulars printed in Quebec, before returning to England in March.

Following the exhumation of Matilda Clover and the autopsy showing strychnine poisoning, the inquest jury

Dr. John Bodkin Adams after his acquittal

Exhumations of
suspected
murder victims.
No evidence of
poisoning was
found but police
still proceeded
with the case

A Doctor's Ordeal:
see page 144

Three prosecution witnesses. Nurses Randall, Stronach and Mason - Ellis. Right, Sir Geoffrey Lawrence QC, the doctor's last chance of survival

A Doctor's Ordeal: see page 144

Arthur Kendrick Ford thought his love potion would make the girls respond to him. Instead, office typists Betty Grant (below) and June Malins, a seaside beauty queen, died in agony. Ford had given them cantharides - better known to the layman as Spanish Fly

'LOVE DRUG' KILLED THE TWO TYPISTS

DAILY MIRROR REPORTER

A "LOVE DRUG" killed the two girl typists who died mysteriously after eating coconut ice.

This was disclosed yesterday by Scotland Yard scientists who have been trying to discover what poisoned the girls and how.

Last night, they were still seeking an answer to the questions: Who gave June Malins, 21, and former seaside beauty...

Clues in tea cups?

A Foolish Dreamer: see page 83

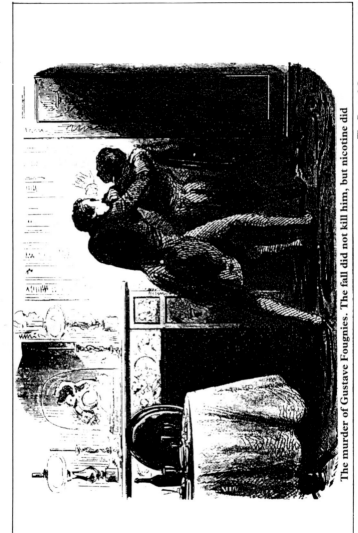

The murder of Gustave Fougnies. The fall did not kill him, but nicotine did

The Busted Count: see page 169

found that Thomas Neill, as he was still known, had administered poison to her with intent to kill. Cream now appeared before Bow Street magistrates on July 21st, the original charge of forgery having been amended to one of murder.

His Old Bailey trial, before Mr Justice Hawkins, began on October 17th, 1892, with the Attorney-General, Sir Charles Russell, prosecuting. Mr Gerald Goeghegan appeared for the defence. Cream was insolent in court, and contemptuous of the proceedings. But the evidence against him was overwhelming: his handwriting on those letters; the strychnine capsules found in his possession; a chemist who testified that Cream had purchased gelatin capsules and strychnine; a letter in his possession in one of the victims' handwriting; witnesses who identified him as having been seen in the company of some of the victims; girls he had tried to get to take his capsules. It was all too much. The jury took just twelve minutes to find Cream guilty, and he was sentenced to death on October 21st.

The judge had criticised the police for failing to act straight away on those anonymous letters, but as a senior officer told him, if Scotland Yard acted on every anonymous letter it received, it would require thousands more detectives.

As Cream lay in the condemned cell, his optician wrote to *The Times* suggesting that the root cause of Cream's moral degeneracy might lie in the fact that his eye defect had not been corrected when he was a child. This was akin to saying perhaps Jack the Ripper had not been breast-fed.

It was reported that he spent the night before his execution pacing his cell, white as a sheet and shaking. But he never made any confession. The forty-two-year old doctor was hanged at Newgate Prison on November 15th, 1892. It has been said that just as the bolt was drawn and the trap opened, he cried out: "I am Jack the – " before death took him. Perhaps he was hoping for a postponement while his claim was investigated, but of all the suspects named as Jack the Ripper, Cream is about the only one who can positively be cleared of the Whitechapel Murders of 1888. He was in Joliet Prison at the time.

As we have seen, Cream virtually turned himself in. Why? There can only be one explanation: his psychopathic streak of vanity. He advertised his murders, brought them to the attention of the authorities and worked hard to bring himself to justice because of that fatal flaw of exhibitionism in his character. After all, what's the point of a practical joke if you can't share it?

30
STRYCHNINE

Killers with a ruthless, sadistic streak tend to choose this lethal, fast-acting poison. Extracted from *Strychnos nux vomica* and other plants found mainly in India, notably St Ignatius's beans, strychnine is not a gentle poison. It causes intense pain and leaves the victim with the back arched so violently that only the head and heels touch the floor. This "bowed" contraction – called opisthotonus by the medical profession – can last for as long as two minutes at a time, with the victim fully conscious and in terribly agony. After several such spasms, exhaustion quickly sets in. The lips are drawn back in a macabre smile – which old textbooks called the "risus sardonicus" – and the face of the corpse has a wild-eyed, staring expression. A fatal dose is about one and a half grains.

Strychnine quickly enters the bloodstream, even from external application, and affects the central nervous system, causing convulsions and difficulty in breathing. The convulsive pains can last for an agonising couple of hours or more, before muscular tension stops the lungs working, resulting in death from respiratory paralysis. Alternatively the poison acts on the medulla area of the brain which is responsible for such reflex actions as the heart-beat, resulting in a welcome death from cardiac arrest.

Incredibly, this poison was once used in quack

preparations – in a dose of about one two-thousandth of a grain – as a cure for impotence, for it tends to increase blood pressure.

The most notable early case was that of Thomas Griffiths Wainewright, a literary gent who also sketched and painted and was friendly with such writers as De Quincey, Hazlitt and Lamb, although he lacked their talent. He wanted to live the life of a dandy, and in doing so ran into financial difficulties. He had married Eliza Frances Ward in 1821, and found marriage an expensive business. Discovering that two cannot live as cheaply as one, he forged the signatures of the trustees who controlled his inheritance, obtaining £2,000 which did not last him long: though he cultivated the appearance of a romantic artist, he had no intention of starving in a garret. In 1829 he was suspected of poisoning his grandfather with strychnine. However, he inherited the old man's fortune, most of which went to pay off pressing debts. Then his mother-in-law, Mrs Abercromby, came to live with him, bringing with her two daughters, Madeleine and Helen.

Mrs Abercromby died in 1830 – possibly another strychnine victim – and Wainewright had by now insured twenty-year-old Helen for £18,000, putting the policies in the name of Madeleine, who then assigned them to him. In December 1830 Helen conveniently died and Wainewright sent Madeleine to collect the insurance money. The insurance companies were suspicious and refused to pay, so Wainewright sued them. The case dragged on for five years and then the verdict went against him.

Named as a poisoner, he fled to France, where he administered strychnine to the father of a girl he knew, having first insured the man's life for £3,000. Wainewright returned to England in 1837, but was recognised by a Bow Street Runner and arrested. Tried only for forgery, he was convicted and sentenced to transportation for life to Tasmania. He died there, aged fifty-eight and still a convict.

His literary acquaintances – including Dickens – visited him in prison before he was shipped out, and when one of them asked him why he had poisoned Helen, he replied: "Yes, it was a dreadful thing to do, but she had very thick ankles." This appealed to Oscar Wilde, who in his essay, "Pen, Pencil and Poison," praises Wainewright as an artist, and seems tacitly to approve of murder on aesthetic grounds.

One of the earliest recorded strychnine poisoners of more modern times was George Hersey, who, on May 3rd, 1860, in Boston, USA, poisoned his pregnant fiancée, twenty-three-year-old Betsy Frances. A few days earlier Hersey had asked a doctor to perform an abortion on Betsey, and when he refused, asked him to supply some strychnine to "kill a dog." The doctor declined to supply the poison.

Then, on the day of her murder, Hersey showed a friend a glass phial of white powder, remarking: "There is something to kill the little one." Betsy was found by her family ill in bed, in such pain that she had bitten through her lip. She began screaming, arching her back in agony, and was dead before a doctor could reach her. Betsy's family at first suspected food poisoning, but then remembered that George Hersey's first wife, and later a girl friend, had both died suddenly, displaying the same symptoms as Betsy. They asked for a post mortem. Hersey objected, saying he did not want his beloved to be mutilated, but the family insisted. They were horrified when the doctor who carried out the autopsy told them that not only had Betsy been three months pregnant, she had also died as a result of strychnine poisoning. Hersey was arrested and charged with murder. At his trial he pleaded not guilty, claiming that Betsy had committed suicide, but after he was convicted of first-degree murder he confessed, although he denied causing the deaths of the other two women. Hersey had been a medical student and had studied chemistry, where he learned the toxic effects of strychnine.

Murder with Venom

Christiana Edmunds appears to have been another compulsive poisoner. This forty-two-year old spinster lived in Brighton with her mother. She developed a passion for the family physician, Dr Beard, who was married, and he had to order her to stop writing florid love letters to him. On August 10th, 1871, she sent Mrs Beard a parcel of cakes through the post, with a note reading: "Those done up are flavoured on purpose for you to enjoy." The Beard family servants ate the cakes and were seriously ill. Dr Beard confronted Miss Edmunds and accused her of trying to kill his wife, and she was arrested and charged with attempted murder. Police inquiries linked her with the murder several months earlier of a four-year-old boy who had died after eating strychnine-laced chocolates. Three anonymous letters sent to the boy's father were in Miss Edmunds' handwriting. It was discovered that she had made several purchases of strychnine from a local chemist, and was in the habit of poisoning sweets, leaving them lying around where she knew children were likely to find them. Several children had been taken ill as a result of her "pranks." Found guilty at her trial and sentenced to death, she was subsequently reprieved.

Jean-Pierre Vaquier was a jealous forty-five-year old Frenchman who poisoned his mistress's husband. Vaquier had met Mabel Theresa Jones when she was on holiday in France. She was the wife of the landlord of the Blue Anchor Hotel at Byfleet in Surrey. Although neither spoke the other's language, they began an intense love affair. When Mrs Jones returned to England, Vaquier followed, staying at a hotel in London, where Mrs Jones visited him.

We do not know if she encouraged him to visit her, but on February 14th, 1924, he booked into the Blue Anchor Hotel. On March 1st he went to London where he bought strychnine for "experiments with wireless." He signed the Poisons' Register with the name "Wanker," returning to the Blue Anchor. On the morning of March 29th, following a party the night before, Mr Jones went to the bar to fetch a bottle of bromo salts he kept there for hangovers. He drank some with water, explaining: "My God! These are bitter!" He became ill almost instantly, and a doctor was called. While the physician was attending Mr Jones, Vaquier ran into the kitchen saying "Medicine, doctor, quick!" and took the bottle of bromo salts away. After Mr Jones's subsequent death, an autopsy revealed strychnine poisoning. That bottle of bromo salts was found empty and washed out in the kitchen, but strychnine was still detectable inside it. Tried for murder at Guildford Assizes in July 1924, Vaquier was convicted, and he was hanged at Wandsworth Prison on August 12th, 1924. The moral? Holiday romances can kill . . .

Eva Rablen poisoned her deaf husband with strychnine in Tuttletown, California, on April 26th, 1929. She liked to dance but her husband could not. He would sit in the car outside the dance-hall, waiting for her. That night she took him out a cup of coffee. Within seconds Carroll Rablen was writhing in agony, unable to get out of the car. His screams brought people running, and before dying he complained about the bitter taste of the coffee. Strychnine was found in the dead man's stomach; a bottle marked "Strychnine" was found in the dance-hall, and traces of the same poison were found in the residue of that cup of coffee. Tried in the open, to accommodate the huge crowd of interested parties, Eva Rablen pleaded guilty and was sentenced to life imprisonment.

The Chevis case remains a classic unsolved poisoning mystery. On June 21st, 1931, Lieutenant Hubert George Chevis, a young artillery officer, died after eating poisoned partridge in his married quarters near Aldershot. His wife had prepared the meal, and although taken ill herself, recovered. The coroner recorded an open verdict, but there was no doubt that Chevis had been murdered. On the day of his funeral, the dead man's father, Sir William Chevis, received a telegram which read simply: "Hooray. Hooray. Hooray." Sent from Dublin, it was signed by a

"J. Hartigan." Sir William received another telegram from the same source later which read: "This is a mystery which will never be solved." Sadly, the writer was correct.

Mark Shank was a lawyer in Kenmore, Ohio, a suburb of Akron. Tall and hawk-nosed, he had been elected mayor of the town and served his term with distinction. Returning to private practice, he was caught out in the stock market crash of 1929, which triggered the great Depression. He was glad to get a client in July 1933, a man who hired him in a civil suit involving $1,000. He won the case, but his client complained that Shank had appropriated a considerable portion of the settlement for himself, and went to the District Attorney. Shank was questioned about two hundred dollars that were missing, and hinted that his assistant, Alvin Colley, might know something about it. The D.A. never got a chance to question Colley, for Shank's assistant disappeared, along with his wife and three children.

He turned up in Malvern, Arkansas, on August 10th, 1933, when a car being driven erratically crashed close to a farm where Tom Steadman was working. He went over to the car and noticed that the driver's face was contorted in a grimace. Beside him sat an unconscious woman, clasping a small boy in her lap. The boy, aged about four, was vomiting. In the back seat were two older boys, their bodies rigid, backs arched, eyes glassy and unseeing. Tom Steadman ran for help.

Sheriff Tom Fisher took the call and drove to the scene. A doctor arrived at the same time who, after taking one look at the five victims, said: "Poison," and began using a stomach pump. The doctor paused long enough to tell the sheriff: "It's strychnine, without a doubt."

The sheriff checked the identification of the victims and found the driver to be Alvin Colley from Akron, Ohio. He questioned the youngest boy, who said the family had been on a picnic. The sheriff drove out to the picnic site and found plates laid out – but with six cups, not five. The purple dregs in the cups suggested grape juice. A cake had been cut into six slices. Who had been the sixth member of the picnic party? The sheriff suspected that it was the poisoner. Where he had sat was a purple patch on the grass where he had poured out his drink, while watching the others quaff their strychnine-laced grape juice. Reasoning that the poisoner must have been one of the party in the car, but had jumped out before it crashed, the sheriff called out men with a bloodhound to track down the mystery man from the point where he had jumped – his deep heel marks were clearly visible. The bloodhound duly tracked down the man, a muddy and exhausted Mark Shank.

Taken to the morgue to view the victims, Shank identified them as being Alvin Colley and family. He said he had been invited to meet the Colleys at the picnic site, but had lost his way. Placing Shank in a cell, the sheriff checked out his lodgings in a cheap hotel in Hot Springs. In a suitcase belonging to Shank strychnine powder was found, and strychnine was also discovered in the picnic cups and in the stomachs of the victims.

After denying any involvement in the murders, Shank was persuaded to confess by his Congressman. "I had no idea that poison would work that way," he said. "I thought it would act quickly, instantly. . . It meant sheer ruin for me if I was found out (in the swindle of his client). My licence to practise would be taken away from me." He had poisoned Colley and his family to stop the honest assistant from talking.

Shank was executed in 1937.

Ethel Lillie Major was a Lincolnshire gamekeeper's daughter who, at the age of forty-three, poisoned her husband with strychnine. He had been violent, and was receiving letters from another woman. On May 22nd, 1934, Arthur Major was taken ill after eating some corned beef. After two days of agony he died, the hospital doctors certifying the cause of death as status epilepticus. Then the police received an anonymous letter alleging that a neighbour's dog had died after eating scraps put out by

Ethel. The dog's body was exhumed, was found to contain strychnine, and Arthur's funeral was halted while a post mortem was carried out. Strychnine was also found in his remains. Tried at Lincoln Assizes in November 1934, his widow was found guilty. She was hanged on December 19th in Hull Prison.

Strychnine was commonly used to destroy dogs, a practice which perhaps gave others the idea of extending the treatment.

31
GRAHAM FREDERICK YOUNG
Death of a Gargoyle

"I am your friendly neighbourhood Frankenstein" – Young,
describing himself in a letter to his sister.
"It was a pity about old Fred" – Young, casually discussing
one of his victims.

Graham Frederick Young, the most notorious mass-poisoner in Britain this century, was found dying in his cell at Parkhurst Prison on the Isle of Wight on the evening of August 1st, 1990. He was forty-two.

An inquest was held within a couple of days, and the coroner was told that Young had died from a heart attack – which was ironic, because of all the poisoners chronicled in these pages, Young was perhaps the most heartless.

There is a Latin phrase which translates as "Do not speak ill of the dead." But no obituary of Graham Young could be written without speaking ill of him. He had not one redeeming feature.

His case demonstrates exactly what a psychopath is, and it shows that the psychopath can never be cured: he simply goes on doing what he does until he is either killed or caught. In a sense, this is not his fault. He has a piece missing, the element which in the rest of us promotes communication and empathy with our fellow-beings. This ability to feel for others cannot be taught, transplanted or injected. The psychopath can never be cured, just as a jigsaw cannot be completed when a piece is missing.

Graham Young was born on September 7th, 1947, in Neasden, north-west London. His mother died that same year and he was raised by an aunt and uncle until his father re-married in 1950. Then the family of son, daughter, father and stepmother, lived together at 768 North Circular Road, Neasden.

The daughter, Winifred, was eight years older than her brother, Graham, and was able to observe him growing up. He appeared to be a normal boy, except that he was a loner who disliked games, and unlike other children, he had no hobby.

As he grew older, he displayed signs of high intelligence, doing well in class-work, especially English and chemistry. What no one realised was that by the age of eleven he had found a pastime which was to last him all his life. He had become obsessed with poisons, and spent hours in the library reading up the subject. He also began to display an intellectually aggressive attitude, always ready to argue against anything, and he was obsessively neat and tidy – traits which are often seen in the mentally disturbed.

Before his teens he became a devotee of Hitler and the Nazi movement. He wore a swastika badge in his lapel, and made himself a crude swastika arm-band which he wore to Braintcroft Junior School. It caused a few raised eyebrows, but only his stepmother appeared to find it odd. When she went to the librarian to complain about the "unhealthy" books that Graham was reading, she was assured that it was nothing to worry about. It was a phase some lads went through and he would soon grow out of it. But Graham never did.

Convinced that Hitler had been a misunderstood genius, Young had become obsessed with power, and nothing gives one more power than a bottle of poison: the power of life and death. Young also developed an interest in black magic and the occult, which claim to offer power over others.

By the age of fourteen he was making explosives in his

garden shed, and he was still doodling those symbols of power, the swastika and the skull and crossbones, on bits of paper. He had a cruel sense of humour, delighting in causing embarrassment or accidents. And he had found another hero to stand alongside Adolf Hitler: the notorious Victorian poisoner, William Palmer, who claimed some fourteen victims.

The teens are an awkward period for most youngsters, experiencing that rush of hormones which causes chemical imbalance and leads to moods and pimples. Young did not develop pimples. In 1961 he began systematically poisoning his family.

His sister was courting by now, and had most of her meals at her fiancé's house, but when she did eat at home she tended to be horribly sick. But not as sick as Molly, the stepmother. She was writhing about in agony in the autumn of 1961. The father was sick too, and even Graham had the odd bout of vomiting – probably because he couldn't remember which item of food he had poisoned.

Their doctor was puzzled by the family's symptoms and suspected that the water supply to the house might be contaminated. He could not have known that upstairs in Young's bedroom there were such works as *The Handbook of Poisons, Poisoners in the Dock,* and so on; or that Young was spending his pocket-money buying antimony, atropine and digitalis from chemists' shops.

But *can* children buy poison? Young simply told chemists that he needed the poisons for science experiments at school, and signed the poisons' register with the name "M.E. Evans." When he was arrested he was found to have enough poisons to kill 300 people.

While experimenting on his immediate family and studying the effects, he also poisoned his only friend, Christopher John Williams, who lived nearby. Early in May 1961, Young gave him three grains of antimony in a cream biscuit. The boy was taken to hospital.

When Young's stepmother died on Easter Saturday,

1962, the post mortem found the cause of death to be a slipped disc at the top of her spinal column and she was cremated. After his arrest, Young confessed to his aunt Winnie that he had been poisoning his stepmother with antimony over a long period, observing her bouts of agony and even nursing her. He had finished her off with 20 grains of thallium in a trifle the night prior to her death. After the funeral, when the mourners came back to the house, Young poisoned his uncle with antimony in a ham sandwich. The victim was violently ill.

Now it was the father's turn to suffer, and he had agonising bouts of sickness and diarrhoea. Young nursed him, Winifred urging him to make sure that their father ate something regularly. Bengers food was what she suggested, and Young had thought of that: the Bengers food was already laced with poison.

Gradually the suspicion of poisoning grew. Aunt Winnie had suspected Graham from the start, knowing of his obsession with poisons. When the father went to hospital for tests, the doctors said that he was suffering from either arsenic or antimony poisoning. Young sneered at the diagnosis: "How can any doctor not tell the difference between the symptoms of arsenic and antimony?" He could. After his father's release from hospital, he sat at his bedside staring at him, studying the results of his experiments.

Meanwhile, the science master at the John Kelly Secondary School, Willesden, was worried by Young's possession of poisons and had a chat with the headmaster about it. As a result a psychiatrist from a Child Guidance Clinic was called in to counsel the boy. Young set out to dazzle the psychiatrist with his expertise, but only damned himself, since his conversation was a form of concealed confession. The police were contacted and the following day Young was arrested.

On May 23rd, 1962, the police were waiting when Young got home from school and they searched him inside the house. In his shirt they found three bottles containing antimony, and they later recovered a quantity of poisons from a nearby hedge.

Following a night in the cells at Harlesden police station, Young made a full confession, admitting poisoning his family and a school-friend. In his statement, he said he "started experimenting at home by putting one and sometimes three grains on prepared foods which my mother, father and sister ate. By September of last year (1961) it had become an obsession with me, and I continued giving members of my family antimony tartrate on prepared foods. My mother lost weight all the time through it, and I stopped giving it to her about February this year. After my mother died, on April 21st, 1962, I started putting antimony tartrate into milk and water my father was drinking. As a result he became critically ill and was taken to hospital. I knew the doses I was giving were not fatal, but I knew I was doing wrong. It grew on me like a drug habit, except that it was not me who was taking the drug."

Antimony potassium tartrate is a sweet-tasting powder which is readily soluble in water. Young described it as his "little friend." While on remand awaiting trial, he made an attempt to commit suicide by hanging himself with his tie. This was not through remorse, but more likely through fear. Interviewed by a psychiatrist prior to his appearance at the Old Bailey, Young said: "I am missing my antimony. I am missing the power it gives me."

On July 5th, 1962, Young appeared at the Old Bailey, at fourteen one of the youngest criminals ever to be tried there. He pleaded guilty to poisoning charges involving his father, sister and a school friend. The issue of his stepmother was never raised, as she had been cremated and there was no evidence to secure a conviction.

Dr Fysh, the senior medical officer at Ashford Remand Centre, told the court: "Poisons have tended to take an extremely prominent place in his mind because of the sense of power they give him." He said that the boy was in need of psychiatric treatment and there was a place available at Broadmoor for him.

For the defence, Miss Jean Southworth pleaded that "like a drug addict he is to be pitied for his obsession, and there was no killer instinct." But Dr Ronald Blair, a consultant psychiatrist, told the court: "I would say he was prepared to take the risk of killing to gratify his interest in poisons. He is obsessed by the sense of power they give him. I fear he will do it again."

Mr Justice Melford Stevenson sentenced Young to be detained at Broadmoor for a minimum of fifteen years, adding the warning: "Such people are always dangerous and are adept at concealing their mad compulsion, which may never be wholly cured."

During his time at Broadmoor, Young continued to take an interest in the Nazi movement. In a letter to his sister giving her news of his imminent release, he described himself as "your friendly neighbourhood Frankenstein."

Young left Broadmoor in February 1971, having served less than ten years of his sentence. The doctors had pronounced him "cured" of his hobby, and the Home Office sent him to a Government Rehabilitation Centre at Slough, where he lived in a hostel, and eventually found him employment with a Hertfordshire photographic laboratory, Hadlands at Bovingdon. The day after he applied for the job, on April 24th, 1971, Young went to a chemist's shop in London and bought 25 grains of antimony, again signing the poisons register as "M.E. Evans." Eleven days later he returned to the shop and bought antimony and thallium. Incredibly, his new employers were not told about his habit of poisoning people.

In his letter to the managing director of Hadlands thanking him for the job offer as an assistant storekeeper, Young wrote: "May I take this opportunity of expressing my gratitude to you for offering me this position notwithstanding my previous infirmity as communicated to you by the placing officer." But both the placing officer and Hadlands were under the impression that Young had recovered from some sort of nervous breakdown.

Young began work at Hadlands on May 10th, 1972, having got himself lodgings in Hemel Hempstead. The head storeman was Bob Egle, aged sixty and looking forward to retirement. By the end of May Mr Egle was suffering from an extremely upset stomach.

Workmates at Hadlands, a small firm with a family atmosphere, found Young to be rather reserved, always with his head in a book. He was not the tea-boy, as some reports have it, but he was always keen to fetch cups of tea and coffee from the trolley for his colleagues.

Mr Egle got worse. He rolled around in agony from pains in his back and stomach, and he experienced a curious numbness in his fingers and feet. He was becoming paralysed, and he was taken into the intensive care unit at St Albans City Hospital, where he died eight days later, on July 19th. Doctors had been treating him for peripheral neuritis.

Everyone at the works was shocked, and Hadlands was represented at the funeral by the managing director and by Mr Egle's closest associate, twenty-three-year-old Graham Young, who laid a wreath. Afterwards Young asked Mr Foster, the managing director, what had been written on the death certificate. Told it had been peripheral neuritis, Young could not resist displaying his erudition. "That's just a general term to cover any damage to the nervous system," he said. "The proper name for it is the Guillan-Barré Syndrome." Mr Foster was to say later: "I was astonished at the depth of Graham's medical knowledge."

Ron Hewitt took over in the stores. Towards the end of June he felt very ill. After having time off with severe stomach pains, he quit his job – and unwittingly saved his life. More and more people at Hadlands were falling ill with what the workers were now calling the "Bovingdon bug." The symptoms were much the same: severe vomiting and diarrhoea.

Mrs Diana Smart was a woman who had got closer to Young than anyone else, and discovered that he liked to talk about the Nazis and horror films, and read books on murder. She first fell ill in July and saw her doctor. Her sickness became worse in August and by October she was having a lot of time off work with the "bug."

Peter Buck, an export manager at Hadlands, was brought a cup of tea by Young on September 20th, and within a quarter of an hour of drinking part of it was very sick and pain-racked.

Jethro Batt, aged thirty-nine, used to give Young a lift back to Hemel Hempstead after work. During the journey Young would talk about poisons and murder. He once said: "It's quite easy to poison somebody and when any doctor does an autopsy afterwards, they'd think they died of natural causes." On October 15th Young got Mr Batt a cup of coffee. He thought it tasted "bitter" but finished it off. Afterwards he was violently sick, his legs went numb and he was continually rushing to the toilet. His illness got worse, until he had to enter hospital.

David Tilson, a clerk, had been brought a cup of tea by Young on October 8th and woke the next day feeling a curious sensation of pins and needles in his feet. He continued to go to work, but his condition deteriorated. There were pains in his chest and stomach, he could not breathe properly and his hair began to drop out. He was admitted to hospital in St Albans and afterwards took five weeks off work to recuperate. He had lost almost two stones in weight and most of his hair.

The staff at the works were becoming increasingly concerned as more and more people went down with the "bug." Mrs Smart was getting worse and Young was very solicitous, getting her to describe in detail the symptoms of her illness.

Fred Biggs, aged fifty-six, another man who worked in the stores, went down with the bug on October 26th. He too became steadily worse. He was eventually admitted to the National Hospital for Nervous Diseases in London, dying nineteen days later.

The management at Hadlands were so concerned

about the epidemic of sickness that they called in the local health department to investigate, and on November 12th a team of doctors arrived at the works to carry out tests of materials used and to question staff. Young asked one doctor if he had considered it might be thallium poisoning . . .

On November 19th, 1971, Dr Arthur Anderson, the firm's doctor and a local general practitioner, spoke to workers in the canteen about the "bug" and reassured them that everything possible was being done to trace the source of the virus. When he asked for any questions at the end of the talk, Young put up his hand.

He asked whether the symptoms of the bug were compatible with some form of heavy-metal industrial poisoning – thallium, for example. The doctor questioned him afterwards, curious about his extensive medical knowledge.

With the "Bovingdon bug" still active, a worker went to the management to tell them that Young had said his hobby was toxicology. The police were called and the first thing detectives did was to make a routine check on all the staff, including the newest recruit, Graham Young. When his record came in over the teletype line, the police were stunned. A mass-poisoner had been released upon an unsuspecting workforce.

Young was promptly arrested, and in the car taking him to the police station he asked: "Which one is it?" Detectives were puzzled. What Young meant was: which of the murders are you arresting me for?

From his lodgings police recovered bottles containing thallium, antimony and aconitine. There was also a drawing which revealed Young's macabre sense of humour. It showed a man with a full head of hair, and beneath the same man was portrayed, now completely bald and wearing a look of astonishment. But the most important find was a diary which Young had been keeping since October. It made riveting reading.

The entry for October 12th revealed a plot to murder

David Tilson by visiting him in hospital and giving him a miniature brandy laced with thallium. But Mr Tilson was not admitted to hospital until October 20th. The entry in the diary had read: "David has not been hospitalised – happy for him – and therefore is free to live out his allotted span. For needless to say, it would be injudicious of me to focus my attention on him for a second time."

Another entry reminded Young: "I must restrain my tendency to over-liberal doses." The entry for October 18th concerned Jethro Batt, and read: "A sad development, and one which I now regret, is that J has now been afflicted. I feel rather ashamed of my action in harming Jeth. I think he is a really nice fellow and the nearest I have to a friend in Hadlands. I have faith he will recover."

The diary entry for Diana Smart read: "Di irritated me intensely yesterday, so I packed her off with an attack of sickness. I only gave her something to shake her up. I now regret I didn't give her a larger dose."

On October 31st, an entry referring to Fred Biggs recorded: "I have administered a fatal dose of the special compound to him and I anticipate a report of his progress on Monday. I gave him three separate doses . . . In a way it seems a shame to condemn such a likable man to such a horrible end, but I have made my decision and therefore he is doomed to premature decease."

November 1st: "A disturbing symptom has occurred in the case of D (David Tilson). He has started losing hair." Two days later, Young was becoming worried that Tilson's hair loss might alert doctors to the real cause of the Bovingdon bug: "The hair loss is almost total and the hospital thinks it might be due to poisoning. I must watch the situation very carefully. If it looks like I will be detected then I shall have to destroy myself. The events of the next few days will prove decisive. They point either to my continuation to live, or my destruction by my own hand."

Young was found to have a phial of thallium in the breast pocket of his jacket when arrested, and when asked why he carried it, he replied: "It was my 'exit' dose, but I didn't have a chance to use it."

The diary continued: "News from other fronts. F is now seriously ill. He is unconscious and it is likely that he will decline in the next few days. It will be a merciful release for him, as if he should survive he will be permanently impaired. It is better that he should die. It will remove one more casualty from the crowded field of battle."

Later entries read: "F must have phenomenal strength to fight the special compound. If he lives it would be inconvenient. It is better he should die. Too many health authorities are being involved for me to press the matter further." The last entry, referring to F, said: "He is surviving too long for my peace of mind."

At Hemel Hempstead police station Young was questioned about his diary, and which people the initials represented. He insisted: "They are figments of my imagination. I was preparing to write a novel and they are my notes . . . You are suggesting I am a monster – some sort of mass-poisoner who poisons people regardless. That is not so."

Later, he admitted the poisonings, and when asked why he had done it, he said: "I suppose I had ceased to see them as people, or more correctly, a part of me had. They became guinea pigs."

Later he said: "It was a pity about old Fred." Told he was to be charged with two murders and the attempted murder of six other people, Young countered: "That's an academic point. I could of killed them had I wished, as I did Biggs and Egle, but I allowed them to live."

Asked if he felt any remorse for what he had done, Young replied: "No, that would be hypocritical. What I feel is the emptiness of my soul."

Young entered the dock at St Albans Crown Court on June 19th, 1972. The trial lasted ten days, as Young insisted on pleading not guilty. At Broadmoor he had collected press cuttings of his earlier crimes. Now he wanted more.

Mr John Leonard QC, prosecuting, told the court that thallium was a rare poison which was not known to have been previously used in the UK for murder.

"Thallium is an accumulative poison which builds up in the body," he said. "One of the symptoms of thallium poisoning is loss of hair, discolouration of the fingernails, abdominal pains and diarrhoea, and degeneration of the nerve fibres resulting in delirium and paralysis."

Mr Leonard described Young as "a young man of considerable intelligence, with a knowledge of toxicology well out of the ordinary. He exhibited a strong interest in the symptoms of his victims, and a possible motive – although a curious one – might be a scientific experimental approach."

Mr Batt testified to having been poisoned by Young. He had received four grains in two separate doses, by Young's own admission. Mr Tilson told of his hair falling out. He had now recovered his hair and the weight he had lost.

Dr Hugh Johnson, a forensic pathologist, told of being telephoned about the death of Fred Biggs. On hearing the symptoms, he had told the police the cause might be thallium poisoning. This was because he had recently read an Agatha Christie novel in which thallium was the poison used.

In *The Pale Horse*, a character talks about thallium, saying: "A lot of workers in a factory died one after the other. The deaths were put down to astonishingly varied causes. . . Thallium is tasteless, soluble, and easy to buy." Young denied having read the book and said he had learned of thallium from a medical paper. He claimed he had supplied Mr Biggs with thallium to kill insects, but had cautioned him to be careful with it, and not allow it to get into contact with naked skin.

He insisted that his diary was merely a collection of notes for a novel. "It was the expression of a theory, a somewhat fanciful one, which I outlined for my own amusement." As for these confessions he had made to the police, "I said nothing of the sort. It sounds like something out of a detective novel."

At the end of the trial the jury found Young guilty of the major counts of murder and attempted murder, but not guilty of administering poison to Peter Buck and Diana Smart. His counsel asked the judge to impose a prison sentence on his client, rather than send him back to Broadmoor.

Sir Arthur Irvine told the judge: "If your lordship is balancing the desirability of a custodial sentence with that of a hospital order, I think it is right that I should say . . . that Young himself thinks the prison sentence would be better for his condition than a return to Broadmoor. The Broadmoor experience has had the tragic consequences of which we have learned in this trial." Young was accordingly jailed for life. There was great public disquiet about Young having been released from Broadmoor, and the authorities came in for much criticism.

Why the chapter-heading "Death of a Gargoyle"? It was the custom to carve gargoyles, or stone devils and imps, on churches to remind the congregation of the terrors of hell, or to drive away evil spirits. Graham Young was like one of those carvings: cold, remote and without feeling.

32
THALLIUM

Discovered by William Crookes in 1861, thallium is a heavy metal, related to lead and mercury, but far more poisonous than either. Thallium sulphate is tasteless, colourless, and soluble in water, and the symptoms of thallium poisoning can be mistaken for complaints like pneumonia, typhus, epilepsy, brain tumour, alcoholism, neuritis, and encephalitis. In a series of thallium poisonings in Holland, these were the various diagnoses. For the killer, thallium is almost the "perfect" poison.

It was once commonly found in pesticides, but this use was banned in the USA in 1972, and later in the UK. It is still used – in the Middle East and Third World countries – to kill vermin. In 1987 hundreds of people in Guyana were affected after drinking milk contaminated by thallium sulphate intended to kill sugar-cane rats. Forty-four people died. In Iraqi it has been used by the security forces to dispose of opponents of the regime, like Abdullah Ali, who in 1988 was found poisoned with thallium while living in exile in Britain. In 1992 a staff colonel in the Iraqi Army and a university professor both fell from favour and became ill. They managed to escape to Damascus and were flown to Britain for treatment, where thallium poisoning was diagnosed.

Once absorbed into the body, thallium takes about a week to work. Since it is mistaken by the body for potassium, an essential nutrient for every cell, it interferes with a number of different systems, upsetting the metabolism and the absorption of calcium, and affecting the nerve cells, leading to phantom pains and numbness in the fingers and other extremities. One of the tell-tale symptoms of thallium poisoning is that the hair drops out – dermatologists formerly used thallium acetate to remove hair in bad cases of ringworm, and for over fifty years thallium was sold over the counter as a depilatory for women.

Agatha Christie is credited with being the first writer to bring thallium to the attention of readers, in *The Pale Horse*, written in 1961. She got the symptoms exactly right, and her novel helped solve the Graham Young case. But she was not the first mystery writer to use thallium as a killing agent. Ngaio Marsh had employed it in 1947, in *Final Curtain*, though she didn't get the symptoms right: her victims dropped dead within minutes of swallowing the poison.

A fatal dose of thallium is about 800mg – less than a quarter of a teaspoon – and the antidote is Prussian blue. This dye used in blue ink is a complex mixture of salt of potassium, iron, and cyanide, and it was first suggested as an antidote twenty years ago by a German pharmacologist, Horst Heydlauf of Karlsruhe.

One notable thallium poisoning case was that of Martha Marek, an Austrian murderess aged thirty-four who was responsible for at least four deaths. An orphan in Vienna, she was adopted by a poor family, but in 1919 was spotted by a wealthy businessman who made her his ward and sent her to finishing schools in England and France. When he died he left her a large sum of money.

In 1924 Martha married Emil Marek, an engineering student, who helped her get through her inheritance much too quickly. They ended up broke and devised an insurance fraud. Emil had himself insured against accident for £10,000, and he promptly had an accident, almost losing his leg in the process. That couldn't have been part of the plan: the limb had to be amputated below the knee. Emil claimed he had been cutting down a tree when the axe slipped, yet doctors found three separate cuts on the leg – no axe slips three times! Cleared of fraud charges, the couple were sentenced to four months for bribing a hospital orderly to say he had seen a doctor tamper with the wounds.

In 1932 Emil died of tuberculosis. A month later Martha's infant daughter died and she went to live with an elderly relative, who died leaving her a fortune. For the second time, Martha quickly got through a bequest, and she was reduced to renting out rooms to make a living. When a female boarder died in mysterious circumstances, poisoning was suspected and the autopsy revealed thallium poisoning. The authorities had Emil, the baby, and the elderly relative exhumed. They too contained thallium which Martha had bought from a local chemist. She was convicted of the murders and beheaded on December 6th, 1938.

LIST OF POISONING CASES

Since I have barely managed to scratch the surface of the subject of poisoning in this book, I have compiled the following list of poison cases known to me, which might be of interest to the reader determined to pursue the poisoner.

The List

(1) Armstrong, John. UK. 1956. Seconal.
(2) Besnard, Marie. France. Arsenic. 1961. Acquitted.
(3) Bocarmé, Count. Belgium. 1851. Nicotine.
(4) Botkin, Cordelia. USA. 1898. Arsenic.
(5) Bowers, Dr. USA. 1885. Phosphorus.
(6) Bravo, Florence. UK. 1876. Antimony. Acquitted.
(7) Brinkley, Richard. UK. 1907. Prussic acid.
(8) Bryant, Charlotte. UK. 1935. Arsenic.
(9) Buchanan, Dr. USA. 1886. Morphine.
(10) Carew, Edith. Japan. 1896. Arsenic.
(11) Chantrelle, Eugène Marie. Scotland. 1878. Opium.
(12) Chapman, George. UK. 1903. Antimony.
(13) Clements, Dr. UK. 1947. Morphine.
(14) Coppolino, Dr. USA. 1967. Succinylcholine chloride.
(15) Cotton, Mary Ann. UK. 1873. Arsenic.
(16) Cream, Dr. UK. 1892. Strychnine.
(17) Mary Creighton & Everett Applegate. USA. 1936. Arsenic.

(18) Crippen, Dr. UK. 1910. Hyoscine.
(19) Cross, Dr. Ireland. 1887. Arsenic.
(20) De la Pommerais, Dr. France. 1864. Digitalis.
(21) De Melker, Daisy Louisa. South Africa. 1932. Arsenic.
(22) Deschamps. Dr. USA. 1889. Chloroform.
(23) Devereux, Arthur. UK. 1905. Chloroform and morphine.
(24. Edmunds, Christiana. UK. 1871. Strychnine.
(25) Friedgood, Dr. USA. 1975. Demerol.
(26) Girard, Dr. France. 1918. Bacteria.
(27) Groesbeek, Maria. South Africa. 1969. Arsenic.
(28) Harris, Carlyle. USA. 1891. Morphine.
(29) Hearn, Annie. UK. 1931. Arsenic. Acquitted.
(30) Hilley, Marie. USA. 1975/8. Arsenic.
(31) Hirasawa, Sadamichi. Japan. 1948. Cyanide.
(32) Hoch, Johann. USA. 1905. Arsenic.
(33) Hofrichter, Adolph. Austria. 1912. Cyanide.
(34) Hyde, Dr. USA. 1909. Strychnine.
(35) Jegado, Hélène. France. 1851. Arsenic.
(36) King, Dr. USA. 1858. Arsenic.
(37) Lafarge, Marie. France. 1840. Arsenic.
(38) Lamson, Dr. UK. 1881. Aconitine.
(39) Major, Ethel. UK. 1934. Strychnine.
(40) Marek, Martha. Austria. 1938. Thallium.
(41) Marymont, Marcus. UK. 1958. Arsenic.
(42) Maybrick, Florence. UK. 1889. Arsenic.
(43) Merrifield, Louisa. UK. 1953. Phosphorus.
(44) Molineux, Roland. USA. 1898. Mercury cyanide.
(45) Moreau, Pierre-Désiré. France. 1874. Copper sulphate.
(46) Palmer, Dr. William. UK. 1856. Antimony.
(47) Patrick, Albert. USA. 1900. Chloroform.
(48) Pritchard, Dr. UK. 1865. Antimony.
(49) Rablen, Eva. USA. 1929. Strychnine.
(50) Seddon, Frederick. UK. 1912. Arsenic.
(51) Smethurst, Dr. UK. 1859. Arsenic.
(52) Smith, Madeleine. UK. 1857. Arsenic. Acquitted.

(53) Tawell, John. UK. 1844. Prussic acid.
(54) Vaquier, Jean-Pierre. UK. 1924. Strychnine.
(55) Waddingham, Dorothea. UK. 1935. Morphia.
(56) Wainewright, Thomas Griffiths. UK. 1830. Strychnine.
(57) Waite, Dr. USA. 1916. Bacteria and arsenic.
(58) Young, Graham. UK. 1971. Thallium.

Fifty-eight people who were tried for poisoning and mainly convicted, the exceptions being Marie Besnard, Florence Bravo, Annie Hearn, and Madeleine Smith. Of the fifty-eight names, twenty-one were women, and eighteen were doctors.

I have not included the classic "unsolved" cases, like the Chevis case, the Croydon poisonings, or the poisonings at Lancaster Castle. Those interested can pursue these cases in other books of this nature.

Bibliography

Bodin, F. & C.F. Chenisse. *Poisons* (Weidenfield & Nicolson. London. 1970).

Browne, Douglas G. & Tullett, Tom *Bernard Spilsbury* (Harrap. London. 1951).

Cullen, Tom. *Crippen, The Mild Murderer* (Bodley Head. London. 1977).

Cuthbert, C.R.M. *Science and the Detection of Crime* (Hutchinson. London. 1958).

Devlin, Patrick. *Easing the Passing* (Faber. London. 1986).

Dickson, Grierson. *Murder by Numbers* (Hale. London 1958).

Dower, Alan. *Crime Chemist: The Life Story of Charles Anthony Taylor, Scientist for the Crown* (John Long. London. 1965).

Duke, Thomas S. *Celebrated Criminal Cases of America* (James H. Barry. San Francisco. 1910).

Eaton, Harold. *Famous Poison Trials* (Collins. London. 1924).

Furneaux, Rupert. *The Medical Murderer* (Elek. London. 1957).

Gaute, J.H.H. & Odell, Robin. *Murder 'Whatdunit'* (Harrap. London. 1982).

Gilbert, Michael. *Dr. Crippen* (Odhams Press. London. 1953).

Glaister, John. *Medical Jurisprudence and Toxicology* (Livingstone. Edinburgh & London. 1953).

Glaister, John. *The Power of Poison* (Christopher Johnson. London. 1954).

Glaser, Hugo. *Poison – The History, Constitution, Uses and Abuses of Poisonous Substances* (Hutchinson. London. 1937).

Huggett, Renée, & Berry, Paul. *Daughters of Cain* (Allen & Unwin. London. 1956).

Jesse, F. Tennyson. *Murder and its Motives* (Harrap. London. 1952).

Jackson, Robert, *The Crime Doctors* (Frederick Muller. London. 1966).

– *Francis Camps. Famous Case Histories of the Most Celebrated Pathologist of our Time* (Hart-Davis, MacGibbon. London. 1975).

Jones, Frank. *Murderous Women* (London. 1990).

Jones, Richard Glyn. (Ed.) *Poison!* (W.H. Allen. 1987).

Kind, Stuart. *The Scientific Investigation of Crime* (Forensic Science Services. Harrogate. 1987).

Marjoribanks, Edward. *Life of Sir Edward Marshall Hall* (Gollancz. London. 1929).

McLaughlin, Terence. *The Coward's Weapon* (Hale. London.)

Morland, Nigel. *Background to Murder* (Werner Laurie. London. 1955).

Morrison, J.T.J. *Poisons* (Benn. London. 1930).

Nash, Jay Robert. *Murder, America* (Harrap. London. 1981).

Notable British Trials. (A series of 83 titles).

Neustatter, W. Lindesay. *The Mind of the Murderer* (Johnson. 1957).

Picton, Bernard. *Murder, Suicide or Accident* (Hale. London. 1971).

Rowland, John. *Poisoner in the Dock* (Arco Publications. London. 1960).

Simpson, Keith. *Forty Years of Murder* (Harrap. London. 1978).

Smith, Edward H. *Famous American Poison Mysteries* (Hurst & Blackett. London. 1927).

Smith, Sydney. *Mostly Murder* (Harrap. London. 1959).

Thompson, C.J.S. *Poison and Poisoners* (Shaylor. London. 1931).

Thompson, John. *Crime Scientist* (Harrap. London. 1980).

Thorwald, Jürgen. *The Century of the Detective* (Harcourt, Brace & World. New York. 1964).

Walls, H.J. *Expert Witness: My Thirty Years in Forensic Science* (John Long. London. 1972).

Wilson, Colin. *Written in Blood* (Equation. London. 1989).

And once again, many thanks to Magazine Design for permission to go through their archives, spanning over forty years.